King of the Southern Diamond No Hits No Runs

Bradsher Hayes

Cover art by Alexis
Book layout by Ned Kandul

This is a work of narrative nonfiction. The events are portrayed to the
best of the author's and his family's memory. The conversations in the
book all come from the author's and his family's recollections, though
they are not written to represent word-for-word transcripts. Rather, the
author has retold them in a way that evokes the feeling and meaning
of what was said, and in all instances, the essence of the dialogue
is accurate. All the statistics and baseball records are substantiated
by box scores, newspaper articles and records received from Duke
University and are factual.

ISBN: 978-1-7334084-6-2

Printed in the United States of America
Perfect Game Publishing.
First Printing October 2019.

Visit arthurbradsher.com to order additional copies.

Love is the most important thing in the world,
but baseball is pretty good, too.
~ Yogi Berra

This book is dedicated to my grandparents,
Arthur and Lizzie,
my parents Fred and Mary,
and my children Bo and Jenny.
~ King of the Southern Diamond

CONTENTS

PREFACE

Untold Stories Are the Best
This Is One That Has Never Been Told
~ Bradsher

BASEBALL WAS KING AT THE TURN OF THE TWENTIETH CENTURY.
America was looking for an idol from the college playing fields
and they found one in Arthur Brown Bradsher, the best pitcher in
the country. He had pinpoint control, movie star looks and cum
laude intelligence. One newspaper reported "Every woman in the
South wanted to marry him and every baseball boss in the country
wanted to own him."

The Trinity College "strikeout king" captured the hearts of
the Southern fans and newspaper reporters after he pitched three
shutouts in eight days in April 1902, striking out forty-three batters
and allowing a total of three hits. This phenomenal performance
remains unmatched in the annals of college baseball.

The legendary John Heisman, nicknamed Arthur Bradsher,
King of the Southern Diamond, after he started the 1904 season
hurling twenty-five consecutive no-hit innings.

In 1905, the pros offered Bradsher $10,000, the highest salary
ever for a college ballplayer. Would it be his love Lizzie or baseball?
Would he pitch for Boston and lose Lizzie? Or would he decide on
a life of love and family.

The narrative non-fiction, enhanced by seventy-six photographs,
depicts much more than the exciting escapades on the ballfield. It
is a tender love story between Trinity college sweethearts Arthur
Bradsher and Lizzie Muse, their deep faith in the Lord, and their
family's adventures on the 100-acre farm, Summerlea.

Two sections in the back of the book, entitled "Extra Innings" and "Full Glossary of Baseball Terms", compliment this work which is well-referenced.

King of the Southern Diamond came from the desire of a grandson to know his grandfather that he never met. It is based on four years of research, 350 newspaper articles, family letters, family conversations, diaries, and hundreds of pictures. Some of which are included for your viewing pleasure with special help from the Duke University library.

Love, God, baseball, family, and adventure ... *King of the Southern Diamond* touches all the bases.

One

STOP THAT TRAIN

*It has been long known that he has a particular fancy
for causing strenuous batsmen to assault the atmosphere
in vain efforts to connect with his goods.*
~ *Macon News,* April 8, 1905

C ATCH THAT TRAIN BOYS, CATCH THAT DAMN TRAIN,"
Coach Stocksdale screamed at his team.

He watched in horror as the Southern 317 chugged down the
tracks from Atlanta Union Station towards Macon without his
Trinity team aboard. Within a minute of the train from Durham
coming to a halt, the entire Trinity ball club, fully dressed out
in their baseball uniforms and spikes, sprang out of the car and
sprinted in hot pursuit to stop the train, their only means to get to
Mercer that day.

Bradsher, Flowers, and Wren led the way in what looked like
a 220-yard dash. They hollered along the way, waved their arms,
and shouted at the top of their lungs, "Stop that train. Stop that
train!" The three most athletic players on the baseball team yelled
at each other to move quickly to catch the train. "Faster, Brad,
faster," Flowers shouted out.

The rest of the Trinity ball club charged down the middle
of the tracks, fifty yards behind Bradsher and his sidekicks, also
screamed. There was no sign the conductor had seen or heard any
of the desperate players.

Otis Stocksdale, the assistant managers, and scorekeepers yelled, "Stop! stop!" They were all flapping their arms. He and Inez Duke blew their managers' whistles with every ounce of breath they had in their lungs. It did not look like the train was going to stop, and the early part of the season would begin with a disastrous start. A failure to catch this train, scheduled to arrive in Macon at 3:45, would result in a forfeit of their first game of the Southern tour.

Seven of the players had run out from under their ball caps. The managers halted to pick them up and then to continue the desperate chase to catch the train. Scorekeeper Huckabee tripped awkwardly on the track as his papers flew from his clipboard, sailing across the ground and swirling into the air.

Gravel churned under their feet as the players gasped for breath. They'd frantically chased the train for a half mile when suddenly, the 317 let out a loud screeching noise.

The conductor slammed on the brakes when he finally saw the Trinity team in mad pursuit chasing down the rail line. Sparks started flying from under and around the front wheels of the train. The intense squealing and screeching noise of metal on metal, unbearable for most people, was a sweet sound to the winded baseball team.

The train finally came to a halt and blew thick smoke through its chimney. It made a long belching sound and emitted a thick smoke cloud. As the team caught up with the train, the players sucked the throat-drying diesel smoke into their lungs. The conductor sounded the horn, and the train continued to hiss as the doors to the passenger car slid open.

The boarding platform dropped, and the Trinity players climbed aboard. Their metal cleats made clickety-clack sounds against the steel stairs. The steward greeted the Trinity contingency with a big smile. "Jump aboard, boys. I understand you've got a game to play. We should be in Macon in two hours." The team and coaches all found seats as the train started to move again.

Chugalug, chugalug, wailed the train. The conductor gave a double pull on the train's whistle as they headed to Macon.

Woo-woo! Woo-woo! It was two o'clock. The heralded southpaw and the Trinity team would be facing its first big challenge of the Southern tour in two hours if they made it in time.

John Heisman named Arthur Bradsher the "King of the Southern Diamond" after he pitched twenty-five consecutive no-hit innings in the first three games of the 1904 season.

He led Trinity to the Southern Intercollegiate Athletic Association's championship by winning thirteen of fourteen games and walking only four batters the entire season. He and the Trinity team had their sights on winning back to back championships.

After ten minutes of heading down the tracks, backup pitcher Webb looked over at Bradsher with a sheepish grin on his face, "How're you feeling, Captain?"

"Never felt better," the Trinity hurler replied.

Webb broke out in a huge rip-roaring laugh.

Bradsher shot back, "What's so funny?"

"Well, I hope you got your best stuff of all time, cap, because we left all our bats and balls on the train in Atlanta." That brought out nervous laughter from the entire Trinity team.

～

The "KING OF THE SOUTHERN DIAMOND" was about to put all his cards on the table. In the next eight days, he would be touting his talents against four of the finest teams in the South. Reporters swarmed to those games like ants on a sticky sucker on a sizzling summer sidewalk.

Baseball was the king of sports in the early 1900s. It was the national pastime and the love of the American sports fan. Standing six feet tall, the Trinity star had a contagious smile and was a straight-A student with movie-star good looks and cum laude intelligence. The college baseball fans at the turn of the century wanted a baseball idol, and they had one in Arthur Brown Bradsher.

While most of the Trinity team engaged in poker on the ride to Macon, Bradsher and his first-year catcher, Wren, huddled up on a corner seat. "I feel good about playing Mercer today," the

Trinity ace said. "I've earned my confidence from my performance two years ago against the Mercer team on this very field. That was my only relief appearance in my career."

~

WEBB PITCHED A GOOD GAME against Mercer that day. Unfortunately, he ran out of gas in the seventh. Mercer exploded for four runs without him getting an out, tying the score at four apiece.

Chadwick signaled to Coach Stocksdale to come to the mound. As the three huddled, he said, "Coach, it's time to get Webb out of the game. They are hitting him like he's throwing grapefruits to the plate."

Stocksdale turned to centerfield and screamed, "Bradsher! Get in here!"

This would be the only game he was ever used as a reliever in his five years with Trinity. His unmatched pitching performance still had the Mercer fans talking two years later. Bradsher came in and pitched six perfect innings, not allowing a single hit or base runner. He struck out twelve of the eighteen batters he faced and sent them cussing and kicking the dirt on the way back to the bench.

~

HE TOLD WREN, "I have already faced four of their players from the 1903 team. Today the fans are going to witness something that they may never see again."

Wren and Bradsher spent forty-five minutes going through the Mercer batting lineup from the leadoff batter all the way to the nine-spot in the order. They discussed the bunters, the curveballs hitters, the fastball hitters, and the bad-ball hitters. They decided who to pitch high and tight, and who to drop the ball off the table down below the knees.

He and his all-star catcher Chadwick had done this ritual thirty times over the 1902-1904 seasons, losing only three games. It was now time for his rookie batterymate Wren to get involved in going over scouting reports before each game.

Coach Stocksdale addressed his team, "Men, I want you to stand up and stretch, for we'll have no warm-up time when we hit the field running at Mercer. We'll be pulling into the train station in twenty-five minutes. Captain Bradsher, before we loosen up, would you please lead us in prayer?"

"Gentlemen," he began, "I'm proud to be a part of this fine baseball team. Let's go out today and win and play in a manner that would make our school and fans proud.

"Fellows, please take off your caps and let's pray." His voice was filled with emotion. He reached out to his teammates. They all joined hands and bowed their heads. The team leader cleared his throat.

"Dear Heavenly Father, we're grateful for all the blessings you have bestowed upon us, and for this opportunity to represent Trinity. We thank you for the unity and friendship on this team. Lord, lead us to play up to our capabilities and display good sportsmanship. In Jesus's name, we pray. Amen."

After Bradsher's prayer, Stocksdale sat down in private and gave his own prayer to the Lord. He reflected on the day. His team had been delayed outside of Greenville with a damaged track resulting from a flash flood the night before.

The Trinity coach was a wreck. He walked back and forth in front of the repair crew with a nasty scowl on his face. *We can't afford to forfeit and lose the first game on the Southern tour if we expect to repeat as champions,* he thought. He barked at the workers! "Come on, fellows, let's pick up the pace. We've got a game to play in Macon at four!" After six hours the repair to the track was completed and there was a ray of sunshine that they might make it to Macon. But would it be in time?

Stocksdale spoke the words in almost a whisper, "Thank you, God, for getting my team this far. I apologize to you, Father, for doubting that you would get us here after my prayers earlier today."

Bradsher sat alone and was bent over in his seat with his head cradled in his hands. It felt strange to be traveling to one of the most important games of the year without his all-stars Chadwick and Wooten, who had not returned to Trinity for their senior year. *Quit feeling sorry for yourself, Bradsher! You can rise above this,* he thought.

~

The SOUTHERN 317 ARRIVED in Macon ten minutes from the scheduled start of the game. As the train did a gentle crawl into the station, the players pounced out like wild cats. They sprinted frantically the two blocks to the field. The clock was ticking.

Would they make it to the field on time or forfeit the most important game of the season and lose a chance to win the SIAA championship for the second year in a row?

Two

THE MIRACLE
AT MERCER

*I have been in the business for a long time, but I've never seen
anything like it before. It was a remarkable game.*
~ Coach Billy Smith, Mercer University

W HERE THE HECK ARE THEY?" COACH BILLY SMITH ASKED.
The Mercer players arrived at Central City Park
at two-thirty on game day and were puzzled why the Trinity team
was nowhere to be seen. Mercer had granted the North Carolina
club warm-up time for batting and fielding practice from one-thirty
to three o'clock.

When the Mercer ball club arrived, the field was vacant.
The staff, players, and coaches had not received word about the
Durham boys' six-hour delay on the tracks outside of Greenville.
They had boarded the train at two in Atlanta and were still
heading down the rail line to Macon.

Ten minutes before game time, Trinity arrived in Macon, and
the players hurried off the train, sprinting to the baseball field.
They looked like wild horses as they galloped to the diamond.
Coach Stocksdale screamed to his team, "Go, boys, go!"

Umpire Stinson directed his comments to Stocksdale, "Coach,
you have five minutes to get your team ready to play, or you will
be faced with forfeiture."

Stocksdale shouted to Mercer coach Smith, "We need to talk! We have an emergency! We have no equipment! In a panic to catch the train, we left all our bats and balls and catcher's gear on the train in Atlanta."

"Holy shit," Smith responded, "You boys have had quite a day." He walked away and then came back.

"Fine, you can share our equipment," Smith said. "Here are three bats and some balls to use for the game. Both teams can use our catcher's equipment. A broken bat will cost you two dollars."

The umpire soon yelled, "Play ball!" The Southern tour was finally underway.

Arthur Bradsher had become a folk hero in the South, and trains full of avid fans followed to watch him perform. One-hundred-and-fifty Trinity fans took the train to the Mercer game and then would take it to Atlanta for the Tech game. They would party for a few days in the big city and then return to Durham. It was spring break and they were looking for some fun.

The fans had brought their K-cards to hold up every time Bradsher struck out an opposing batter. Seven-hundred fans were sitting on the edge of their seats ready for one of the most anticipated games of the year.

The first three innings Bradsher was as sharp as he had ever been. He sent a message to Mercer by striking out the side in the first inning.

In the second inning, the clean-up hitter, Popper, reached first on an error by Smith, the shortstop for Trinity. On the next pitch, he stole second base. Bradsher took several deep breaths.

This is getting serious quickly. It's time for a visit from my nasty curveball, Uncle Charles.

Six out of the next eight pitches he delivered were nasty benders. The next two batters, Smith and Mundy, swung helplessly on the way to Bradsher's fifth and sixth strikeouts. The next batter, Dwyer, grounded out weakly on a comebacker to the mound.

In the third inning, he struck out the side again and had the fans' attention by striking out eight out of the nine batters he'd faced in the first three innings, without allowing a single hit or walk. Eight excited Trinity fans waived their K-cards in the air.

By the fifth inning, the game had become a little bit like a carnival. The fans realized they were witnessing the finest game ever pitched in the history of college baseball.

The Trinity Twirler was in perfect control, and inning after inning, he mowed down the Mercer team without walking a single batter. The crowd broke into cheers repeatedly. They were ringing cowbells, blowing whistles, and stomping the wooden bleachers.

Some fans were betting whether the North Carolina wonder would strike out the side in upcoming innings. One overweight Mercer fan stomped so hard that he snapped the bleacher board in half and fell through the stands, hitting the ground. The Trinity fans howled.

By the sixth inning, the no-hitter fever had taken hold of the spectators who had now become delirious. Bradsher had won the Mercer fans over. They gave him a standing ovation when he came up to bat. The "strikeout girls" held up their K-cards every time the Trinity ace whiffed a Mercer batter. By the end of the sixth inning, there were twelve fans sitting in a single row holding up the K-cards.

In the eighth inning, Bradsher faced the middle of the order, Smith, Mundy, and Dwyer. He stepped off the mound and took a deep breath. *Don't let up and make every pitch as perfect as possible.*

The Trinity Twirler achieved something in the eighth frame which was very rare to accomplish in baseball. He pitched "the immaculate inning." He threw the minimum of nine pitches, all being strikes, and struck out the three batters he faced.

The ninth inning offered a deserved ray of sunshine for Bradsher and the Trinity blue team. With one out, Trinity's Armfield reached first on a Mercer error. Kendrick bobbled the ground ball and then threw wide to first, which allowed Armfield to get to second base. He reached third base on a Webb weak ground-out and was stranded at third as Wren hit a comebacker to the pitcher Gates.

Shadows were everywhere as darkness was creeping into

Central City Park. Umpire Stinson yelled to both teams, "We'll play one more!" In the top of the tenth inning, Gates retired Trinity's first, second, and third batters. Trinity's weak hitting would haunt them today and for the rest of the season.

The bottom of the tenth truly showed Bradsher's resilience and character. He had already thrown 170 pitches. His heavy wool uniform was soaked in sweat, but he still had plenty of wind in his sails. Coming up to bat to face Bradsher in the bottom of the tenth inning was the heart of the Mercer batting order: McCathern, Crawford, and Popper.

Bradsher smiled, *this is the "murderers' row" in the lineup. Don't get careless here.*

The first batter to face Bradsher in the tenth was McCathern. He was a hitter that if you left the ball out over the plate, he loved to burn you to the opposite field. He was also known to crowd the plate. There was tension and concern on the fans' faces. They had squinted faces and clenched fists. Could Bradsher continue with his magic and close out Mercer with his no-hitter intact?

It's time to back him up off the plate a little bit with a high inside fastball and show him who's boss. I am going to give him some chin music.

The pitch climbed the ladder to right under his jaw. He bailed out and ended up on his rear end in the red brick dust around home plate. The small contingency of the Mercer fans booed loudly. He came right back with a called strike fastball on the inside corner and a foul ball for strike two. It was time to dispose of the pesky Mercer hitter.

The Trinity ace delivered a twelve-six drop ball that broke so severely that McCathern missed it by a foot and a half.

A cute brunette with the pigtails waived her K-card in delight of the strikeout and displayed it proudly along with the nineteen held by those sitting next to her.

Crawford, the hard-working little catcher, had failed to do anything with his bat so far in the game. Bradsher knew all too well that he could be a troublesome hitter.

You're not going to spoil my day, buster! Get ready for my best!

He started him off with two swing-and-a miss curveballs and then wasted one six inches outside of the strike zone, down at the knees. Bradsher's next pitch was a beauty: a rising two-seamer heater on the letters that Crawford couldn't catch up with. The umpire threw his right fist forward and screamed, "Strike three!"

Both sides of the stands were screaming, "Bradsher, Bradsher, Bradsher," in support and respect for the North Carolina star pitcher.

Crawford slammed his bat to the ground and returned to the bench cussing all the way. A girl in a pink sweater raised her K-card for the Trinity phenom's twenty-first strikeout of the day. The fans screamed and hollered with joy.

One more strikeout and let's go get a steak, Bradsher thought.

Popper was their clean-up power hitter. He loved high balls. Problem was he couldn't hit them, and he couldn't lay off them.

He started him off with a letter-high inside fastball which Popper swung at in vain. He followed with a high outside smoking fastball. Again, Popper missed it by a foot. The Mercer hitter slammed his bat to the ground.

Common sense would tell me to throw him another high fastball.

The Trinity strikeout king took a deep breath and sent the nastiest drop ball he had thrown all day. It so fooled Popper that he never swung at it. The umpire yelled, "Strike three. You're out!"

Popper turned to the ump and said, "How is anybody in the world supposed to hit that shit?" He walked off kicking the dirt in disgust.

The umpire screamed out, "Ballgame!" The game ended with neither team scoring a run. The exhausted ump called the game because of darkness. It would become known as the "Miracle at Mercer."

Bradsher walked over to the Mercer bench and congratulated Big Gates, the Mercer hurler, and shook Coach Smith's hand. "Great game, coach! I enjoyed playing against your men these last three years."

"We did too, Brad. Your sensational pitching challenged us to raise the level of our play. Good luck to you the rest of the way."

As he walked towards the hotel, he overheard Smith tell a reporter, "I've been in the business a long time, but I've never seen anything like it before. It was a remarkable game."

Out of the shadows and the darkness emerged an immense figure at around six feet, three inches, and weighing two-hundred-and-thirty pounds. He stepped in front of Arthur Bradsher and extended his right hand.

"Great game, kid," Cy Young said. "Son, that's the finest game I've ever seen pitched, except for the perfect game I threw against New York last May. You were exceptional today. I was sitting up there on the hill and I watched your every pitch. I wanted to remove myself from being close to the field, so as not to be a distraction."

Young continued, "Let me know if I can offer you any future advice concerning the lifestyle in the major leagues. You can contact me at any time in Boston. I'll give your coach the best way to reach me. You should expect some calls from the owners soon. I believe you could start right out of the gates next year."

"I thank you, Mr. Young," Bradsher responded. "Good luck to you and the Boston ball club this season."

He turned to cross the street to head to the Lanier House Hotel for a needed meal and shower. As he caught up with his team, he said, "Let's get to the hotel fellows. We need to get some rest before the second game with Mercer tomorrow. And then, it's on to Atlanta to whip those Tech boys and John Heisman."

The 1905 Southern Tour was now in full swing and it would produce some of the finest baseball games and heroics ever seen in the South.

MIRACLE AT MERCER

ARTHUR BRADSHER PITCHES A 10 INNING NO-HITTER
STRIKES OUT 22 MERCER BATTERS
MISSES PERFECT GAME BY ERROR IN SECOND.

A LONG TIE GAME AT MACON.

**Bradsher, of the Trinity Team, Struck
Out Twenty-Two Mercer Bat-
ters in Ten Innings.**

Macon, Ga., April 7.—(Special.)—Darkness brought to a close this afternoon
one of the prettiest games of the season,
when Mercer and Trinity battled for ten
innings without a single run being made.

Bradsher, of Trinity, the best-known
college twirler in the south, held Mercer
at his mercy, striking out twenty-two
of her best men during the progress of
the game.

Tomlinson, the Mercer twirler, was also
in great shape, and fine work of infielders and outfielders aiding the pitcher,
saved Mercer from a defeat.

Trinity will play in Macon again tomorrow afternoon. The Mercer boys are
highly enthused over their splendid showing against Bradsher's team, and hope
to win the last game.

~ Courtesy of *The Atlanta Constitution*
Atlanta, Georgia
April 11, 1905 - Page 10

Arthur Bradsher gives his two-year-old granddaughter,
Patti, a ride in the wheelbarrow at the farm, Summerlea.
~ Courtesy of the Bradsher Family.

Three

GRANDFATHER'S FARM ON THE NEUSE RIVER

Your family and love must be cultivated like a garden.
Time, effort, and imagination must be summoned
constantly to keep any relationship flourishing and growing.
~ Jim Rohn

S IXTY-SEVEN YEARS AFTER THEIR GRANDFATHER'S DEATH, A
brother and sister stood at the edge of the bluff looking
down at the magnificent Neuse River. There is no brilliant sunrise
or sunset at this moment to show off its beauty like a brand-new
dress on an attractive woman.

It had been raining, and the water was a dull grey. It looked
like God had taken his brushes after he painted the gloomy sky and
washed them in the river.

The year was 2017 and they had come to New Bern and
then would go to Morehead City for a family reunion to
relive childhood memories of their summers spent at the farm,
Summerlea. The two stood in silence, in awe, both reflecting on the
remembrances it served up to them, as the river slowly crept to the
ocean.

Brad spoke first. "Grandfather died when I was three
months old, but Liz, your stories about his farm and the family's
adventures on the river have brought this place alive to me. I can
picture the spear as it pierces the flounder's brain and taste the

saltiness of the river crabs. I feel the mussels under our toes that felt like stones as the family walked through the mushy silt while gigging for flounder and crabbing in the darkness of the night."

Liz responded, "Brad, I stand here looking into the mouth of the river, and I think of our grandparents, and the deep love they held in their hearts for each other. Mom would say to me, 'those two acted like love-birds whenever they were together.' They always displayed a warm affection for each other when we were around them during the summers of our childhood."

She continued, "I think of Grandfather asking our little five-year-old sister, Dottie, 'Well, young lady, what do you plan to accomplish today?' Always with a gentle voice. He was never intimidating."

Brad, the ballplayer in the family, said, "I imagine him throwing the ball to Kirk and the others. It brings me back to his great baseball days, and the stories when he was playing for Trinity. He was a folk hero in the South. My goodness, Liz, when he finished his career at Trinity in 1905, they hung his portrait in the library between those of Abraham Lincoln and Washington Duke.

"In the following thirty years that I played ball after his death, when I heard a crack of the bat that echoed across the playing field, I knew it wasn't Grandfather pitching that day.

"Liz, he was a loving father and husband, a tobacco executive, a devout Christian leader, a gentleman farmer, and perhaps the greatest pitcher of his era in college baseball. I think his story is one that should be told.

"Let's walk the property and you can describe some of your experiences," Brad said. "What first defined Grandfather to you?"

"Walk down the stairs to the river with me and I'll tell you a story about him. I was eleven years old, and Mom was pregnant with you."

They walked down the old wooden steps and continued to the path to the river. It was blocked by an overgrowth of sawgrass. "This's where it happened." Her face displayed fear. Liz pointed her finger and said, "It's a morning none of us would ever forget," she said in a mysterious voice. "Let me take you back sixty-eight years to that day."

Liz recounted the happenings of that morning. "Ten of the grandchildren were huddled around him. A box had been delivered by the postman. Grandfather opened it with his fishing knife that had a handsome bone handle. The finely sharpened blade cut through the package like it was soft butter. He pulled out thirteen blue Duke baseball caps, with a white-scripted D on them."

"Now my lineup is going to look like a ball club," he said proudly. "I also take comfort that you're playing for the right team," he said, smiling at his grandchildren.

"Let's enjoy a fine breakfast prepared by Aunti Pearl, and afterward, go down to the river to fish and swim."

The housekeeper carried out platters filled with scrambled eggs, bacon, homemade biscuits, grits, vine-ripened sliced tomatoes, and milk from the farm's only cow, Bessie.

"It sure looks good," Dottie said as she hugged Aunti Pearl's leg.

"Let's be seated children, Teddy will lead us in prayer," he said. The whole family and Aunti Pearl reached out to hold hands.

"Our Father ... We thank you for this wonderful family and all the blessings you've bestowed upon us. We're so grateful for this fine meal our Lord has provided, and the farm that you created for us to enjoy. I thank you for our grandparents and our parents, and for Bessie the cow, all our chickens, and our dog, Dusty. In Jesus' name, we pray, Amen."

As they ate the hearty Southern meal, the grandfather gave out instructions for the morning. "Kids get the fishing poles and the tackle box. Kirk, bring down the fly rod and let's spend a few minutes to practice our casting. Get your swimsuits on and bring a couple of towels.

Entrance sign for the Farm/River
house Summerlea.
~ Courtesy of Kirk Voorhees

Children having fun on the Neuse River
~ Courtesy of the Bradsher Family

"Liz and Kirk, I want you to be responsible for everyone's safety going down the steep stairs. When you get to the path, everyone needs to stop! Don't go on it without me!" he instructed. "I'll come down to join you shortly."

"Yes, sir," the two older grandchildren responded in unison.

A few minutes later, all the children were filing out of the house and heading to the stairs at the edge of the bluff.

Arthur walked over to Lizzie and gave her a warm kiss and said, "I love you, my dearest."

"I love you with all my heart, Arthur," she replied with sparkling eyes.

He then walked to the highest cabinet in the kitchen and unlocked it with a small key. He reached for his baseball glove and told Lizzie, "We'll be back at lunchtime."

When the family patriarch reached the bottom of the stairs, he saw that Liz had all the children lined up in single file to go down the path to the river. He was holding his baseball glove folded shut in his right hand. He parted the dense sawgrass and entered, disappearing. Fifteen seconds passed without a sound, and then it happened!

~

Bam! THE SOUND ECHOED ACROSS THE WATER and up to the river house. Some of the children screamed in horror. The others laughed hysterically because they thought Grandfather had set off a firecracker. He reappeared with a smoking gun and said to Kirk, "Hand me the gigging spear, please, son." He went back in and came out again with two rattlesnakes at the end of the spear. Their two heads were blown to smithereens.

The snakes had been coiled up tightly on the path. He had shot two snakes with one bullet. He cut off the rattlers with his pocketknife and handed them to Liz.

~

"That's WHAT FIRST DEFINED my grandfather to me," Liz said with a chuckle. "I felt he was a superhero that could do anything, and, being with him, we'd always be safe."

The two siblings returned up the stairs to the farm. They walked over to a standing chimney. "It's the only thing that remained from the fire in the river house in 1950," Liz offered with a saddened look. "Grandfather carried Grandmother through the smoke and the flames through the front door. He was gasping for air and collapsed in the yard. The fire burned and smoldered for a day and a half, and they never found her wedding ring."

They spent another hour walking the property, and Liz pointed out many things about the farm that her brother had never experienced. They walked past the driveway which brought them into the hundred-acre farm.

"This is where our brother learned to drive. Freddie was thirteen and could barely see over the wheel. Dottie and I sat in the backseat, laughing as he struggled to keep the car on the mile-long driveway. Each bump Freddie hit while driving down the dirt road unsettled him. It took him a while to get used to the brakes," Liz said with a chuckle.

"Grandfather's dog was chasing us the whole way. We're yelling out the backseat windows, 'Come on, Dusty, come on! Good boy, Dusty, good boy!'"

"You're a great storyteller, Liz. It's like watching a movie of your memories coming alive."

"This is the exact spot where his tomato garden was," she explained. "He taught us how to plant, starting from a rough plot of land and working and improving the soil until it was ready to plant. For the tomato garden, the process included tilling the soil, adding chicken manure, homemade peat moss, a small amount of lime, and potash from the firepit. He would plant each tomato plant midway up, burying half the branches to promote stronger root growth.

"I'll never forget my grandfather picking a deep red tomato from the vine and cutting a slice with his pocketknife and handing it to me."

Her grandfather told her, "Bite into it, Liz, and tell me what you taste."

"I taste a beautiful and refreshing sweetness," she answered.

Liz continued with her memories of the garden, "In front of the two rows of tomatoes, we planted cucumbers, potatoes, and beans. Some of those cucumbers were used to make bread-and-butter pickles by Aunti Pearl." Liz laughed. "The cucumbers were so fresh they were great to eat with just salt and pepper. Once I ate so many that way, I got a stomach ache.

"Brad, our dad never had a garden growing up in Boston. Grandfather taught him how to plant potatoes from cuttings in a sandy loamy soil. When it came time to harvest the potatoes, we would stick our arm down into the soil at about the depth of your elbow, wiggle our fingers until you felt purple new-potato treasures."

Liz pointed in the distance and said, "That's where the cornfield was located. The back house over there was where the kids all played cards, and over here was where we threw horseshoes. We sure had fun at the farm. We were kids of the outdoors.

"The boys loved to play home run derby with a wooden bat and baseball. They pretended to be the greats of all time: Joe DiMaggio, Lou Gehrig, Ted Williams, Jimmie Fox, Willie Mays, and others. If you hit the ball into the four rows of the cornfield, you were awarded a round-tripper, and you could take that joyous trip around the bases lauding your greatness all the way."

"Wow, I wish I had been born ten years earlier, so I could've played," Brad said.

Liz continued, "Uncle Arthur was thirty-five and he loved to join in. He had played football at Duke and had a stocky build with a bit of a gut. He joyfully called himself the sultan of swat. He resembled the Babe.

"Before the first pitch was thrown to him, he would shout out, 'Now batting, the great Bambino, the one and only Babe Ruth.' He hit many balls into the cornfield and over it. Each time he yelled, 'Back, back, back. ... This one's long ... gone!' I will never forget Grandfather's smile as he watched his son gleefully tromp around the bases.

"Those were some fond memories. Let's head to Morehead City for the reunion. There are a lot of delightful stories to be shared about our grandparents."

Brad's Jeep Grand Cherokee started down the long and straight driveway but came to a sudden stop. The brother and sister exited the car and stood side by side. The two reached out for each other and held hands. They took their last look of the farm with tears in their eyes.

That would be their last visit ever to their grandfather's farm.

Four

THE REUNION

Every parting is a form of death,
as every reunion is a type of heaven.
~ Tryon Edwards

T HEY PULLED OUT OF THE FARM ONTO THE TWO-LANE
highway to the beach to spend the weekend with the
Bradsher family. "Liz said we will be at Morehead in an hour. Tell
me more about your research on grandfather."

The eight-foot bonfire blazed on the beach. It towered over the
twenty descendants of Arthur Brown Bradsher. The waves from
the Atlantic Ocean pounded the sand. A half-dozen tanned great-
grandchildren were surfcasting in the waters off Morehead City.
The grandchildren had been called together for a family reunion to
celebrate their grandfather.

Brad stood, popped open a Coke can, took a long sip, and
addressed his eleven first cousins. "Family, I want to go down two
roads in our conversations about Grandfather. Going down one, I
want to tell the story of some of his exceptional accomplishments
on the baseball diamond for Trinity. It is an untold story. Duke said
there were no records for two years that he pitched for Trinity. I
spent three years researching this project and dug up over three-
hundred newspaper articles about him. I uncovered an article on

every one of the fifty-eight games he pitched in his five years at Trinity.

"He pitched in seven no-hit contests, five of which were complete games. This is a record that has never been matched in the history of college baseball. He also pitched three one-hitters and three two-hitters. Another example of his power on the mound is the fact in the year 1904 in one-hundred-and-twenty-nine innings, he walked only four batters for the entire season. He finished his career with five-hundred-and-eighty-two recorded strikeouts, twenty under the all-time NCAA record. In fifty-eight games he started, he pitched fifty-seven complete games, and he always was a gentleman on the playing field."

"That is some incredible stuff. Fantastic job, cousin," Chad added.

Brad pulled a file card out of his pocket and said, "I want to read something about Grandfather that I discovered from the *Raleigh Morning Post*. 'On the walls of the reading room of the Trinity library hang the portraits of Washington Duke; Col. A.C. Alspaugh of Winston, another of Trinity's benefactors; Isaac Erwin Avery the late gifted journalist who was a Trinity man; Arthur B. Bradsher, called the greatest college baseball pitcher in the South, who for five years pitched for the Trinity team; and Abraham Lincoln, given to the college by his son, Robert Lincoln.'"

ABB 111 chuckled and exclaimed, "He sure did keep good company." The rest of the family laughed with him.

Brad continued. "In 1943, Wilbur Wade Card, Bradsher's good friend and his athletic director, was presented a portrait of himself painted by a former Trinity student, Paul Whitener of Hickory. Card presented it to the university, stipulating that it be hung in the gymnasium flanked by the portraits of Arthur Bradsher and Bob Gantt, two of his favorite players that pitched a combined eight no-hitters.

"Bradsher and Card died two years apart and their burial plots are only fifty feet apart in the Durham Maplewood Cemetery."

David asked, "Have you heard from Duke whether he is going to be put on the ballot for the Hall of Fame?"

"I've great news!" Brad exclaimed. "Duke University has selected him for the ballot one-hundred-and-fifteen years after he had played for Trinity. The university has recognized twenty-one of his pitching records, and they are now published in the Duke Baseball Media Guide."

"This is incredible!" Janey shouted.

"I'm writing an account about his life, entitled King of the Southern Diamond. Going down the second road, I am asking all of you to share stories about your memories of the six summers spent at Summerlea. After dinner please share your remembrances of him. Our family needs to pull together to make this happen. For us to be successful, it's all about teamwork."

"Let's eat!" Chad shouted as he poured the contents of his ten-quart pot on the long wooden table covered with a plastic tablecloth. Steamer clams, mussels, lobsters, corn, shrimp, sausage, and red potatoes rolled out of the clambake pot onto the table with the aromatic smell of butter, lemon halves, and fresh herbs.

~

BRAD SAT DOWN to eat his seafood dinner with his favorite cousin. "It's good to see you, Cuz." The two were born from their Arthur Bradsher's first and last-born daughters, Mary and Millie, on the same day, four hours apart. Fifteen years separated the two sisters, but despite the difference in age, they had been close and best friends.

Bradsher taught both of his daughters to fish in the Neuse River. They were brought up to be very strong women. They learned how to finesse a fly rod and a spinning reel and passed down those fishing skills to their sons, David and Brad. The two cousins had fished together for eight summers in Morehead City. They surfcast at the edge of the ocean in the mornings, and then again from the piers in the early summer evenings. They caught pompano and bluefish ankle-deep in the surf. The two favorite cousins caught Spanish mackerel, sea bass, and striped bass off the piers as the sun went down in the evening.

~

DOTTIE ROSE TO OFFER a memory of the farm. "We went to the Summerlea during spring break in 1949. I was five years old. I will never forget the first time I saw the seeds he planted break through the soil, fourteen days after planting them. We left for Atlanta the next day, and on the long ride home I couldn't get the miracle of the garden off my mind. The birth of many seedlings, a colt, and dozens of baby chickens were unique to us. We witnessed all God's gifts on his hundred-acre farm."

Teddy, the oldest of the grandchildren, began, "One of the primary reasons he bought the farm after his retirement was to spend his last years with his family. During the five summers at the farm, he would teach each one of us something new every day. And in that newness, there would be an adventure for each of us. I'll never forget when he stopped the car when we were coming back from the country store. He got out and walked over to a willow tree and broke off a small branch. He proceeded to carve a whistle out of that branch and handed it to me. I still have that whistle in a small box with other special treasures.

"We gigged for flounder, crabbed in the river, explored the chicken coup for freshly laid eggs, and pickled cucumbers with Aunti Pearl. He taught us how to gently tug and squeeze his cow Bessie's teats to retrieve fresh milk. He loved that black-and-white marbled cow. Not a day passed that didn't find us fishing and swimming in the Neuse River. We even shot a few rattlesnakes."

Liz had the most vivid memories of her grandfather. "There was not a question or a fear running through our bodies that we didn't hesitate to ask our grandfather for the answer. He always reacted calmly. He was not just our patriarch; he was a friend we trusted."

Arthur Bradsher with granddaughter, Patti,
at the farm, and his youngest daughter Millie.
~ Courtesy of the Bradsher Family

Marien joined in, "Sleeping late on summer mornings wasn't in Grandfather's playbook. His morning hours with us was valuable time, and he wanted to enjoy every possible minute with his grandchildren."

Teddy spoke next, "His goal with us city kids was to teach us where the food on our tables came from. He wanted us to have an appreciation of how much work the farmers had to put forth to raise a crop and get it to us."

Marien smiled and spoke. "He set a high bar in what he expected from all of us, but he never pushed us in a crass way. He simply stated what he would like to see us accomplish on any given day. We seemed to always respond because of our love and total respect for him. We found out years later this was close to his relationship and how his players on his Trinity team responded to him. Throughout his life, he seemed to bring out the best of people."

Wow, Brad thought, *it is being revealed this night how much the grandchildren love and adore their grandfather.*

Susan shared, "He gave us valuable life lessons that could

never be taken away from us. Some of us used them as a blueprint for our lives and some others didn't."

"The garden was our meeting place," Artie began. "Even though I was only six years old in the summer of 1950, he left a definite impression on me. When we met to till and improve the soil, plant, and harvest, we would talk and ask each other many questions. There were twelve of us present that summer. When he asked one of us to help, he made us feel important and grown-up."

Kirk added, "Everything about him was based on teamwork. If you were truly doing your best and you stumbled, it made him smile. He felt sometimes the effort was much more important than the stumble. He treated his ballplayers on the Trinity team the same way.

"Every night, the dozen or so children could be heard delightfully squealing as they played kick the can, roll the bat, hide-and-go-seek, or dodgeball. He loved to challenge us in horseshoes. He was a real ringer. We were kids of the outdoors and roamed the farm in the evenings with mason jars in hand to catch the yellow-blinking lightning bugs."

Sandy added to the conversation, "We loved our card games. The girls loved to play canasta, and it wasn't unusual to have eight decks of cards laid out on the long wooden table in the backyard guesthouse at one time."

"Gosh, the food sure was good we had at the farm," Thor offered. "Our dinners were healthy and right out of the garden or the river. We ate a variety of fish and shellfish, including flounder, red striped bass, sea trout, soft-shelled crab, and occasional oysters. The corn he grew was the sweetest, and the green beans Aunti Pearl cooked with bacon were unforgettable."

Liz joined in, "One of my favorite thoughts of the farm was story times. After dinner, the family congregated on the screened porch overlooking the river. Grandfather had the best tales and Grandmother would sing her favorite hymns. She would request my older brother, Freddie, to play the piano when she sang. He was a very accomplished pianist and a perfect complement to her beautiful voice."

Dottie finished with a sad look. Her brother, Freddie, was deceased. "We gathered in our basket of experiences from the summers spent at Summerlea many things. His stories were not just about baseball and the good times. In fact, I don't ever remember him bragging about his extraordinary accomplishments on the field. Many of the things we heard on the porch those summers were invaluable lessons that would be passed down to our children."

Artie raised his wine glass and addressed his cousins, "I toast the love affair between our grandparents. One of my favorite remembrances of Grandfather was the story of when he returned to Petersburg after a week of business travel. As soon as the Southern 322 pulled into the terminal, he hopped off the train and told the porter, 'Watch my bags and I'll be back in an hour.'

Artie (4) and Grandfather at Summerlea
~ Courtesy of Art Gill

"He was so anxious to see his family that he took off running down the middle of Main Street in his three-piece suit and dress shoes to his home on South Sycamore. He would always find Lizzie and the children waiting for him on the benches on each side of the front porch."

Kirk cracked open a cold beer and offered an observation. "I never saw him sick or showing a foul temperament. Even after his first heart attack, which detained him in Cuba for three months, he returned to the States to attend Mom's wedding. They say he walked her down the aisle with a wide grin on his face, looking perfectly healthy. I will never forget when he climbed a forty-foot pine tree with his spikes on to hang a clothesline for Grandmother. They strung it from the second story of the river house to the tree with a pulley on it."

Sandy stood, stretched, and offered a memory. "Sleep came easy those summer nights in the big house. Grandfather built wooden screens for all the windows on the second level of the house. Every window was fully opened on the upstairs level waiting for a refreshing breeze to find its way to us from the waters of the Neuse. He built and repaired things every day. He was a Renaissance man.

"After prayers and good-night hugs, we all faded into a deep sleep. We were exhausted, very contented, and knew we were in the right place with our grandparents."

Brad clapped his hands and said. "Speaking of sleep. I think it's about time to call it a night."

"Uncle Brad, before we turn in can you please tell us about the famous Ga. Tech contest?" Chad asked. "I heard they called that game the "greatest game ever played in Dixieland."

"You are so right Chad. The battle against John Heisman and his fine ballclub was one of the most notable games to ever to be played in college baseball. Let me tell all of you how the story unfolded. It all started with Heisman bragging in the newspapers he had a shocking surprise for Bradsher and the Trinity Blue.

Brad threw a maple log on the fire and began to tell the last story of the night. "This baseball thriller occurred on a beautiful spring day in 1905 three days after the famous *Miracle at Mercer* contest."

Five

GREATEST GAME EVER PLAYED IN DIXIELAND

When you find your opponent's weak spot, hammer it.
~ John Heisman

TWO DAYS EARLIER, ARTHUR BRADSHER'S TWENTY-TWO strike-out, no-hitter caught the attention of every baseball fan in the country. His performance, referred to as the "Miracle at Mercer," was unprecedented in the history of college baseball.

The baseball game between Trinity College and Georgia Tech in April 1905 was being billed as, "The greatest game ever to be played in Dixieland." Reporters from the major newspapers had come to Atlanta from all over the South to cover this highly touted game. Two of the South's best teams prepared for an epic face-off.

Excited students walked from the Tech campus to the ballfield.

The fans came to Brisbane Park by different ways of transportation. Some rode the streetcar, others came on their horses and bicycles, and many arrived by horse-and-buggy.

The large oak and maple trees along North Avenue had greened up, and the leaves were magnificent, forming a dense canopy. The overhang of large limbs offered a comfortable, shady walk for the fans coming to the game.

They were full of enthusiasm and looks of fashion. North

Avenue was flooded with a sea of hats on the fans walking to attend the much-anticipated baseball game.

The women wore long and non-corseted flowing dresses. Their colorful outfits were trimmed with ribbons and lace. Most of them wore long sweeping hats and over-the-ankle boots.

Almost every man sported a hat, either a straw boater with a two-inch band or a newsboy cap. An occasional bowler hat could be spotted in the crowd.

Blazers were a primary fashion worn by the men. They were made from navy, brightly colored, or striped materials. They had patch pockets and brass buttons. The blazers were cut like sack coats. Many males coming to a casual ball game wore striped shirts and suspenders for more comfort. Most men wore vests.

The vendors were busy hawking refreshments to the crowd. The smell of freshly popped corn drifted through the stands. The loud sizzle from the grill beckoned the fans to come and get a cooked hot dog with a partially burned skin and a juicy inside.

Roasted peanuts were a big hit at baseball games. If you wanted an order, all you had to do is to yell out, "Peanuts!" After you passed your money down the row to the salesman, he would toss you a bag.

The favorite beverage was a Coca Cola, invented in Atlanta in 1896. In 1905, the company's advertising slogan was "the most refreshing drink in the world." It was the perfect beverage to wash down the peanuts, hot dogs and popcorn, and a great complement to your meal at the ballpark. Each sold for a nickel.

Word had spread from Macon to Atlanta about Bradsher's amazing no-hit performance two days earlier against Mercer. John Heisman, the increasingly famous coach at Georgia Tech, had promised he had a surprise in this game planned for Bradsher and the rest of his Trinity nine.

Before the season began, many of the experts felt that this might be the most important game played in the 1905 campaign. The winner of this contest would be the favorite bet to win the SIAA conference.

On game day, this looked to be true as Trinity came into

Atlanta with an eight-two record. Bradsher was pitching brilliantly as he entered the contest. In five games, he had struck out 11.4 batters per game and allowed just 2.8 hits per outing. The Trinity southpaw had given up only four earned runs in the first five games of the season.

The crowd was buzzing, and conversations were going back and forth about the excellent job Heisman was doing at Georgia Tech. The excitement was building for the fans who yearned to see the "King of the Southern Diamond" pitch.

As he took his warm-up throws prior to the start of the game, seventy-five spectators stood within ten feet of the Trinity Twirler, marveling at his perfect control and variety of pitches.

The number one question traveling through the stands on both sides was, *what is the shocking surprise John Heisman has for Bradsher and the Trinity baseball team?*

~

JOHN HEISMAN was euphoric in his second year at Georgia Tech, and it was looking like his baseball team was going to have one of the best years ever. Heisman had coached Clemson from 1900 to 1903. He had an outstanding baseball record of twenty wins and seven losses during his three years there.

Georgia Tech had lured Heisman away from Clemson to coach the Gold-and-White in football, baseball, basketball, and be Tech's athletic director. Most people in the know recognized that this was the most important game in his career as a baseball coach.

No one prepared more to go into battle with an opponent than Heisman. He had a great scouting advantage over every other coach in the South. *The Atlanta Constitution* had offered him a salary to write an article on every baseball team in the South prior to the season's start. Heisman knew every strength and shortcoming of each player. If there was a weakness, he would exploit it. He was being paid on both sides of the coin: one by Georgia Tech to coach and win, and by *The Atlanta Constitution* to report on every team.

~

TICKET PRICES had been raised to twenty-five cents for students and fifty cents for adults. It was the hottest ticket in town. About 700 stirred-up fans were expected to attend. Both clubs had announced their lineups, which included two of the best pitchers in the South.

Heisman named Bradsher the "King of the Southern Diamond" the previous year after he started off the season with twenty-five no-hit innings. The North Carolina wonder would bring the heat for Trinity. He had finished the 1904 season with a record of thirteen wins and one loss and led Trinity to the SIAA championship. He was selected as the player of the year.

Craig Day, coming off an impressive performance against Georgia would pitch for Tech. Both pitchers would be pitching on two days' rest.

There were blue skies in Atlanta, and it was a perfect day for baseball. At exactly four p.m., the umpire screamed, "Play ball!"

Little Tommy McMillan led off the inning. The feisty five-foot–three-inch all-star shortstop was a very tough target to throw to. He worked Bradsher for a walk after a dozen pitches.

Hamilton, the next batter, filed off the first three balls delivered by the southpaw as McMillan broke to second base on every pitch. John Heisman screamed through his megaphone, "Go! Go! Go!"

John Heisman with his megaphone.
~ Courtesy of Ga. Tech

Something is not right here, Bradsher thought, *no team attempts a steal on every pitch.*

McMillan did. He successfully stole second base on a ball in the dirt when Bradsher struck out Hamilton.

I need to give my struggling catcher an advantage. I'll put my next pitch a foot off the plate, so Wren can get a jump on the runner with his throw.

On the very next pitch, McMillan took off to steal third base, and Wren threw wildly over third-baseman Webb's outstretched glove. McMillan trotted home with the first run of the game. The bleachers were filled with moans and groans from the diehard Trinity fans.

The Tech fans were in a state of hysteria. They were stomping the stands and ringing their cowbells. Their loud cheers could be heard two blocks away. They outnumbered the Trinity fans by four to one.

It had become obvious to Bradsher and all the fans that Tech was going to steal on every pitch each time they got on base. John Heisman had found a crack in his opponent's armor. It was catcher Wren's lack of arm strength and his inaccuracy. He was incapable of throwing out the runners for Georgia Tech who were running on every delivery.

The quote by Heisman rang true on this day. "When you find your opponent's weak spot, hammer it." The reporter for the Atlanta newspaper wrote, "Seven stolen bases show the correctness of this criticism."

The two unearned runs and relentless base-stealing had brought chaos on the field. Bradsher remained calm as usual, but he was pitching in a three-ring circus.

In the third inning, Trinity evened the score. With two out, shortstop Smith laced a single in the hole between short and third. The next batter, Bradsher, strolled to the plate. The fans were screaming his name repeatedly. He looked confident and smiled.

He scalded the first ball from Day and sent a scorching double down the line, and Smith scored all the way from first base with Trinity's first run. The one-to-one score held up until Tech batted in the fifth inning.

Tech scored again in the fifth. center fielder Gager singled for Tech's second hit of the game. He advanced to second on a passed ball by Wren.

The Trinity lefty watched the Tech runner lead off second and thought, *I've got to get Gager off the base paths. It's time for the pickoff play. After I give the signal to my trusty shortstop and rest my glove on my chest, he will break for the bag on the three-count.*

He scratched his nose, positioned his glove, Smith broke, and the Trinity wizard turned and wheeled. After his throw was launched, he saw it was a perfect strike to second base.

We got him!

Gager slid under the tag and the umpire pounded the ground with his fist and screamed, "Safe!" The Trinity fans were irate and booed the call and screamed, "Home cooking."

Bradsher slapped his leg!

On the next pitch, the pesky base runner stole the bag at third. He scored on a passed ball by catcher Wren. Georgia Tech had scored their second run without hitting the ball past the pitcher's mound.

Bradsher smiled and thought, *help me, Lord.*

He closed out the sixth inning by striking out two more Tech batters and fielding a weak comebacker and throwing the runner out at first.

Trinity fought back and tied the game in the sixth inning. Bradsher led off the inning, receiving a free pass to first. He was one of the fastest men on the team and had great instincts on the base paths. On the second pitch by Day, he swiped second base.

Webb was up next, and he was overdue. Before stepping in the batter's box, he hitched up his pants, spit on his palms, and rubbed dirt on the bat handle. The fans screamed in delight. On the third pitch, Webb stroked a fastball for a single, scoring Bradsher to tie the score at two apiece.

The Trinity Blue were back in the game, and the small brigade of the Durham hopefuls were delirious. Bradsher and Day were locked into a battle like two strong gladiators.

A determined Arthur Bradsher
~ Courtesy of Duke University Library and Archives

Six

HEISMAN STEALS
THE GAME

*If anyone had told me before the game started that any college
pitcher could, in the space of one game, strike out sixteen
of my men, I would have called him a complete fool.*
~ John Heisman

BRADSHER MURDERED THE FIRST PITCH THROWN TO HIM BY
Day to lead off the twelfth inning. He smashed the ball
over first baseman Myrick's head. As soon as he bolted out of the
batter's box, he was thinking two bases. His sharp cleats dug into
the ground on every stride. As he rounded first at full speed and
digging for second base, clogs of red clay flew in the air behind
him.

The throw and the Trinity southpaw arrived at the same time.
He made a perfect hook slide avoiding the shortstop's tag. The
umpire following the play was right on top of the action, and
he waived his arms out and screamed, "Safe!" Bradsher, with
his second double of the game, had given Trinity an excellent
opportunity to win the game.

The two-bagger brought the Trinity fans to their feet. They
screamed, "Bradsher, Bradsher, Bradsher."

"That's a hell of a slide," McMillian said to Bradsher. He
extended his hand to pull him up from the ground. After he helped
him to his feet, he gave him a friendly slap on the back.

"Thanks, Tommy," he said with a smile, as he brushed off the dirt from his uniform.

The cleanup hitter, Armfield, followed Bradsher to bat. They desperately needed to move up the runner into scoring position to third base. The fans from Durham were stomping the bleachers unmercifully with their feet as Armfield walked to the plate.

Before stepping into the batter's box, he reached to the ground and grabbed a handful of brick dust. He opened his hand and spit a couple of ounces of tobacco juice on the red dust and proceeded to grind the spit and dirt onto the handle on his bat. He tugged at his crotch, wiped the nasty tobacco substance on his jersey, and stepped up to the plate.

This is a great time to surprise Tech and lay down a bunt to get me to third, Bradsher thought.

He raised his hand to get the umpire's attention. "Ump," he screamed, "I need a minute with my coach."

The umpire saw him signaling and walked out to speak with him. "Mr. Bradsher, what can I help you with?"

"I think I've pulled a muscle in my leg coming into the bag and I need to speak to Stocksdale," he said with a nasty scowl on his face.

"Make it quick. It's getting dark," the grumpy ump, Ely, responded.

The portly Stocksdale jogged out to his star hurler at second base. Before Stocksdale could say a word, the Trinity pitcher said in a stern voice, "Coach, let's surprise them. We need to bunt Armfield to get me to third. He is struggling getting his bat on the ball, and we need a run here. You get me this run and I will win the game for you."

"I'm going to let him swing away," he said, indifferent to Bradsher's suggestion. He turned to head back to the bench.

Holy crap, Bradsher thought.

He watched his manager waddle back to the bench.

He certainly wasn't bunting and swung vainly at the first pitch. It was painful to watch Day pitch to Armfield and toy with his ego.

It is a trick Bradsher used often against hitters who thought they could win the game with one big swing.

The Trinity team captain was running on the next pitch from Day. He slid under the tag at third base for his second stolen base of the game. "Safe!" the umpire screamed.

The umpire looked over at Bradsher with a puzzled look on his face and shook his head. The ump mumbled as he left the play at third, "Pulled muscle, you say, huh!"

The Trinity star was only ninety feet from putting Trinity in the lead. He was now looking for Armfield just to put the ball in play or for a wild pitch from Day.

There was no such luck to be had. Armfield took a violent swing, missing the final pitch for the first out in the inning. He slammed his bat to the ground on the walk of shame back to the bench. He was cussing, spitting, and talking to himself. "Damn, damn, damn!" he hollered.

Day was working hard to close out Trinity in the twelfth, getting the second out with a pop up in the infield by Webb. The Georgia Tech hurler got the final out on a weak comebacker from pitcher to first, retiring Wren.

Trinity's weak hitting team failed to produce when it was critical. After a lead-off double, they had failed to get the ball past the pitcher's mound for the rest of the inning.

The Trinity workhorse had thrown over 175 pitches, and his heavy wool uniform and baseball cap were soaked in sweat. As he walked to the mound, he recited the twenty-third Psalm. "Yea, though I walk through the valley of the shadow of death, I will fear no evil: for thou art with me: thy rod and thy staff they comfort me." It always assured him and gave him a feeling of trust and calmness during challenging times on the pitcher's mound.

The first batter to face him in the twelfth was Gager, who batted third in the lineup. After battling the Trinity hurler deep into in the count, he got his second hit of the game, the third hit of the day for Tech.

With Gager on first, Heisman stuck with his game plan to run off Wren. On the first pitch, he cleanly stole second base. Bradsher got the cleanup hitter and pitcher Day to line out to third base. Webb almost doubled off Gager, who was leaning towards third.

Bradsher desperately needed a strikeout now. He threw a rising fastball up the ladder on the first pitch that Daniels couldn't catch up with, and the umpire screamed, "Strike one!"

The Trinity sensation thought, *It is time for a visit from my trusty curveball, Uncle Charles.*

He reared back and delivered a sweeping curveball that caught the outside corner. The nasty pitch froze Daniels, and the umpire hollered, "Strike two!"

The next pitch jammed Daniels on the hands on the next pitch. The ball moved in on the bat handle and Daniels laid down a swinging bunt. Gager was breaking for home on the pitch and scored easily as Webb bobbled the ball.

The greatest game ever played in Dixieland was over!

He looked to the heavens to thank God for this day. He walked to shake hands with Coach Heisman, opposing pitcher Day, and the rest of the Tech team before he and his Trinity teammates boarded the train. Their next game on the Southern tour would be played against Clemson in two days.

The pitchers on both sides had done an excellent job bringing their teams to the twelfth inning. In comparing the two all-star pitcher's performances, Bradsher had clearly out-dueled and out-hit Day.

He pitched twelve innings, giving just three hits, and struck out sixteen Tech batsmen. He had successfully picked off two Tech runners in the game with his quick step and accurate left-handed move to first. He had two doubles and stole a couple of bases.

He walked four batsmen in the contest. It was rare that he would ever issue more than one base on balls in a ballgame. The Trinity hurler had only walked a total of four batters the entire previous season in 129 pitched innings.

Day pitched the twelve innings and allowed ten hits, walked one, and struck out six Trinity batters.

After the game, reporters ran in the direction of Bradsher. He walked with the Trinity team to the locker room and to Heisman and his Tech squad. Bradsher wanted to forego the press, but they were relentless. They screamed out questions for the *King of the Southern Diamond.*

"Tell me, how does it feel to lose this hard-fought game?" the reporter, Danny Davis, with the newsboy cap, asked.

"It's worse than having to kiss your sister." Bradsher wasn't smiling.

When pushed by the press for a comment about the outcome of the game, he answered, "I want to congratulate the Tech team for a great game and compliment Craig Day on his well-pitched performance.

"I would like to recognize Coach Heisman for a superb job in coaching his men." Bradsher closed by saying, "Tech is the fastest team we have faced." It was a comment to take the spotlight off him and take the blame off his catcher and battery mate, who had a tough day.

"Thank you, gentlemen." He turned to head to the locker room.

~

JOHN HEISMAN was surrounded by reporters from at least six states. It was a huge moment for him. He had made a genius coaching-decision on how to defeat the best college baseball player in the South. He complimented his team and pitcher Day for staying in the game until the very end.

"But I want to change course here and say something about Trinity's baseball team and their extraordinary pitcher, Bradsher. Somebody had to win this game and I won't go as far as to say the best team won today," the Tech coach said.

"Coach, is Bradsher pro material?" one of the reporters asked.

"If anyone had told me before the game started that any college pitcher could, in the space of one game, strike out sixteen of my men, I would have called him a fool, for I fancy that I can teach men how to bat if nothing else."

Heisman continued, "Yet this North Carolina wonder did the very thing I believed impossible and for this reason, knowing the batting strength of my own team, I must pay tribute to his skill. He's undoubtedly the most talented college twirler I've seen in my years of coaching in Dixie. I believe that he's more than ready for big league company and could hold his own with ease."

Arthur Bradsher knew nothing of Heisman's comments as they left Atlanta and would not hear them until three days later when they reached Durham. The players on his team and their success meant more to Bradsher than his own glory. They boarded the train to Anderson to play Clemson, which Heisman had coached the previous year.

~

BRADSHER SAT next to the team's scorekeeper, John Huckabee. "Are you okay, Brad? That was a tough one."

"Huck, it's like having your heart ripped out of your chest when you lose such an important game you came so close to winning. People don't realize how bad it hurts, but I've been raised to keep my calm and not show negative emotion."

"You'll win the next one, Brad."

The train chugged down the track to Anderson. Was another cliffhanger in the near future for Bradsher and the Trinity team?

Box score Trinity vs. Georgia Tech
~ Courtesy of *The Atlanta Constitution*
Atlanta, Georgia
April 11, 1905, P. 10

The official score follows:

TECH—	ab.	r.	h.	po.	a.	e.
McMillan, ss.	3	1	0	2	3	1
Hamilton, cf.	4	0	0	3	0	1
Gager, lf.	4	2	1	0	0	0
Day, p.	5	0	1	1	7	0
Daniels, 3b.	3	1	0	1	4	0
Brown, 2b.	3	0	0	3	6	0
Cannon, rf.	4	0	0	0	0	0
Myrick, 1b.	4	0	0	18	3	0
Hyde, c.	3	0	0	5	4	0
Totals	33	3	3	36	27	2
TRINITY—	ab.	r.	h.	po.	a.	e.
Justis, rf.	5	0	0	0	0	0
Smith, ss.	5	1	1	1	2	0
Bradsher, p.	4	1	2	2	6	0
Armfield, 1b.	4	0	1	9	1	0
Webb, 3b.	4	0	1	3	2	0
Wrenn, c.	5	0	1	18	0	1
Flowers, cf.	5	0	2	2	0	0
Berringer, lf.	5	0	1	1	0	0
Hutchinson, 2b.	5	0	1	0	0	0
Totals	42	2	10	*34	13	1

*One Tech man out when winning run was made.

Score by innings:
Tech . . . . 1 0 0 0 1 0 0 0 0 0 1—3
Trinity . . . 0 0 1 0 0 1 0 0 0 0 0—2

Summary: Two-base hits, Bradsher 2, Flowers; struck out, by Bradsher 16, by Day 6; bases on balls, off Bradsher 4, off Day 1; hit by pitcher, by Bradsher 1, by Day 1; double plays, Wrenn to Webb, McMillan to Brown; Stolen bases, Bradsher, McMillan, Gager 3, Day, Daniels, Hyde; passed balls, Wrenn 2, Hyde 1; time, 1:50; umpire, Ely; attendance 400.

Seven

NEVER, NEVER GIVE UP

You just can't beat the person who never gives up.
~ Babe Ruth

I T WAS THE SUMMER OF 1949 AND THE FAMILY HAD LISTENED TO Red Barber's account on the radio of the day's events in Major League Baseball. The date was July 13, and on that day Cincinnati Reds catcher Walker Cooper went six for seven, with three home runs, three singles, five runs scored, and ten RBI in a 23-4 win against the Cubs.

Arthur Bradsher took a sip of coffee and prepared to tell his family about some of the tough times he had experienced at Trinity College. He had never shared with his grandchildren any hardships he had suffered in his lifetime. This would be a new experience for both.

The sixty-six-year-old patriarch sat back in his chair with a solemn expression on his face. His granddaughter, Trinka, asked, "Is everything okay, Grandfather?"

"I'm fine, my dear child. I appreciate your asking."

He began by saying, "When I came to Trinity as a freshman, I knew two things. I would be a dedicated student and would bring straight A's home to my mother on my report cards. Secondly, I had a burning desire in my heart to play sports. I wanted to be a pitcher on the baseball team."

He continued, "Most people are shocked to learn I was never officially on the baseball team in high school. I had only pitched in one game prior to coming to Trinity. As it turns out, the high school pitcher was hurt, and they needed someone to pitch that afternoon.

"My friend, Chadwick, volunteered me and I pitched. I got slaughtered twelve to nothing by Bingham Park."

"How'd you make the Trinity team?" Kirk asked.

"Ever determined to play baseball, I tried out for the varsity team and even though I'd no experience as a pitcher, I worked very hard and made the team. I took the mound in ten out of the eleven games."

Bradsher said with a downturned expression on his face, "Boy, did I get kicked around that first season. It was a lonely, humiliating, and painful experience. Most people don't know my father died when I was four and I never had a big brother to coach or guide me along in sports.

"After hurling a shutout against Wake, I developed a sore arm. It took a toll on me. My arm stiffened up on me. I had thrown in three games and twenty-seven innings in eight days.

"Children, what I'll tell you next will show you that sometimes a bright and sunny day can change into a dark and dangerous storm without much notice," he said with concern in his voice.

The children edged closer to their beloved patriarch.

"What happened, Grandfather?" Patti asked. "We've only heard what a star hurler you always were at Trinity."

"Patti, I knew nothing about the mechanics and philosophy of pitching. Without the proper training, I was clueless against the batters." He frowned and continued, "Our next game was against Lehigh, and I asked the coach to sit me out. I couldn't even lift my arm, there was so much pain."

He grabbed his left arm and grimaced.

"Captain Anderson insisted I start, and I did so, allowing eight runs in three innings, before taking myself out after the third inning. I'd struck out only one batter."

"Did your arm heal?" Dottie asked.

"I had a six-day break before our next game and my arm felt better.

"The fifth game I pitched in 1901 was against Harvard. They called the Harvard Nine the greatest college baseball team of all time. They finished the season with a record of eighteen and two. Three of the players on that team ended up in the Harvard Varsity Club Hall of Fame.

"Pitching against Harvard, as an unlearned freshman pitcher, was like offering a young lamb into a lion's den. They got six hits and six runs in the first inning before I could retire the side. In nine innings, I threw 170 pitches. It was ugly. I cried in my room that night. I felt so ashamed, I wanted to quit the team."

1901 Trinity Team.
~ Courtesy of Duke University Library and Archives

The children could see the pain in their grandfather's face and edged closer to comfort him.

"I'd lost my third straight game against Wake Forest in a rain-soaked contest that probably should never have been played. I called it the 'flop in the slop.' I was ready to quit and needed to talk with someone," he continued. "I remember the long walk over to President Kilgo's office. Each step I took to his office was one of regret. 'I am not a quitter,' I told myself.

"During the walk to the chancellor's office, I felt I was betraying myself and my college."

"What happened next, Grandfather?" Liz asked

"I stood on the doorstep of the president's office. I was rain and tear-soaked."

Trinka suddenly stood up and walked over to her grandfather. "I'm sorry you were crying, Grandfather. I love you so much." She turned and returned to her spot on the floor with the other children.

"The president's door swung open and he extended his right hand to me."

He remembered the meeting in detail.

Kilgo declared, "Arthur, what has happened to you? You look terrible! Come in and let's get you dried off." He retrieved a towel from his office's private powder room. "How can I help you?"

"I appreciate your seeing me, sir. My original purpose in coming today was to discuss my quitting the baseball team. The long walk over here has given me time to clear my head and reshape my thinking. I've decided that I don't want to quit the team but improve it.

"I'm a Trinity man. I'll never quit on you," Bradsher said with earnest.

"Arthur, we appreciate you so much at Trinity College," the school president began. "Your competitive spirit, willingness to work hard and gentlemanly demeanor sets a fine example for all that watch you perform."

The two of them made an agreement to support each other with some positive changes.

"Son, you are making the right decision in sticking with the team," Kilgo said. "We will be making some improvements to the program next year. We will be hiring Otis Stocksdale to coach the team."

Bradsher told the children: "At season's end, I managed to escape with a respectable record of six wins against four defeats. That summer and fall I worked every day with my best friend,

Walter, on the mechanics of pitching."

Five-year-old Dottie asked, "What does the mechanics mean?"

Bradsher stood up. He had a baseball in his hand. He began to explain to his precious granddaughter. "It's how to grip a ball and how to properly deliver a pitch," he said. He leaned over and displayed the ball within six inches of her face. "See how my fingers are positioned on the various places of the horseshoe stitching of the ball?"

He had Dottie's and the other children's attention.

"How do you spin the ball?" Liz asked.

"Once I have the right grip on the ball, I set my wrist and come straight over the top like I do when I deliver my fastball." He did a mock wind up and brought his arm through like he just threw his famous drop ball.

When he finished, the children all screamed: "Strike!"

Grandfather continued, "Walter intended to be the starting catcher for Trinity the next season. He taught me the importance of being able to locate my pitches and how to throw a curveball in three separate ways. We worked hundreds of hours together.

"No one worked harder than I did those next ten months to perfect my control. I mastered locating the fastball on the corners and pinpoint control when delivering my curveballs. We spent hours talking about the philosophy of pitching.

"Great things happened after that," he said with a big smile. "I ended my sophomore season with a record of seven and two."

The children started applauding him, cheering, "Go, Grandfather, go!"

"Thank you, children," he said as he clapped back.

"I guess the lesson learned that day was a blow to my pride, shouldn't be deeded a severe injury. Do not let your ego and some bumps along your journey in life send you home. Also, children, sometimes we do not know what we don't know," he said with a chuckle. "Stick around until you know more of the facts, and push and play through hard times."

He smiled at the children and looked over and winked at his wife. Little Bradsher was sound asleep. He stood and said to the children, "Let's get some sleep. We've got fish to catch in the morning. Get your pajamas on, and I'll be up for good night prayers in a couple of minutes."

~

AN HOUR LATER, his wife heard his footsteps coming down the central staircase of their beautiful river house. As she listened to him walk through the living room, she seemed to notice a slower pace in his gait. She heard a chair move in the hallway and her husband sit for a couple of minutes. She was worried about his heart condition.

He entered their bedroom with a pleasant smile on his face. He looked deeply into her eyes and spoke softly, "My dearest, we're so blessed to have had such fine children and grandchildren. By talking, listening to each other, and respecting each other, we have made incredible decisions together. Our right choices have led to a joyous and successful life."

"I thank God every day for the blessings you've brought to this family," she said and reached for his hand.

"My love, I know I don't tell you enough, but I feel lucky to have you as my wife, my friend, and my love. You are truly one of God's special blessings and the true love of my life. Let's go to bed. I want to lay with you, embrace you and fall asleep with you in my arms."

He turned off the oil lantern and turned towards his loving wife, looked into her beautiful eyes, and kissed her softly.

Eight

THE LETTER

An investment in knowledge pays the best interest
~ Benjamin Franklin

T HE FIFTEEN-YEAR-OLD, FIVE-FOOT, PETITE AND EXTREMELY attractive high school senior sang the last verses of the hymn *I'm a Child of God* with great emotion. The students of her high school graduation assembly gave her a loud round of applause.

It had been a remarkable day for Lizzie Chadwick Muse, daughter of William and Helen Muse and the oldest of the family of eight children. Earlier in the commencement program of 1901, she was awarded the honor of being the valedictorian of the senior class.

After the graduation ceremonies, Lizzie walked hand in hand with her parents, followed by six of her brothers and sisters. Mary, the second oldest of the Muse family pushed the stroller with one-year-old baby Sarah resting comfortably. They prepared to cross the road to their Craftsman style home on Morris Street when Lizzie let go of their grip and sprinted across to the mailbox.

She reached inside to an empty mailbox and scowled. There was no letter.

Lizzie was worried sick. The letter of admissions from Trinity

College had not arrived five days after her school year ended. There was nothing more important at this time in her life than attending Trinity. She had diligently prepared for twelve years for this moment of starting her studies at an institution with high academic standards.

~

"FATHER, MOTHER!" LIZZIE SHOUTED OUT, "The letter has finally arrived from Trinity." With an excited look on her face, she rushed through the parlor and into the study and nervously handed the envelope to her father. It was addressed to Lizzie and the Muse Family.

"Open it, Father! Please open it now."

The patriarch reached into the top drawer of his mahogany writing desk, retrieved a sterling silver letter opener, and slid it through the top of the envelope. Before taking the letter out, he glanced at his oldest daughter. She anxiously shuffled her feet, and her hands were clenched together. She forced a smile.

The letter was written by the Trinity chancellor, Dr. John Carlisle Kilgo, on a rich ivory parchment paper. The calligraphy on the stationary was elegant in its classic Palmer style, slanted with large and small ornamental loops.

Mr. Muse peered at the letter over his rounded metal spectacles. He silently read the correspondence. He continued reading to himself for several minutes, showing an occasional smile and also a look of concern. He looked up, directed his attention to his daughter, and spoke. "My dearest, do you want the good news or the bad news first?"

Her mother crossed the room to comfort her daughter and grasped her hand, which had started to perspire. She stroked her daughter's forehead and whispered the words, "Everything will work out."

She had a frown on her face and spoke to her father in a slightly stuttering voice. "Pl ... plea ... please give me the sad news first."

He looked at her and began to read the sentiments of Dr. Kilgo.

"The unfortunate news I have to express to you today ..." Mr. Muse paused and glanced over at his daughter.

Lizzie's heart was racing. She had never liked the word unfortunate, and tears started to well up in her eyes.

He continued, "... is that you have been turned down," he stopped and shook his head.

Oh my God, she thought, *turned down for admission to Trinity College.*

"... turned down for a scholarship for your freshman year at Trinity College," were her father's next words.

"Father, please tell me the good news. I cannot wait any longer."

He smiled. "The good news is you have been accepted to Trinity, and Dr. Kilgo states that the school will offer you a full scholarship for your second year, and I quote, 'If you have performed in an honorable fashion.'"

Lizzie had a troubled look on her face. She feared without the scholarship; it would be impossible for her to go to college. With seven brothers and sisters, it seemed improbable the family would be able to afford it.

"Daughter, are you okay?" he asked, reaching out to her in a concerned voice.

"Father, can we afford my going to Trinity without financial aid from the school?"

Mr. Muse smiled and spoke in a calm, even tone. "Lizzie, you have always been at the top of your class in the Durham public school system. I have some exceptional news for you."

"What is it, Father?"

"Seeing how hard you have always worked on your studies and helping your mother around the house, I made the decision that you would definitely be my first child to attend college. I started a savings account for you four years ago and have steadfastly deposited five dollars a month for that period of time. As of today, you have two hundred and fifty dollars in your account at the Durham Bank and Trust. This will be enough to pay for your first year's expenses."

Lizzie stood, tears streaming down her face, and walked over to her father and hugged him lovingly. She didn't want to let go and said, "Oh, Father, I am so appreciative of what you and Mother do for our family. I love you both so very much."

"Thank you, your words mean a lot to me. Now go sit down next to your mother and let me read the entire letter from Dr. Kilgo." It read:

June 5, 1901

>*Dear Lizzie,*

>*Congratulations! Trinity College officially accepts you for admission to our school in the fall of 1901. Orientation will begin on August 15th and the first day of school will be September 5th, 1901. You will be the eleventh female to attend our college and I believe the youngest.*

>*I have followed your successes in the Durham Public High School system, and my staff and I welcome you with open arms and lofty expectations of you to our fine school. One of our goals at Trinity is to attract more female students to the college and we feel you will set a fine example for those considering our institution.*

>*I am only sorry we cannot offer you financial aid for your first year, but if your grades compare with your high school marks and you have performed in an honorable fashion, which I have all the confidence you will, we will strongly consider offering you a full scholarship for your sophomore year.*

>*Attached, please find a list of expenses you will incur for the full year. Here is a quick summation: Tuition is $64, the enrollment fee is $139, textbook costs for seven subjects-approximately $21, school supplies-$10, and a hundred and twenty meals at twenty-five cents a meal-$30. Those costs total $254. Our lunches served from the Trinity cafeteria are exceptional.*

>*I have reviewed your application and the seven courses you plan to take for each semester in your freshman year. These*

include four languages, chemistry, mathematics, and Bible study. That is a massive curriculum of study. May I suggest we arrange a meeting next week with me, Trinity's academic advisor, your parents and a couple of professors to explore your goals and expectations. I do not want to see you get in over your head in your first year at Trinity.

Before I close, I understand you will be spending two weeks of your summer vacation in Wrightsville Beach to attend the Sunday school teachers preparatory camp. Give my best to Professor H. M. Hamill of Nashville as she is a personal friend. Enjoy yourself. It is a great program.

I have enjoyed meeting with your parents and discussing their religious convictions which are common to mine.

You seem to have a very clear vision of your academic goals for college and your commitment to serve the Lord. I commend you.

I look forward to spending time with you and your parents in future weeks.

With Kindest Regards and Best Wishes, I am,

Yours sincerely,

Dr. John Carlisle Kilgo
Chancellor of Trinity College

William Muse handed Lizzie the letter. She spent several minutes re-reading it and smiled. "His handwriting is remarkable, and he seems very interested and committed to my success at Trinity."

Lizzie Muse at sixteen years old.
~ Courtesy of the Bradsher Family

Save that letter. It will be a treasure for your children to read someday. We will go and see the chancellor next week.

Little did Lizzie realize that Dr. Kilgo would someday perform the ceremony of her marriage to her future husband, and the two would name their first-born son with Kilgo being his middle name.

Nine

HITTING THE CORNERS

*The pitcher that paints the corners the entire game
will end up with a masterpiece.*
~ Bradsher

FIND ME AN OLD MATTRESS AND WE CAN GET STARTED TEACHING you how to pitch," Chadwick demanded.

Bradsher was puzzled and asked his best friend, "Why do we need a mattress?"

"Don't ask questions, Brad. Just find me a single mattress. Ask your mother if she has one that she's in need of throwing out in her boarding house, and I'll see you at the end of the week." He turned to run home.

~

ARTHUR WENT to his mother that evening and asked her, "Mom, are you going to get rid of a single mattress anytime in the future?"

"It's funny you should ask," she replied.

She wondered, *why does he want an old mattress?*

"Son, I may have one mattress I need to get rid of. I have asked Mr. Williams, my upstairs tenant, to pack his bags and leave by the end of the week. He is a heavy drinker and has turned into a bedwetter. I cannot have this in my boarding house. Why don't you go upstairs on Friday afternoon and bring it down?"

Bradsher's best friend, Walter, showed up on Friday at Elm Street at four in the afternoon. He had his baseball mitt and an old canvas bag with a zipper on it. He was pleased to hear the news about the mattress.

"What's in the bag?" Brad asked.

"I'll show you when we get the mattress out to the backyard. Let's get this over with. I bet the mattress smells to high heaven." He smirked.

They dragged the mattress down the stairs and leaned it against the back of the boarding house. "Are you ready to get started, Brad?" his mentor asked.

Bradsher answered enthusiastically, "I'm ready!"

"You asked me what's this for? Brad, we are going to create a strike zone on the mattress. This will give a target to throw to and put in the necessary work when I'm not here." Chadwick walked over to the stained mattress leaning up against the house, dipped a rag in a bucket of water with bleach, and started wiping it down. "Let this dry out for a couple of days."

Chadwick unzipped the bag and poured twenty baseballs, a small can of paint, and a paint brush out on the ground. "These baseballs are a gift to you. Throw them ten thousand times at the special target we'll create. Do it in the right way, and it will help you become one of the best pitchers in the South. You are going to throw to it until you can hit the edges of the paint on almost every ball you deliver.

"Today we're just going to talk about the role of the pitcher and the catcher in baseball. We'll discuss what is it going to take for you to learn to be a superlative pitcher. What will help you increase your strikeouts, win games, and have some fun? Take notes and be committed to the process, and I know you'll do great.

"First, let me ask you a question, Brad. Tell me what three things every great pitcher must have to be highly successful? Give it to me in three simple words." Before he could answer, Chadwick boldly said the three words: "Control, composure, and creativity.

"The ability to put the baseball wherever you want it, with differing speeds, should be the goal of any pitcher. I'll take a guy that's not as hard a thrower who can hit his spots on every pitch over the flame thrower who throws the ball down the middle of the plate anytime. Perfect control, location, and movement are three key principles to be a successful pitcher.

"Sometimes you will hit the top left edge, sometimes the lower left edge of the tape. It's called hitting and living on the corners. Every pitch you throw will be on the inside or outside edges of the plate.

"Great pitchers pitch to and hit the black edge of the plate consistently with an assortment of at least three pitches."

"How do I get better at spotting my pitches?" Brad asked.

"Ultimately, it is in good mechanics that will help you produce better velocity, accuracy, and command of your arsenal of pitches. There is an enormous difference between grooving a fastball or curveball and putting a good fastball with movement, or a quick and sharp breaking ball on the corner of the plate. Sometimes you will try to lure the batter with a pitch two inches off the plate. It's called wasting a pitch."

"What comes next?" Brad asked.

"Once you get your mechanics down and you're totally in command of your three pitches, I'll teach you to become a thinking pitcher, not just a thrower. I'll explain ways you can get in the mind of the hitter and mix him up."

Gosh, Walter is a baseball genius, Brad thought.

"A great pitcher will know why he's throwing a pitch to a batter when he does. He knows what the hitter is looking for."

"How do I know what the hitter is thinking?" Bradsher asked.

"We'll scout each team we play next year to find out their hitter's tendencies. We'll know going into the game which batters are fastball hitters or curveball hitters, which batters like to jump on the first pitch, and which ones like to work the count," Chadwick said with authority.

"Once you go through a team's lineup for the first time, it should teach you a good bit about your opponent's strengths and weaknesses. This will help you be more effective and efficient with your pitches.

"You'll be a hurler that always mixes up his pitches. Sometimes, no two in a single at-bat may look the same. You'll move the balls you deliver in and out and up and down. Balls commanded from you will come at the hitter in all different speeds and from varying angles. You want to put the batter constantly off balance and wreck his timing. Your job is to make your adversary feel uncomfortable."

Great game plan. This's going to be fun, the Trinity hurler thought.

"Brad, I think this is enough talk for today. We will start tomorrow. Thank your mother for the mattress and ask her if she has a yardstick. If she asks you what the mattress is for, tell her that your good friend is making you something that's going to help you become one of the best college pitchers in the South." Chadwick slapped his leg and laughed.

"Let's go for a run over to Hanes Field," he suggested. The two best friends sprinted down Elm Street, laughing and talking about baseball. It took them about ten minutes to reach the Trinity diamond.

The two ballplayers walked to the middle of the pitcher's mound. Walter said, "We will duplicate this in your backyard."

He handed the end of the measuring tape to Arthur. "Take it to the other side of the mound," he directed. He backed up to the other side of the oval mound area. A standard pitcher's mound needs to be fifteen inches in height with the rubber being exactly sixty feet-six inches from the front edge of home plate."

"What are the other dimensions of the mound?" Brad asked.

"It is approximately eight feet in width by twelve feet in depth. Let's start early in the morning. That's a lot of red clay we're going to dig up to build your pitcher's mound.

Let's stop for today. Get us a couple of shovels, a pickaxe, and we'll get started in the morning," Chadwick instructed.

He turned to run home. He'd gone about fifty yards when Bradsher yelled to him. "Wait up, Walter!" He ran to catch up.

He looked him straight in the eyes and said, "Thanks for being my friend and really caring about me."

"No sweat, buddy," Chadwick said, giving his best friend a bear hug. He slapped his sidekick on the back and took off again.

Brad stood and watched him disappear at the hill on Noble Street. Walter had become the brother that he'd never had.

Ten

BUILDING THE FUTURE

Hitting is timing. Pitching is upsetting timing.
~ Warren Spahn

WHEN CHADWICK ARRIVED AT THE BOARDING HOUSE THE next day, he found his best friend covered in sweat and red clay brick dust. He'd been up since sunrise working on constructing his pitcher's mound.

"Holy cow!" Walter exclaimed, "You've been busy!" The mound was almost eight inches high with another seven inches of dirt needed to reach the regulation height.

"Grab that other shovel and give me a hand," Bradsher said. "Start breaking up the clay with the pickaxe." The dense red clay was hard to negotiate, and it wasn't long until he'd broken out in a full sweat. For the next two hours, the batterymates matched each other shovel for shovel. After filling five-wheel barrows full, they would flip their shovels over and pounded until it was hard-packed.

Chadwick explained, "The pitcher's mound should to be very hard-packed to ensure that the pitcher has a solid landing area when he steps to the plate with one leg and follows through with the other to deliver his pitch." They were determined to make this pitcher's mound to a level equivalent to game day conditions.

After four more hours of hard labor, they took a few steps back to admire their work. Chadwick exclaimed, "It's a real work of art,

Arthur, no pun intended; great job!"

He seemed delighted with his little play on words. "Let's work on putting the strike zone on the mattress. Do you have the tape measure and the yardstick?" He instructed Bradsher to stand in front of him. He measured the distance from the ground to the middle of his knee. "Your knee is twenty-one and my knee is nineteen inches from the ground. Let's split the difference and put the bottom of the strike zone at twenty inches."

Next, he measured the distance from the knee to breastbone height of the team name letters across the jersey. Their two measurements were thirty-three and thirty-one inches, so they split the difference with the top of the zone being thirty-two inches from the knee.

"The other key measurement is the width of home plate, and its width is twenty-one precious inches." Chadwick pressed the knob of the bat into the dirt in front of the mattress and drew an outline of a home plate

He handed the can of black paint and paintbrush to Bradsher. They lifted the mattress and leaned it upright against the back wall of the boarding house. Chadwick instructed his friend; I'll go first and draw a two-inch-wide outline of the strike zone with this chalk and you follow and paint over it.

~

THIRTY MINUTES LATER, Chadwick beamed approvingly. "There's your strike zone. It will always be twenty-one by thirty-one, even though in some games it will seem to get smaller. Those are the times you need to breathe through your nose, relax, and re-focus."

They both laughed. Bradsher thought, *this is going to be a journey that will entail a lot of work, but it's going to be a very fulfilling experience. Let's make this fun.*

"Grab your glove, ace, and let's throw a few."

Bradsher walked to the mound and his catcher took his place in a crouched position in front of the mattress with the painted strike zone. After warming up for ten minutes, he started getting a little more specific in the location he wanted to receive the pitches from the southpaw.

He called out, one by one, an assortment of pitches he wanted the lefty to throw. "First pitch, curveball low at the knees and on the outside corner. Next pitch, a fastball at the letters on the outside corner. Next, throw low at the knees. Deliver the next ball inside and jam the hitter on the hands," he yelled.

As he threw, Bradsher saw that his receiver was signaling for pitches on every edge of the plate and no two pitches were alike or the same speeds. "Take a little off it!" Walter hollered. When he missed his outside corner location and threw it down the middle of the plate, his catcher went crazy! "No, no, no! Not down the middle, put it on the corners! Brad, the middle is nothing more than a life of misery!" he shouted

He stepped to the side of the mattress. "I'm going to stand here like I'm a left-handed hitter. Now you pitch to the target on the mattress and your imaginary catcher. What are you going to throw me? How're you going to get me out?"

"I don't know," he muttered with a lack of confidence.

"You've seen me bat, what kind of hitter am I? What would I like to see on the first pitch?" his cocky catcher questioned.

Bradsher answered him, "I've watched you hit. You like a fastball on the first pitch."

"Great then, what're you going to throw me, ace? Are you going to throw me a fastball on the first pitch?" he asked sarcastically.

Bradsher was getting a little irritated and excited. Chadwick was starting to build a fire of emotion in the pitcher's belly. "Hell no," he answered. "I'm going to throw you a sharp breaking ball for a strike in on your wrists. You like to extend your arms when you swing and I'm going to force you to shorten it up."

"Okay. Tell me about the next pitch from the Great One," he said, egging on his pitcher.

The crafty southpaw was now ready to go after his belligerent catcher. "Well, you know that I love to throw the curveball, so that's what you'll be looking for. Even though you like fastballs,

I'm going to climb the ladder on you coming in high and tight, but right on the edge of the painted line for a strike," Bradsher said, his voice elevated.

"I've got you right where I want you now!" He was now enjoying himself. "I'll do one of two things next. I'll waste one, three inches out of the strike zone, high and away on a pitch so many batters love to chase. Or, I'm going to simply finish you off with a twelve-six drop ball that falls off the table so rapidly you swing hard and miss it by a good fourteen inches."

"Good, Bradsher, good! Now you are thinking like a pitcher,"

"I'll throw the nastiest sinker you've ever seen and change speeds on the pitch. You're way ahead of it and whiff helplessly."

Bradsher had a big smile on his face. "Oh, by the way, did I mention that after I strike you out, you slam your bat down in disgust and kick the dirt as you're walking back to the bench, talking to yourself?"

"Screw you!" Chadwick responded.

They both laughed so hard their sides almost split open.

Eleven

THE STRIKE ZONE
AND THE MATTRESS

Practice does not make perfect.
Only perfect practice makes perfect.
~ Vince Lombardi

BRADSHER, YOU'RE PROBABLY A THOUSAND THROWS AWAY FROM being an all-star pitcher. Perfection comes from rightly executed repetition," Chadwick instructed. "Do it right, or don't do it at all!

"Why don't you hurl for a few minutes to the strike zone on the mattress while I watch areas of your mechanics you might improve upon. Once again, don't just go out there and throw. Go to the mound and pitch intelligently. Mix your repertoire of pitches and work on hitting the corners every time."

Eager to learn, the southpaw took the canvas bag of Spaldings and emptied them out on the mound.

"There is nothing pretty about those two-dozen old, scuffed-up baseballs," his best friend said. "Make them pretty. Throw twenty-five perfectly placed fastballs and curveballs."

As he started each windup, his mentor screamed at his friend, "Hit the paint, Big B! Hit the paint!" With that new understanding *that every pitch was important,* he was hitting the corners almost every time he delivered.

"Holy crap! Bradsher, you are hitting the black edge on five out of six pitches.

"Brad, we need to clearly understand our roles and how we can most effectively support each other for the next four years. My projection for you next year is if you do the work required, you'll become a star pitcher in the college game.

"After I get through working on your mechanics, you'll be royalty on the mound. You're the big cheese, the center of attention, and the one that wins games and the hearts of the fans."

Brad laughed and rolled his eyes.

"You'll be the star of the show. The guy that always gets the girl."

"Sounds like a dream," his pitcher said, displaying a wide smile.

"Fans will flock to see you because you're a winner that can perform magic with a baseball."

Chadwick continued, "My role is to help you get there. I'll be your negotiator with the umpires. I'll call the pitches that will keep the hitters off-balance and chasing pitches they can never hit.

"Your job is to stay calm on the mound. Let me do the worrying. Do not ever show an ounce of frustration with the umpires, or it will come back to haunt you. I'm your ambassador. Let me fight your battles. You want to win the respect from the umpire from the very first pitch. If the umpire sees you are sharp from the start, he'll give you some strikes on the marginal calls."

The cocky catcher bragged, "One thing that makes me a great catcher is I'm an effective communicator. I will let you know from the very beginning of the game which way the umpire is calling the pitches. Does he like a low strike zone, or is he going to be a little more liberal in calling a ball just off the plate?

"Sometimes, I just flat out ask the umpire, 'What's it going to take to make you happy?'"

Bradsher laughed. "Now that you've become chummy with the ump, what does he tell you?"

"And on occasion, he will offer it to me by saying, 'Your boy, Bradsher, better get his pitches up a little higher in the zone or it's going to be a very long day for him.' I'll be framing pitches for you throughout the game."

"Explain framing, Walter."

"Oh, Lord, I knew you'd ask. I don't guess your catcher gave you much help last season." Chadwick laughed. "You've got a lot to learn, Brad, but with your determination and brains, we'll get there.

"Framing is very subtle sliding that ball back into the strike zone, so the umpire will call it a strike. The catcher needs to work with the finesse of a highly skilled jewel thief." Chadwick put his hands against his chest with his thumbs touching. He quickly moved them two inches to the left. "I'll be stealing balls that are off the plate and making them look like strikes to the ump. I call them strikeballs.

"A great catcher frames his batterymate's pitches like a magician. The catcher moves his body in front of the pitch and leaves the catcher's mitt close to his chest, never jabbing at it, which is a strong indication that the ball is not over the plate.

"By framing your pitches in a nine-inning game, I may get a strikeout or two a game, save a walk, and sometimes, save a critical game-deciding run. Are you okay with what we're setting out to accomplish?"

"Heck yes, I'm pumped! Walter, I can't thank you enough for helping me."

Chadwick broke out in a big smile. "My friend, I'm trying to help us both. I have the feeling you and I are going to be stuck with each other for four more years. I'm going to thank your mother for the mattress. Why don't you throw a couple of dozen balls without me and then we'll stop for the day?"

~

THE EIGHTEEN-YEAR OLD SOUTHPAW stood in silence with a sorrowful look on his face. He was recounting the Harvard game in which they had massacred him by a score of 12-0. The Crimson Nine slammed fifteen hits during nine hurtful innings in his first year as a raw unskilled rookie at Trinity. It was the worst day of his college career.

As he focused on the painted-on strike zone on the mattress, he imagined and, in his mind, saw Big Man Reid of Harvard stepping up to the plate. The imaginary slugger banged his bat against the corners of the plate with the huge barrel lumber. He had hit a bases-loaded double against Bradsher in the contest earlier in the year, driving in three runs. The score was 6-0 before he could escape the inning.

Veins were protruding from the forehead, neck, and arms of the six-foot-two inch, 220-pound hulk of a man. He flexed his rock-solid forearms, and with an arrogant smile on his face, pointed his finger at Bradsher.

The Trinity Twirler grinned and pounded his glove two times with his fist. Bradsher heard himself talking to the imaginary figure he envisioned so clearly in his mind. *That was then and now is now. You aren't facing a scared boy this time. You are going against a tough pitcher that has grown into a man. After I take care of you, Big Man, I want you to walk back to the bench and tell Story and Frantz that I'm gunning for them.*

Reid had an appetite for first-pitch fastballs, and he loved to crowd the plate.

It's time to keep him honest and let him know who is in control.

He backed him off the plate with a sizzling brushback fastball that whistled under his chin. Reid yanked his head back and bailed out from the pitch so abruptly, he landed on his backside in the red clay. "Holy shit!" He scoffed at the North Carolina hurler.

You haven't seen anything yet.

He jammed the Harvard slugger with another heater that handcuffed him on the fists. Reid couldn't get his bat extended and fouled it off into the dirt.

This is starting to get fun.

Bradsher brought his wicked curveball and landed it on the outside corner at the knees. It froze Reid for a called "Strike two!"

Let's waste one and see if the Big Man will go fishing for a fastball.

He fired his pitch high and away, three inches outside of the strike zone. He lunged, started his swing, but held up at the last second. Reid had a good eye.

It's time for the knockout pitch and this one is going to be a doozy.

The Trinity strikeout king reared back, raised his leg, cocked his arm, and delivered the pitch straight over the top. The Harvard clean-up hitter saw the drop ball perfectly at his waist and swung so hard that if he had hit it, would surely have ended up over the fence. He missed it by a foot. The ball dropped severely into the dirt. Reid fell to the ground and got up cussing. As he left the batter's box, he pounded his bat into the ground.

True to his word, he shot down the Harvard murderous sluggers, Story and Frantz, with an assortment of fastballs, and nasty drop balls and benders. It took a total of eleven pitches to bury both Crimson greats. No two pitches looked alike, and each ended up on the edge of the plate. The lefty was living on the corners, and this was the best inning of his career-one he would draw from in the future.

Bradsher's eyes followed Frantz as he made his long walk from the plate to the bench. When he returned his look to the mattress, no one was there.

He walked to his mother's house beaming ear to ear. He was greeted by Chadwick and his mother at the back door.

"How are you doing, son?"

"Great! Mom, I just pitched the best inning of my life."

Both Walter and Corah Carver gazed at Arthur with a puzzled look.

"I'll tell you both about it later."

Chadwick laughed. "Let's take tomorrow off. Get some rest and I'll see you on Monday." Walter gave his best friend a hug. "We're going to win a lot of games, buddy." He took off in a sprint down Noble Street, towards his own house. It was time for dinner and some rest.

~

AFTER DINNER WITH HIS MOTHER, Arthur dropped to his knees and offered a prayer of thankfulness.

He laid his head down on his soft down-filled pillow. His mind and heart were full of big dreams. In a couple of days, he would tell Chadwick about his strikeouts of Big Man Reid, Story, and Frantz.

Twelve

CURVEBALL

Carrots might be good for my eyes,
but they won't straighten out the curveball.
~ Carl Furillo

YOUR CURVEBALL IS TOO FLAT, BRADSHER! THAT IS WHY THE hitters beat you up last year," Chadwick told his best friend. "It's time to change your grip. Your sweeping curveball is staying in the strike zone too long. Hold your hand out," his mentor insisted. He slapped a baseball in the palm of his batterymate. "Now, show me your grip," he demanded.

Bradsher placed his fingers on the ball and asked, "How's this?"

"No, no, no!" the feisty catcher's voice rang out. "You're doing it all wrong!"

"How the heck am I supposed to grasp it?" Bradsher asked.

"Do you see the horseshoe-like stitching on the baseball?" He placed his finger on the top right-hand side of the horseshoe. "Put your middle finger where I've put mine. Next, dig your index finger into the middle of the ball. Locate your thumb at the stitching at the bottom of the left side of the baseball."

"Boy, this is totally different than how I've been gripping the baseball and it feels awkward," the Trinity Twirler exclaimed.

"It'll feel very strange for a couple of weeks until you've thrown a couple of hundred pitches with this new grip. It's the same type of feeling of the awkwardness of first learning to ride a bike. Don't worry, Brad, we'll work on this every day and you'll pick it up quickly."

He extended his hand to his demanding teacher. He had the grip on the baseball just as Walter instructed. "How's this?"

"Fantastic! You're a fast learner.

"You've mastered the control of your fastball. It is time to perfect command of your breaking balls." He slapped Arthur's back, "When I get through with you, you'll have the nastiest curveball ever been thrown in college baseball. Unlike most pitchers that have played the game, you'll have pinpoint control over the pitch that others call the hook, the twelve-six, the deuce, and the bender."

"I'm willing to work as hard and long as it takes to get this done," Bradsher said wholeheartedly.

~

CHADWICK SMILED. "Let's change horses for a few minutes. "How is your love life going?"

Bradsher smiled back." I have several young women at Trinity and the University of North Carolina pursuing me. One of the gals at UNC attended the first two games of the 1902 season and sat on the front row holding up the K-cards. What a beauty. She is five feet seven, blonde, thin waisted, full-breasted, and one of the most striking girls I've ever meet. She's three years older than me and a senior at Carolina, twelve miles up the road. I dated her for four months before we had our big talk. She expressed that she wanted to be my full-time girlfriend and entertain marriage someday.

"Walter, I have promised my mother that I'll make straight A' s at Trinity and committed to you to learn the mechanics and put in the work to be the best pitcher in the South. I don't think it's in my best interests to get into a committed relationship right now. One thing I know in my heart is that I never want to lead a woman on when I don't feel it will be healthy for us in the long run. I had a talk with Louise about this yesterday. It was a painful breakup.

"Down the road, I feel I will meet the woman that will sweep me off my feet and that I will want to marry. The time is just not right now."

"She is a hell of a looker," Walter said with a big smile on his face. "Tell her next time you speak, tell her that you've got a friend that would be a great catch."

"You're the consummate playboy, Walter."

"Yes indeed," he said, slapping his knee. "Are we going to spend the rest of the afternoon talking about your curvy ex, or are we going to settle down and let me teach you how to throw a curveball?

"It's time to get back to the mechanics of throwing the drop ball for a few minutes," Chadwick began. "I want you to bring your throwing arm back close to your ear and release the pitch straight over the top. Snap your wrist when you let go of the ball," his mentor said.

"Now, let's try the new grip," he demanded. "Work the stitches, Brad, work the stitches," he shouted. "Begin with the drop ball.

This is like learning to pitch from a manual, Bradsher thought.

"Which one, the slow drop or the fast drop?"

His catcher squatted down and flashed three fingers in front of his crotch. He discreetly pointed his index finger to the left. "Throw me the slow drop ball and put it on the left corner of the plate."

The southpaw reeled off six slow drops and his pitches bent like never. The balls started at the height of the letters and ended just below the knees and drifted slowly to the plate. Each pitch dropped so severely it looked like it rolled off a table and dropped to the ground.

"Holy Toledo!" Bradsher shouted. "I've never thrown a ball that broke this much."

"The slow speed of the ball traveling to the plate makes the pitch look irresistible to the hitter," his trusty backstop said. "At the same time, it keeps the hitter off balance. With the severe dip of the pitch, it's very difficult to get the bat in the right plane to hit it."

Chadwick snapped his fingers right in front of his pitcher's face. "Now, let's really screw the hitter up, and throw with more speed your dipper and really snap your wrist when you release it. Don't be afraid to get the ball dirty."

"What do you mean?" Bradsher asked.

Chadwick slapped the ground. "Start your big dipping twelve-six at the belt of the batter and have it end up his ankles. If it hits the dirt, that's okay. I will be in front of the pitch and bring it into my mitt."

The lefty reared back, coiled his leg, brought his hand back up near his ear, pushed off with his left foot, and delivered. The fast-tight spin on the ball caused it to break at the last minute and drop severely in the dirt. He threw seven more fast-moving drop balls. Ball after ball broke so sharply, half ended up bouncing in front of the plate.

"Holy cow! This'll be my knockout punch when I get my control down pat," he said excitedly.

"The control of your breaking ball has to be perfect," Chadwick said. "You'll be in such command of those pitches, you won't be afraid to throw your benders with three balls on the batter. Then, we'll start perfecting the control of your money pitch. Try coming straight over the top like you do when you throw your fastball. We want your twelve-six drop ball to look like a fastball because of the increased velocity, versus your conventual curveball traveling at much slower speeds.

"This's where the fun begins." Chadwick laughed and slapped his thigh. "The tightly coiled batter sees a fastball coming to the middle of the plate thinking it's a straight-lined fastball, and the hitter starts to explode his swing. Suddenly, the bottom drops out and he misses the pitch by a foot. Whiff. It'll not only be your strikeout pitch, it'll have the batters swinging wildly like a drunk at your drop ball." His best friend mimicked a fooled hitter waiving his bat at an imaginary ball. He looked so off balance he almost fell.

"I'm getting it," Bradsher said.

"It can be your set-up pitch for your sweeping curveball and fastball. Now you have four completely different weapons in your arsenal that will keep hitters guessing what you are going to throw next. The batters will feel like they are losing their minds. One of your main goals is to make the batter feel uncomfortable at all times."

"How do we make this happen?" Bradsher asked.

"Like we always do. You're going to work your ass off every day until you have perfect control of your four pitches. I say you throw thirty curveballs and your two varieties of drop balls every day for the next six weeks. That's the time we have left before we play Guilford and Wake Forest twice, in the most important games of the year. God almighty, Bradsher, we don't have much time!"

"I'm willing to do whatever it takes to make this happen."

"Brad, you have a great heater. When you perfect your curveball and the two different drop balls, you'll become the best hurler in college baseball."

"Let's get busy! Time is of the essence!"

Trinity Catcher Walter Chadwick.
~ Courtesy of Duke University Library and Archives.

Thirteen

CHADWICK

The catcher is in the middle of everything. He sees it best.
~ Johnny Bench

AFTER THE 6-2 LOSS TO DAVIDSON, BRADSHER STOOD BEFORE Coach Stocksdale with his fists clenched. The veins protruded from his forehead. "Coach, the current situation at catcher isn't working for the team or me. We need to make a change immediately. Get Chadwick in the lineup!"

Walter Chadwick joined the Trinity team late for the 1902 season. When he did arrive, a day before the first game, he found himself sitting on the bench. It would take Bradsher's best efforts to convince the coach to move his friend behind the plate.

"Tell me why he should be our first-string catcher," Stocksdale demanded.

The Trinity ace slapped his hand on his coach's desk. "He's a strong-armed catcher, and his throw to second is a frozen rope. He's not one prone to errors, mental mistakes, or passed balls. He's quick as a cat. He frames pitches, fields bunts, and blocks balls in the dirt better than any catcher I've seen.

"One of the reasons we're getting beat this year is opponents are playing small ball against us. They bunt and steal and then they repeat the process. Nobody fields a bunt and throws out a baserunner better than Chadwick."

"You're getting my attention. Tell me more."

"Coach, it's time for someone to step forward and inspire and lead this team. Standing five feet and eight inches and weighing a hundred-and-fifty pounds, he's a fierce and gritty competitor. He's not afraid to kick a teammate's butt if he's not giving one-hundred-and-ten percent. Coach, Chadwick's moxie and swagger will wake this team up," Bradsher said, smacking his hands together.

"Can he hit?"

"Oh boy, can he sock the ball!" Bradsher answered. "I watched him hit in every one of Trinity Park's home games last year. He bats from the left side of the plate and really beats up right-handed pitchers. He blisters the ball with hot shots down the line. He goes to the opposite field effectively against left-handers with a quick slap of the bat."

"Thanks, Arthur." The Trinity coach beamed to his star southpaw. "I'll consider everything you've told me today. I agree with you. It's time for some changes."

~

STOCKSDALE MET Chadwick at Hanes Field at eight a.m. with a bat and a bag of balls. "Loosen up and then I am going to throw you a couple of dozen pitches and see if you're the hitter Bradsher says you are." Five minutes later, Stocksdale rifled pitch after pitch to his hopeful catcher. Bam! He hammered the first ball delivered from his coach and almost took his head off.

"Holy shit, Chadwick! Go easy on me."

Chadwick didn't. *Whack, crack, bam!* He sprayed the ball all over the diamond with sharply hit line drives. He hit the Hanes field fence twice. The sound of wood meeting leather echoed across the ballfield. Chadwick pointed his finger at Stocksdale and, red-faced, he shouted, "Bring it, Coach. Don't hold back." This was developing into a confrontation between two strong competitors. Chadwick smashed every pitch thrown to him.

The Trinity coach exclaimed, "Walter, I'm impressed. Let's call it a morning. I'm starting to fear for my life."

~

THE NEXT DAY, Stocksdale walked into the locker room with a clipboard in his hand. "Listen up, gentlemen," he barked at his squad, "there's a new sheriff in town. It's Walter Chadwick, and he's our starting catcher from here on out. He'll be batting cleanup."

Chadwick's leadership and fiery swagger created an uplifted spirit on the Trinity team. As a freshman, he wasn't afraid to stand up to the upperclassman and admonish them for their lack of hustle and effort.

From his first game in the lineup, the team went on a tear. Bradsher pitched a nifty three-hitter against a strong Hobart College team. His spunky catcher was brilliant in his pitch-calling and framing of pitches in the contest. He threw out the only baserunner trying to steal second base.

Trinity played A&M in the next game and they committed ten errors through the first seven innings. In the eighth inning, the infield committed two more miscues. It was a critical moment in the contest, and a defeat for Trinity looked like a great possibility.

Chadwick raised his right hand, got out of his crouch, and spun to face the man in blue. "Ump, can we stop for a minute? I need to talk with my boy."

The agitated umpire responded, "Go ahead, but make it quick."

He stood, toe to toe, directly in front of his rattled pitcher. He was within six inches of Bradsher's sweat-covered face. So close the pitcher, Bradsher could feel his excited catcher's breath on his neck.

He displayed a crazy looking grin on his face. He looked up to Bradsher and raised both of his palms skyward and shook them. Bradsher exclaimed, "Jesus Christ, how do you stay so calm through this horrendous play of your teammates?"

Before he could answer, the Trinity receiver said, "Forget them and focus on me, the corners of the strike zone, and the mitt! We will get through this, Brad! The score may not be pretty, but we'll win this game!"

He slapped the southpaw on his chest and returned to the plate. The Trinity Twirler kept his composure and continued to pitch calmly through the messy game. They got through the error-filled ballgame and won by a score of ten to seven.

~

IN THE LOCKER ROOM thirty minutes after the ballgame ended, Chadwick screamed at his teammates for their uninspiring play. "Men, you're better than this," were his last words as he kicked over a trash can and stormed out of the exit.

After the victory, the Trinity ball club went on an amazing streak. It started on April 14, 1902. The next eight days would draw the attention of every newspaper reporter in the South and many more throughout the entire country.

~

A WEEK BEFORE the famous streak began, Bradsher and Chadwick started a routine that they would follow for the next three years. They would go over a scouting report of each team they played. It would begin with the Wake Forest game.

They met at Murphy's Cafe, and each had a yellow pad and pencil. Chadwick laid out newspaper clippings on the table.

Bradsher picked them up and asked, "What are these for?"

"These are box scores I cut out of the *News and Observer*." He tapped his finger on the account from the newspaper and said, "This is the probable lineup we'll face against Wake Forest tomorrow."

Chadwick ran his index finger down the clipping. "We're going through the entire lineup from their leadoff man through their number-nine hitter. Let's evaluate each player's strengths and weaknesses. We'll decide how to pitch to each batter."

The waiter approached the table and welcomed the two teammates with a pleasant smile. "What will you have, fellows?"

Chadwick ordered first. "I'll have a corned beef sandwich on toasted marble rye bread, fried potatoes, and a Coca-Cola." He waived his menu at his sidekick. "How about you, Brad, what meets your fancy?"

"I'll have the cheeseburger with lettuce and tomato. Also, bring me the fried potatoes, and a Coca-Cola. Thanks."

"Okay, here're some of the box scores from games Wake has played this year," Chadwick explained. "Here's the lineup in the game you pitched against them last year. We play them twice in the next eight days, so let's get ready for them." Chadwick held up four fingers and said, "Four of the players you faced last year are still playing. In effect, we're going to pre-pitch tomorrow's game today as we eat our lunch."

"It's a great plan, Walter. Let's get started."

Chadwick raised his index finger and wiggled it right to left. He began with their leadoff hitter, Mull. "He's their center fielder, and he loves to bunt." He put both hands in front of himself, chest level, and faked a bunt.

He elevated his voice, and he continued, "I'll be looking for him to bunt. If he lays one down, I'm on it like a cat on a mouse, so stay out of my way. Don't walk him. He's very fast. If you let him on base, with his speed, it'll cost you!

"Their next hitter is Harris," his backstop said, as he leaned forward over the table. "He crowds the plate to try and rattle the pitcher and draw a walk. Come in high and tight on a first-pitch fastball. Give him some chin music, and move him off the dish," he said as he moved the flat of his right hand under his chin.

"What'd we do with the meat of the order?" Bradsher asked.

His outspoken catcher slapped his right thigh and howled, "This is where it gets interesting and you earn your stay."

Fourteen

THE MEAT OF
THE ORDER

The most important part of a player's body is above his shoulders.
~ Ty Cobb

THE WAITER SET THE PLATTERS OUTFITTED WITH THE CORNED beef sandwich and cheeseburger meals in front of Chadwick and Bradsher. "Here are your condiments, pickles, and a small bowl of chopped onions. "Do you guys need anything else?"

"Thanks, we've got everything for now."

"Please bless this meal, Walter," Arthur said.

He responded quickly, "Good Lord, good meat. I bless this food, good Lord. Let's eat ... Amen."

Bradsher could do nothing with his response but roll his eyes and shake his head.

As he looked down to get a grip on his thick cheeseburger, he heard the first bite out of Chadwick's corned beef sandwich. It was a crisp crunch sound.

"How's your sandwich?"

"Frigging fabulous!" he exclaimed wholeheartedly. "Murphy buys the freshest corned beef available and he bakes his bread here in his kitchen. This marbled rye is a work of art," Chadwick said with a broad grin. He licked his lips.

"I went back to the kitchen and watched Murphy make the corned beef sandwich last time I was here. First, he butters the rye bread on the outer side of the top and bottom of the sandwich and lays them on a piece of wax paper.

"At this point, he builds the sandwich in layers: pickles, swiss cheese, corned beef, and his special sauce. He embellishes his sauce with horseradish, which gives the sandwich a real kick. Umm good," Chadwick said with a broad smile on his face.

He continued his praise of the sandwich-maker. "He's an artesian when preparing his food. He gently lays his body of work in the heavy iron skillet for about three minutes until the bread is golden brown and the cheese is melted. The sandwich becomes one when he finishes."

Bradsher bit into his one-inch thick juicy cheeseburger and took a big sip of his Coca-Cola. Both batterymates loved the fried potatoes. The juices of the hamburger drizzled out of the bun onto his plate as his teeth cut through the beef.

The waiter brought out a platter of the fries made two different ways: some thick cut and others curly. They dressed the crispy potatoes with plenty of salt and ketchup. Not a word was spoken for the next ten minutes as the two best friends devoured their meals.

"Pun intended, let's discuss the meat of the order of the Wake lineup that we'll face in their three, four, and five hitters. This's where the fun begins, as these guys are the toughest sonofabitches, you'll face all day," Chadwick said with a look of terror on his face. He flashed three fingers, then four fingers, then five fingers.

"These three hitters feed off fastballs and swing the big lumber in the lineup. You'll live or die against these three batters, depending on how effective you are with your curveball, changeup, and drop ball.

"Don't be afraid to get the ball dirty," his catcher exclaimed.

"What'd you mean by that?" Bradsher asked.

"Mix your pitches up between your curveball, fastball. When you get two strikes on one of their sluggers, throw your sharp breaking drop ball and start it just above the knees.

"It's a pitch a big swinger can't lay off; and if located properly, he can't hit. Your ball should end up bouncing in the dirt and I'll be in front of it to block it." He raised his fist in the air to mimic the umpire's motion for a strike call. "You're out of here!" he hollered.

Bradsher couldn't help but laugh at Chadwick's demonstrative antics with his hands.

"One of the biggest mistakes most pitchers make when facing the heart of the order is feeling they need to overpower them with the fastball. Don't get trapped in that spider web or you'll find yourself getting bit by the long ball. Never leave the ball over the plate with a fastball against the big hitters."

He raised three fingers. "Let's start with Wake's three-hitter, Mull. Their third baseman is very disciplined. He'll take a walk just as well as he'll take a base hit. You must throw him strikes and mix up your pitches. Change up your speeds and vary the level.

"Start him off with a sharp breaking drop ball for a strike. Throw the eighty-seven mile-per-hour pitch with the tighter spin. It'll look more like a fastball when it starts on its path to him," he added as he snapped his wrist.

"On the next ball you throw, Mull will be expecting a fastball. Double up on him and throw him another twelve-six, but in a different location than the first. Waste your next pitch high and wide. Sometimes a hitter behind in the count will chase that bad boy." He smiled now as he continued. "Now you've got him right where you want him.

"Mull now has that last pitch set in his mind, so what do we throw now?" he asked his batterymate.

"We put him to sleep with a nasty change-up drop ball that ends up in the dirt!" the Trinity strikeout-king answered.

"Bingo!" his catcher shouted as he slapped the table.

"Their clean-up hitter and first baseman, Dunn, hits the ball a country mile," the Trinity catcher said loudly as he pointed across the room. "You don't want him sitting on your fastball. Move your pitches up and down on him and in and out.

"You want to mess with his timing and keep him off balance.

Keep changing speeds and keep the ball on the corners. Your knockout punch against Dunn will be your curveball low and away."

Chadwick is a genius and he is teaching me to pitch at the highest level, the Trinity southpaw thought.

"Their fifth hitter is the pitcher, Hobgood, and he's a smart hitter. Don't give him a hanging fastball over the plate, as he loves to hit to the opposite field. Jam him on the first pitch but make the pitch a strike. From there, mix your pitches with fastballs, curveballs, and changeups."

"I get it, Walter. If you leave the ball over the plate, it allows the hitter to fully extend his arms and then, pow!"

"Murphy makes a damn good corned beef sandwich," Chadwick exclaimed. He lathered the meat with a spoonful of mustard. He took another crunchy bite of the sandwich and then washed it down with a big swig of Coca-Cola.

"Who's next?" Arthur asked.

"Wake's sixth, seventh, and eighth hitters are nothing to write home about. You do not want to get careless with them, and it would be a sin to walk one of these guys.

"Throw your fastballs high and outside and then low and inside. Jam them and don't put anything out over the middle of the plate. Your drop ball will be your most effective pitch against Cadell, Dowd, and Pace. Lead with the fastball and finish them off with your drop ball and curveball in the dirt," he shouted as he smacked the restaurant's floor with his foot.

"How about their ninth hitter?" Brad asked.

"Rounding out their starting lineup is Edwards. He'll probably play second base tomorrow, but he's also Wake's second-string pitcher," the excited backstop continued. "Overpower him on your first pitch with a cross-seamed fastball and then mix it up from there.

"If he bunts, stay out of my way, and I'll take care of him," he bragged.

The two best friends finished their sandwiches, and there were only a handful of French fries left. Chadwick salted the remaining fries one last time and poured some additional salt in the palm of his hand. He laughed as he tossed it over his left shoulder. "That's for luck tomorrow, Bradsher. Not that you'll need it, the way you're pitching."

They finished their meal and stood to walk back to campus. "This meal is on me," Bradsher said. He left a one-dollar bill and some change on the table. "After I pitch my shutout tomorrow, Walter, you can buy me a steak dinner." They both laughed.

As they reached the dorm, Bradsher smiled broadly. "What's so funny?" Chadwick asked.

"Thanks for your help today, Walter. The way you talk with your hands is hilarious."

He pointed his index finger directly at Bradsher's face and said, "I'll see you tomorrow." He turned for his run home.

~

WHAT WOULD HAPPEN in the next eight days in the baseball world in the state of North Carolina would reach the front pages of every sports section in the South. It would be one of the most amazing weeks in college baseball's history.

Fifteen

EIGHT DAYS IN APRIL

If I'd known I was gonna pitch a no-hitter today,
I would have gotten a haircut.
~ Bo Belinsky

ARTHUR BRADSHER'S NO-HITTER AND NINETEEN STRIKEOUTS against Wake Forest caught the attention of every sports writer in the South.

His stunning performance was his first induction into the elite No-No Club. His, and Chadwick's, preparation for the contest really paid big dividends. Bradsher started the game striking out the first five batters he faced. He struck out the side four times.

As shadows set in in the bottom of the ninth, he looked as strong as he did at the beginning of the game.

Don't get careless and focus on every pitch, Brad thought. *Let's reel in my first no-hitter.*

The North Carolina marvel struck out the side, securing the seven to nothing shutout.

When the dust settled, there were nineteen students sitting in a row, holding their K signs for each of his strikeouts. The Trinity Twirler had the Wake team off-balance all day long with his movement, change of speeds, and placement of pitches. He struck out nineteen frustrated batters without walking a single hitter or allowing a single base hit.

~

Two days later, reporters from Raleigh, Durham, Charlotte, Greenville, Anderson, and Spartanburg stood next to the fence by the bullpen. Half the press had cigarettes dangling from their lips, and they all wore hats. They stood a mere five feet from Bradsher. They watched him fire well-placed fastballs and three varieties of his sharp breaking curveballs and drop balls to his all-star catcher.

Chadwick barked out different pitches he wanted to be thrown by his star southpaw: "Drop ball on the outside corner at the knees, and fastball high and tight under the chin." His catcher would reposition himself on every pitch and shouted like a drill sergeant. "Hit the black edge before every ball that was thrown."

Pitch after pitch hit Chadwick's mitt with a loud slapping sound. He hit the middle of the target every time.

"Holy crap!" said Walter Jones of *The Morning Post*. "The kid doesn't miss. He puts the pitch at the precise spot every time."

"You aren't kidding," answered Fred Spatz of *The Durham Sun*. "He refuses to go to the middle of the plate. If he mixes his pitches like he's doing now, no one will hit him," the reporter said as he took a long draw on his cigarette.

Jack Wilson of *The Charlotte Observer* chipped into the conversation. "I've never seen a pitcher with the command of his curveball, drop ball, and change of pace like Bradsher possesses."

"No two pitches look alike, and balls come to the hitter at all different speeds," his sassy receiver bragged to the reporters. "This North Carolina wonder is a strikeout artist that can paint the corners of the plate with every pitch. He can put a strike on a flea's butt and isn't afraid to throw his curveball with a three-two count. It's his knockout punch."

His cocky catcher stood from his crouched position and reached for the water bucket a few feet away. He set it in the center of home plate and turned to walk to the bench. After he walked twenty feet with his back to his star pitcher, he yelled, "Put the ball in the bucket with your twelve-six."

Bradsher started his wind-up, brought his arm back, coiled his leg, and let the ball fly. He released the ball straight off the top, and its intense spin took the ball from six feet high down to the height of the bucket of fourteen inches.

Chadwick never looked back, but when he heard the splash in the bucket, he lifted both hands in the air and flapped them excitingly, shouting, "Yes!"

The Trinity ace smiled sheepishly as he walked past the bug-eyed reporters, a few still staring in disbelief at the bucket and the baseball bobbing up and down in it.

"Good afternoon, gentleman. I hope you enjoy the ball game today."

~

NINE MONTHS BEFORE the Guilford game, Bradsher and Chadwick made a pact. Chadwick agreed to teach Bradsher how to pitch: the relationship between a catcher and his pitcher, the mechanics of pitching, the steps necessary to become the best pitcher in the game.

After three weeks of intense training sessions on the art of pitching, Chadwick abruptly held up his hands. "Brad, let's stop and talk for a minute. Tell me how good you want to be in the game of baseball."

The hard-working lefty took in a deep breath, then raised his voice. "I don't want to be good. I want to be great! I will work until I'm absolutely the best pitcher in the college game. As you say, Walter, 'the big cheese' that dominates the opposition."

"Let me give you a few morsels of advice," Chadwick began. "Besides the daily hard work and discipline, which you've shown every day you're willing to do, there's an important mindset any great pitcher needs to have every time he throws a baseball.

"You need to concentrate on *every* pitch you ever throw. You need to learn that every pitch matters. You'll never win a game with four or five good pitches, but it's very easy to lose a game on four or five bad ones."

"Thank you, Walter, for everything you're doing for me. Let's take a run to the ballfield."

~

THE UMPIRE, Mr. Williams, screamed, "Play Ball." Bradsher was ready to face a very good Guilford team. The reporters from three states were chomping at the bit. After watching his amazing warm-up session, they had their pads and pens ready to record another great game thrown by the strikeout-king of the South.

Chadwick was in a crouched position ready for the start of the game when the umpire bent over the plate to brush it off. His rear end was pointed in the direction of the pitcher's mound, and he found himself looking into the backstop's stare. The two sets of eyes were less than twenty-four inches apart, so close the catcher could smell the tobacco on the ump's breath.

Chadwick reached towards the plate and with his index finger tapped it on the edge. "Mr. Williams, my boy, Bradsher is going to put his balls on the black edge all day long."

"I hear you, Walter," he said with a grin.

From the beginning of the game, it became evident that Guilford was no match for Trinity and Bradsher. The southpaw sensation struck out the first three batters he faced. The contingency of fans who had traveled from Durham became delirious early.

The boys from Greensboro couldn't catch up with his ninety-two-mile-an-hour fastball. He froze the batters with his curveball and made them look silly.

After going through the Guilford starting nine for the first time, he could tell what the hitters were thinking by the way they swung at the ball the first time around. By the sixth inning, the Trinity southpaw had struck out eight batters and seemed to get almost every close call from the umpire. Chadwick was a great ambassador between his star pitcher and the ump.

Bradsher retired the first eighteen batters he'd faced. As he walked to the mound to begin the seventh inning, a couple of enthusiastic fans rolled six hard-boiled eggs out on the field in the direction of the mound. They screamed, "Goose eggs, goose eggs, goose eggs," in anticipation of another shutout from their southpaw star.

The Trinity ace smiled at the fans' antics and thought, *Only nine more outs for the second no-hitter in two days. I can do this.*

With two outs in the seventh inning, the catcher, Sellers, lifted a weak pop behind the first baseman, Smith. The ball was Smith's play to make, but he hesitated on it. He was late getting to the ball, and it popped out of his mitt and fell to the ground. *Holy crap,* Bradsher thought. *These fellows with these small mitts must learn to use both hands on every ball they go after.*

"No harm was done," Chadwick yelled out to his batterymate. Everything is okay. The no-hitter is still intact. Let's get this last batter in the inning and regroup, he thought. "Throw him the dark ball, Brad, throw him the dark ball." He directed his next comment to the batter. "Get ready, Camie, you are about to get a visit from Uncle Charles."

The Trinity southpaw closed out the inning by striking out the pitcher, Cameron, on a wicked breaking ball.

As the players made their way to the bench, the scorekeeper climbed his rickety ladder to put another goose egg on the board. To the astonishment of everyone, he put a one in the hits column.

The fans booed for ten minutes. A half-dozen fans threw their hot dogs, bags of popcorn, and soft drinks onto the field.

Other fans were screaming, "Home cooking, good ol' home cooking. What'd you think, we weren't looking?" They shouted the slogan over and over for five minutes.

Chadwick was livid. He walked over to the almost empty water bucket and kicked it fifteen feet.

He turned next to first basemen, Smith. With veins bulging on his neck and his fists clenched, he screamed at Smith, "You can do better than that. Your pitcher deserves more than that sorry effort you made on that ball!"

Next, the angry catcher sprinted over to the scorekeeper's table. He slammed his fist on the table and snarled at the terrified young man that had scored the dropped pop-up as a hit. "That was no hit, that was no hit," he shouted.

The terrified scorekeeper felt his warm urine running down his leg.

The next thing Chadwick knew, he was being muscled by someone from behind, who wrapped his arms around him to contain and settle him down. "Everything is okay, Walter," Bradsher said in a calm voice. "Let's finish the game and catch the train back to Durham."

Trinity and Bradsher did just that. The sophomore strikeout king held Guilford hitless the rest of the way. He finished the day with eleven strikeouts and a 13-0 victory.

~

ON THE TRAIN ride back to Durham, Bradsher said to Chadwick, "We're different and sometimes I don't understand what you say and do. Walter, you are my best friend. I know you always have my best interests in your heart. I thank you for your caring and willingness to fight for me."

Sixteen

BEST FRIENDS

My best friend is the man who in wishing me well
wishes it for my sake.
~ Aristotle

I T IS OBVIOUS IN WHOSE CORNER WALTER CHADWICK STOOD IN. Minutes before the second battle against Wake Forest, he walked down the first base line with his pitcher. "You've got this, Brad. We have gone over their lineup and we know these guys like the back of our hands. Follow our game plan and concentrate on every pitch. Put everything on the black edge of the plate and nothing down the middle."

Bradsher's near perfection of his control on his drop ball thrown at two varying speeds made him almost unhittable. The combination of these two pitches, with his ninety-two-mph fastball, served as lethal weapons against the Guilford and Wake Forest teams.

In the entire game, the crafty lefty had Wake at his mercy and sent batter after batter cussing and moaning after they swung helplessly at his assortment of curveballs and perfectly placed fastballs. He finished the day with thirteen strikeouts, allowing just two hits. The two singles came in the ninth inning. Trinity prevailed, 8-0.

The Trinity hurler continued to put the ball on the black edge of the plate and followed his catcher's lead. As he pitched, the fans noticed a slight smile on his face. It's a happy smile, not one that portrayed cockiness. Chadwick had told him this game of baseball would become fun. He was now having the time of his life.

The Trinity ace had turned the corner and had his game in place. Months of throwing at that old, ratty mattress and working with his best friend every day, for a year, had brought him tremendous rewards: three shutouts in eight days.

~

AFTER SHAKING THE HANDS of the opposing ball club, Bradsher said to his batterymate. "Walter, I need to go meet with the press, why don't you join me today?"

"Hot damn … I mean, sure thing!" he responded.

As they walked to the press tent, he turned and looked Bradsher in the eyes. "You may not see it as clearly as I do, but a star has been born. Performing as you have in the last eight days are the feats of legends. I predict you will become a folk hero in the South. Thousands of fans will want to see you perform and are going to follow you on trains across the state for years to come."

"I couldn't have done any of this without you, Walter." He slung his arm around his best friend's shoulder. "We've got a lot of work to do in the future. For now, let's go meet with the press."

Chadwick laughed and said, "They're hungry as vultures to ask you questions about the last eight days and have their story printed in tomorrow's paper."

The press tent was packed with more than a half dozen excited reporters. They swarmed Bradsher and Chadwick, rifling one question after another at the two batterymates.

Bill Boggs with *The Greenville Times* waived his right hand frantically as he stepped in front of Bradsher. "Today was the fourth shutout of your sophomore season. How would you measure your success?"

The star hurler was quick to answer. "By the number of hits, runs, strikeouts, and whether we won the game or not. To be honest with you, Bill, the stats don't count for a hill of beans if you don't win the game."

O. Maxwell Gardner of the *Raleigh News and Observer* politely and calmly raised his hand. Gardner was a class act. Bradsher smiled and pointed at him. "Max, you're next. Fire away."

"Bradsher, your performance this past week has been one that has never been matched in college in the South. To what do you attribute your incredible effectiveness and the opposition's lack of being able to put the bat on the ball?"

"Max, thanks for your question. I perfected my two drop ball pitches in the past two months. I feel my ability to deliver a variation of pitches with pinpoint control gives me a big advantage over the hitter. Over the last eight days, my team's great defense and Walter's leadership behind the plate have made my job a lot easier."

The reporters screamed out Bradsher's name. Each one attempted to yell over each other to get his attention. Several story-hungry writers were starting to shove each other to get closer.

Gene Floyd, of *The Charlotte Observer*, was picked next and he stepped in front of Bradsher. He was able to speak with a cigarette dangling from his lips. "After pitching the nineteen-strikeout, no-hitter against Wake, how does it feel to have two no-hitters spoiled late in the seventh and ninth innings against Guilford and Wake?"

The Trinity southpaw gritted his teeth and responded, "It stings and is very disappointing. No-hit opportunities are usually very rare for a pitcher. Gene, I look at the whole body of work for the last eight days, and I'm very pleased. Also, I believe my catcher owes me a couple of steak dinners."

"Chadwick, Chadwick, what's it like catching Bradsher?" Bill Harvey of *The Atlanta Constitution* shouted out. "When he is performing like he has been for the last eight days."

"It is like sitting on the back seat of a canoe on a mirror-like calm lake and having him paddle us to the other side. All I have to do is steer a little bit."

Chadwick laughed out loud. "Bradsher's strikeout streaks

are like picking grapes off the vine. They come in bunches. It's fun being part of the show when his control is so perfect and the strikeouts start piling up. But this is getting expensive! At the beginning of the week, I told him I would buy him a steak dinner for every shutout he pitched. It looks like now I'm going to have to buy him the whole cow!"

The room exploded with laughter. "Gentlemen, there's another part of the story on Bradsher I think you should be writing. Most of you don't know that he never was on a high school team. They asked him to pitch one time as a fill-in to avoid a forfeit. He was a walk-on at Trinity his freshman year and knew very little about the mechanics and the mental approach of pitching."

His outspoken catcher continued, "Part of your story should be about the sacrifices he's made to get to this high-performance level. I know, fellows, because I've worked with him almost every day for the last year, teaching him to pitch and helping him hone his skills. His mechanics, control, composure, change of speeds, and intelligent decisions on the mound has never been equaled in college baseball since Christy Mathewson."

He raised his index finger. "There's another aspect of our work ethic that's making our team successful. Brad and I scout every team we play. The genius of John Heisman inspired us to implement this in our approach to each game. We discuss the strengths and weaknesses of every player we'll face."

"You guys are in the hunt for the SIAA championship. Where do you go from here?" Jack Francis from the *Durham Times* asked.

"We'll work our rear ends off every day and expect our teammates to do the same. We will have to develop our secondary starters if we are going to make it to the big dance. Bradsher can't do it all against the tough schedule we face."

Chadwick had captured the reporters' attention. They feverishly wrote on their pads.

"Gentlemen, go out tomorrow and buy some more yellow pads, a fresh batch of pencils and plenty of ink for your pens. All of you are going to have plenty to write about, and some powerful headlines to post over the next three years."

Bradsher stepped forward and addressed the writers. "We're going to need to call it an afternoon. It's time for us to get to the depot and catch the train. We play the professional team, the Durham Tobacconists in an exhibition game in three days."

"It'll be their first game ever played in the league and we're chosen because of Bradsher's drawing power to bring attention to their new franchise," Chadwick chimed in.

As the two comrades left the journalists pool, Arthur turned to his catcher and said, "Thanks for what you said back there. You have always stood behind me and tried to help. You possess one of the greatest traits of being a loyal friend."

"What's that, Arthur?"

"You always have my best interests at heart. You want what's best for me. I feel very fortunate to have a best friend in you."

Seventeen

A WALK AND TALK
WITH CAP CARD

*Baseball was, is and always will be to me
the best game in the world.*
~ Babe Ruth

Y OU NEED TO GO SEE ARTHUR BRADSHER THIS WEEK,"
President Kilgo said to his new athletic director, Wilbur
Wade, who had just arrived on campus in September 1903. "This
is your first order of business at Trinity.

"His winning style and leadership are drawing tremendous
attention to Trinity College. This young man is one of the most
unique individuals to ever attend our school. Go see him tomorrow
morning, get back to me, and tell me what you think," Kilgo said.

Wilbur thought to himself, *Is he the one?*

~

WILBUR WADE CARD was a past star athlete at Trinity. He
was a hard-hitting outfielder who set several batting records. He
was the team Captain in the 1899 season when the Trinity blue
went twelve and six, and he acquired the nickname "Cap."

Upon graduating in 1900, Card attended the School of Physical
Education at Harvard University. After receiving his degree from

Harvard in 1902, President John Kilgo invited Card to return to his alma mater and become the director of the new physical education program.

Wilbur Wade (Cap) Card. Trinity star ballplayer in 1898 and Athletic Director from 1903-1946.
~ Courtesy of Duke University Library and Archives

Kilgo wanted Card to get to know Bradsher. "Tell me if you think our star pitcher would be a formidable team Captain for his next three years," Kilgo demanded. "Bradsher's heroics on the field, fine example of sportsmanship, and competitiveness to show up every time he crosses the white lines and steps onto the baseball field.

"Ask him what ideas he has to improve our baseball program. With football having been banned at Trinity, baseball is now at center stage."

~

WHEN CARD ARRIVED at Bradsher's dorm, he was standing outside. He was met by Arthur's wide and friendly smile, and a strong handshake. "You must be Mr. Card," he said warmly.

"Yes, I am, Arthur, and you can call me Cap," replied Mr. Card.

He pointed down the street. "Let's walk and talk and get to know each other." Their first meeting would be the beginning of a close relationship. Both would leave a substantial mark on Trinity College and Duke University's history.

Card needed to hear from the star hurler about his first-year experience and learn more about his second-year turnaround.

"How did your first year go, Arthur? I understand Coach Schock pitched you in ten games and you won six of them."

"Well, Cap, I got a little roughed up along the way. I guess this is to be expected for a greenhorn who had never pitched on an organized ball team before coming to college," he answered with a wide grin.

"I also had problems coming into the Lehigh game after pitching three games in five days. I could barely raise my arm up to the letters on my uniform because my arm was so sore. I asked to sit out the game. Coach Schock and Captain Anderson insisted I pitch, and I agreed. I got my clock cleaned five days later by Harvard, the number one team in the country. Then lost ten to seven to Wake Forest, in the pouring rain. What a miserable stretch! I came close to quitting the team after the flop in the slop against Wake.

"Cap, I've always believed that adversity can teach you many lessons and make you stronger. Following a raging storm, there's always calmer waters. I tried in the 1901 season never to be overcome with disappointment, but to keep pushing forward and getting better. I felt blessed that I had been given the opportunity to pitch ten games as a first-year pitcher, with no previous experience."

He continued, "Cap, I carried a small three-by-five notebook in my back pocket during the 1901 season. After every game, I jotted down notes and reflections on my strong points and weaknesses where I needed to improve."

Card rubbed his chin and reflected, *Bradsher is not a quitter and has a plan for success.*

"I realized early I had a lot to learn. I knew if I worked on every aspect of my pitching and even hitting, I would ultimately excel. It's one of the things I love about college athletics. It gives me the opportunity to set goals and work until I reach them."

Good answer, Cap Card thought. *This young man is willing to learn and grow.*

He pitched another question to Bradsher. "Let's talk about your second year. You had a breakout season, including four shutouts that electrified baseball fans in the South. Your ERA dropped drastically, as did your hits and walks given up. One of your shutouts was a no-hitter, in when you struck out nineteen batters against Wake. Wow! How did you get there?"

"I was fortunate my best friend, Walter Chadwick, spent the entire summer and fall teaching me how to pitch. He caught at Trinity Park in 1901. Chadwick is a baseball genius and really knows the game. I had specific goals for the upcoming 1902 season and a strong determination to achieve them. Walter held me accountable every day to reach them.

"I knew to achieve my goals to become one of the finest pitchers in the league, I would need to master my control, hitting the corners consistently and keep a calm temperament in any game situation. My batterymate and I set a goal not to give up more than one walk in a nine-inning contest. If my control was near-perfect, I knew I would be the one in command and not the opposing batters. The strikeouts would take care of themselves."

Wow! One walk per nine innings is unheard of!

"Mr. Card, by the early spring of 1902, I had a perfect command of four pitches. If I could take every team into the ninth inning, allowing just one run, we'd have a good chance to win in every game we played."

This is an intelligent, hardworking, and goal-setting young man, Card thought.

He continued, "It took me four games into the 1902 season to convince Coach Stocksdale that Chadwick should be our catcher. After he was announced as our starter, for the Hobart game, we began to rally. My best friend led us to eleven straight victories."

This sounds like an unbeatable combination. I better make a point to go see Chadwick next, he thought.

"I love baseball. It's the greatest game in the world. After putting in all the work with Walter and pitching the three straight shutouts in eight days in April 1902, I was having the time of my life."

"You look fit, tell me about your exercise regime."

"Cap, I keep care of myself. I don't drink, don't smoke, and do push-ups every day. I lift an old wooden chair by gripping one of the chair legs and raising it into the air fifty times to strengthen my back and pitching arm."

It was evident that he was speaking to a mature and well-grounded young man. Having lost his father to tuberculous at age four, he had been forced to grow up faster than most boys.

Card asked him another question. "Tell me about your faith, Arthur."

"My faith in the Lord is strong and is strengthened every day by spending ten minutes a day reading the Bible. My Christian beliefs help me stay calm, peaceful, and focused when I walk into troubled waters. I know I am an instrument of Christ. My favorite Psalm is the Twenty-Third, and my favorite verses are Philippians four-six."

He recited the Philippians 4:6 verse to Cap Card. "Do not be anxious about anything, but in every situation, by prayer and petition, with thanksgiving, present your requests to God."

Card responded, "It's obvious that you're strong in your beliefs. When the time is right for you, find a wife who is equally yoked in your love for the Lord."

It was revealed in the brief time he'd spent with Arthur, he had a wonderful attitude, great pitching credentials, high morals, and leadership qualities. He was a talented, rising star. He could lead

Trinity College as Captain and to win the SIAA championship.

Baseball was king in the South in 1902. Little did Card know that standing right in front of him was a prince that would in a few years become a king on the Southern diamond.

"Cap, I think I'm going to jog back from here. I try to run every day. We have spent too much time talking about me. I hope on our next visit when we get together, you'll tell me a little bit about yourself, and we can start to build a strong and lasting friendship."

"It's been a real pleasure to meet you, Arthur. We'll meet up again soon."

"You can count on me to be loyal to the Trinity program and always give you my all." He extended his hand to Cap and gave him a firm handshake.

Card watched Bradsher sprinting down Broad Street until he disappeared behind the maple trees that lined Hanes Field.

~

At four-thirty, W.W. Card found himself sitting across from the large, antique mahogany desk of Dr. Kilgo. He looked directly into the president's eyes and told him emphatically, "Sir, you have a one-of-a-kind student leader and ball player in Arthur Brown Bradsher.

"In all my years of athletics, I've never met a better athlete suited to Captain a team than this special young man. He is the one that will put Trinity on the map as one of the finest colleges in the South. He will be a real drawing card.

"He is the one!"

Eighteen

A BRIGHT ORANGE MOON

You let go of my hand to hold on to my heart
Distance grasps us tight now that we are apart.
~ Munia Khan

I T WAS A WARM, SUMMER NIGHT AT SUMMERLEA IN 1950, WITH A slight breeze blowing in from the river. A bright orange moon stared down into the faces of all nine of Bradsher's grandchildren, and they stared back in awe. At story time after dinner, all the children sat on the heart pine floor of the screened porch in a half circle around their grandparents. Little Bradsher sat in Grandmother Lizzie's lap. They both held each other tight.

"Why are we here?" ten-year-old Elizabeth asked her grandfather. He loved the inquisitiveness of his grandchildren, or his ball team, as he called them. They were coachable and always willing to learn new things.

Grandfather smiled with such love in his eyes and replied softly, "Why do you think we're here, my dear child?"

Elizabeth quickly blurted out her answer. "So, we can play ball, eat fresh corn and tomatoes, go crabbing, fish, and swim in the river."

His tone when speaking to his grandchildren was always calm. He hesitated for a second or two, carefully pondering, before giving what was a wise and assuring answer to one of them. He made them feel important.

"Sometimes the answers to your questions are right in front of you. Look around, Elizabeth. What do you see?" She turned in a full circle and looked at her brother, sister, and cousins, one by one. She stood up and walked to the back of the porch and looked out at the full moon and the bluff hovering over the Neuse River. She turned and stepped back and sat down in her place in front of her grandfather.

As she began to speak, she reached out and took her cousin Patti's hand. The children on the floor seemed to follow her cue and reached out to the cousin or sibling sitting next to them. "I see my family, my cousins, my little brother, and my very special and dear grandparents I love so much. I see the moon lighting up the sky. I see the stairs going down to the river. The lower stairs and river are hidden by the darkness of the night, and that troubles me."

Grandfather said, with crinkles around his eyes, "What you're seeing and capturing in your heart, at this special moment, is there's nothing more important in this world than your family. You see this close circle, and in it, there is something to love, to understand, support and cherish for the rest of your life, as I have." The grandchildren's grips got tighter. Nine sets of eyes were fixed on the sixty-seven-year-old patriarch.

He pointed towards the river and the magnificent full moon brightly hovering over the water. "Children, as we look at the moon and gaze at its beauty, we witness one of God's beautiful creations. His presence is undeniable to me, and that gives me a great deal of peace.

"What you can't see is the stairs leading down from the bluff, and the river itself that is hidden in the darkness." The wise man continued. "The stairs represent the new opportunities that each of you will be presented with during your life. While some of those new experiences may seem scary because they are hidden in the shadows, they can materialize into positive things if you keep stepping forward to seize the opportunity."

"Thank you, Grandfather, I'll remember your words always,"

Elizabeth responded.

"Sandy, you've been mighty quiet tonight. Is there something on your mind?" Grandmother asked.

"Yes, Granny, will you sing 'How Great Thou Art,' to us?"

"Why I'd be honored to sing that endearing hymn for all my sweet grandchildren," she answered. "It is your grandfather's and my favorite." She stood and walked over to Freddie, her oldest grandchild. She placed her petite hands on either side of his face, kissed his forehead, and asked in a soft, caring voice, "Will you please accompany me on the piano?"

Freddie had played Bach, Mozart, Gershwin, and special hymns for his grandmother many times. They both shared a love for music, and he adored her.

"I'd love to, Grandmother."

She walked to back of the porch, which offered a sensational view for all present.

The children turned to face her, the moon and stars cascading over the Neuse River. The moon rays reflected over Grandmother's beautiful face as she began to sing the lyrics of one of the family's favorite hymns. Freddie began to play "How Great Thou Art" and Grandmother began to sing. The words seemed to be formed by the voice of an angel as Lizzie began:

> *O Lord my God, when I'm in awesome wonder,*
> *Consider all the worlds Thy hands have made;*
> *I see the stars, I hear the rolling thunder,*
> *Thy power throughout the universe displayed.*
> *Then sings my soul, my Savior God, to Thee,*
> *How great Thou art! How great Thou art!*

Lizzie's faced glowed with happiness as she continued.

> *Then sings my soul, my Savior God, to Thee,*
> *How great Thou art! How great Thou art!*

After she had finished her lovely rendition of the hymn, all the children stood and clapped in great exhilaration. Each of the grandchildren walked over and gave his or her grandmother a big hug.

Grandfather said to his children and grandchildren. "While I have you standing, let's hold hands and say the Twenty-Third Psalm together." Everyone reached out for each other and formed a circle and began to recite one of his favorite Psalms:

The Lord is my shepherd. I shall not want.
He maketh me lie down in green pastures.
He leadeth me beside the still waters.
He restoreth my soul.
He leadeth in the paths of righteousness
For his name's sake.
Yea though I walk through the valley
Of the shadow of death,
I will fear no evil for Thou art with me.
Thy rod and staff comfort me.
Thou preparest a table before me.
In the presence of mine enemies
Thou anointest my head with oil.
My cup runneth over.
Surely goodness and mercy shall follow me
All of the days of my life.
And I shall dwell in the house of the Lord forever.

~

EVERYONE SAT DOWN afterward. They were greeted by Aunti Pearl, who had a tray of goodies for the children: small pastries stuffed with apples, miniature pecan pies, and a glass of cold milk. As they munched on the snacks, Kirk joined in, "Will you tell us about the famous Mercer game?"

He asked Aunti Pearl, "Would you please get me the box off the mantle in the living room?"

She returned with a handsome heart pine box that had twelve stones in it. Grandmother had painted each with words that Arthur and Lizzie hoped would convey a special message to each of the grandchildren. They would spend summer nights discussing them in the future.

The words on the stones were as follows: Faith. Forgiveness. Hope. Passion. Laughter. Courage. Tenderness. Grace. Love. Gratitude. Joy. The last stone had the two words, *Never Quit*.

Grandfather reached into the wooden box and took out a flat stone that Lizzie had painted three words on: Time Is Precious. "I'm going to save this stone for a special night this summer. I want each of you to keep the one you have selected, and over the next few days, think about what the stone you picked means to you."

"On future summer nights, I want you to explain to everyone what you hold in your heart for that word on the stone.

"Now, let's get upstairs, wash your faces, brush your teeth, and get in bed. I will be up to say prayers. The last one up the stairs is a rotten egg."

Nine laughing children raced through the living room to the central stairwell. They had inherited their competitiveness from their grandfather.

Nineteen

THE ORDER OF
THE TOMBS

Sports do not build character. They reveal it.
~ Heywood Hale Broun

A S ARTHUR JOGGED TO DR. KILGO'S OFFICE, HE ORGANIZED HIS thoughts he would share with the president of Trinity College. The maple trees that lined Trinity Place were fully leafed and bursting with rich yellow, orange, and red colors. The air was crisp and felt refreshing as it entered Bradsher's expanding lungs. It was a magnificent fall day in October 1902.

The first thing that grabbed Arthur's attention was the desk of the president. He ran his finger along with the inlay on the top edge of the antique walnut desk. "It's very handsome."

Kilgo smiled. "It surely is. This Italian Renaissance executive desk was a gift from Washington Duke to Trinity in 1900.

"It will remain in the president's office for many years to come," he said. "Sit down and make yourself comfortable. It's so good to see you." The two had developed a deep friendship beginning in the early part of the year 1901 when Bradsher was considering leaving the baseball team.

"Arthur, congratulations on being chosen as Captain next year. I appreciate everything you've done and are doing for our college on and off the baseball field. What can I help you with?"

"Sir, I have a proposal. It will benefit Trinity and enrich the lives of the student body."

"Tell me more."

"I want to start an athletic fraternity where students that excel in athletics, academics, debate, editorial activities, and other important campus life would be asked to join. We will be called the 'Tombs.'"

Interesting name, Kilgo thought.

Bradsher continued, "The goals of the Tombs are the furtherance of brotherhood, leadership, and athletics. We'll set out to foster a finer spirit of sportsmanship on campus, but also, we'll attempt to cement and strengthen our relationships with other schools."

"Those are excellent aspirations. Where do you start to make this happen?"

"I'll begin defining the rules of membership to qualify to join the Tombs. We will invite and initiate juniors only. That will give the individual a two-year window to serve Trinity. It also gives the selection board an opportunity to see two years of a student's contributions to the school."

The president leaned forward. "Where do you see the Tombs in twenty years?"

"I feel it'll grow and shed light on the merits of athletics in college life. It will be serving a vastly expanded sports agenda at Trinity which will include basketball and football teams being added. If we recruit men who are not only fine athletes, but also superlative in their academics and activities on campus, the Tombs will become one of our strongest organizations."

Bradsher looked directly into Dr. Kilgo's eyes. "I also see the possibility of something that most people don't envision. Trinity is an attractive environment for women to attend college. As women's attendance grows, so will the athletic opportunities for them to get involved. I believe in fifteen or twenty years, a women's sister society to the Tombs will be proposed."

"Arthur, your ideas are great. I want to start the Tombs organization at Trinity. First, I will have to run it past our board members. One of the first questions they will ask is, who will comprise the first order of the Tombs, and what are the qualifications? Who's your starting lineup to get the Tombs off the ground?"

Bradsher chuckled. "It's funny that you use the word lineup because I propose that our first Tombs class will have nine members. The first initiation will take place in March of 1903."

He slid a piece of paper across the desk. "Most of the men have either excelled in academics or are leaders of important organizations outside of the classroom. All the Tombs candidates on that list have a love for college athletics. Several are varsity players, participate on their class teams, and a few editorialize the sports happening on campus."

The Trinity president looked over the sheet of qualifications of the first pledge class. He raised his eyebrows and stared sternly at Arthur when he spoke. "I'm concerned. There seems to be one person on the list that has had few contributions during his time at Trinity. Why is John Walker being considered for the Tombs?"

"I got to know John when we both attended Durham High School. They nicknamed him 'Little John' because of his small stature. Some of the kids used to make fun of him because of his size, and they'd rough him up. I came to his defense several times until the hooligans realized if they're going to mess with Little John, they'd have to deal with me, also," Bradsher said, slapping his hand on Dr. Kilgo's desk.

"You're right, sir, his resume pales in comparison to the others on the list.

"John Baily is on the debate team and the class baseball team, not the varsity. That's not a whole lot in most people's minds," he continued. "Sometimes our life shouldn't be judged on our good deeds or accomplishments alone. Some are passed over when maybe they should've been given a chance to succeed or be included."

The tone of his voice became stronger. "I believe in Little John and feel the Tombs can be a life-changer for him. There's no better feeling than to be wanted as part of a team. Many times, when you give someone an unexpected opportunity to participate, it creates loyalty and an important level of appreciation. Those two qualities can make remarkable things happen."

"It's a point well taken, Arthur."

"I hope John accepts my invitation to join the Tombs. I believe he'll do wonderful things for the college before he graduates."

"Good for you Arthur, I agree with you. You have my complete support. I'll get back with you after I've talked with the board."

They both stood. Arthur shook Dr. Kilgo's hand and turned to leave.

The president looked out of his office window and smiled. He watched his prized student-athlete jog down Trinity Place.

Cap was right by saying, *He is the one, he is truly the one!*

The 1937 Tombs continued to foster the spirit of finer sportsmanship on the campus and to cement firmly the relationship between Duke and other universities and schools in the field of Sports. Between 1903-1943 the Tombs initiated over 1,100 members. Tombs members were required to wear their letter sweaters ever Friday on campus. The Tombs were successful in passing a resolution to ban smoking in the Card basketball gymnasium. The Tombs sponsored card stunts at football games and provided entertainment and entertainment and hospitality for visitor teams. They took charge of inner-scholastic basketball and track competition on campus.

~ Courtesy of Duke University Library and Archives

Tombs 1909 class with their bowlers and formalwear.
"Big Bob" Gantt is in the top row, third from the left.
~ Courtesy of Duke University Library and Archives

Twenty

TOMBS STARTING NINE

*The worst kind of group for an organization that
wants to be innovative and creative is
one in which everyone is alike and gets along too well.*

~ Margaret A. Neale

BRADSHER BEGAN, "FELLOWS, I'VE ASKED YOU HERE TONIGHT to invite you to join an honorary society new to Trinity College. I have met with President Kilgo and he's given me his full blessings to start this organization."

"I've provided him a list of potential Tombs members, on which your name is included. He and the Trinity board members are very excited that you'll be part of the team that will change Trinity history."

Bradsher stepped forward and placed a basketball and a football on the table. "The start of basketball is right around the corner. We don't know the future of football. I've heard that Card is going to start a basketball team program in the next couple of years.

"As the sports programs grow at Trinity, the Tombs will be deeply committed to promoting the betterment of athletics on all levels, both varsity and the college class teams.

"Let's go around the room and I'd like everybody to share a

little about themselves. Any creative ideas on how you can serve the student body and Trinity College would be appreciated. We need officers for leadership, recording the minutes, managing the budget, with public relations, and suggestions to make membership in the Tombs a fun and unforgettable experience.

"Jesse Frizzell, will you be the leadoff hitter? We'll go clockwise around the table. I understand some of your classmates have nicknamed you 'the hot-headed debater.'" He chuckled.

"That's right. Debating is what I do best, and I have won several debate medals. I was the recording secretary for the Hesperian Society. I'm in the Kappa Alpha fraternity, the 9019, and Tau H Beta Kappa Honorary Societies. I don't play sports, but I'm an avid fan. I have really enjoyed watching you pitch this season. I would like to volunteer to record the minutes for the order of the Tombs. Let's make this meaningful for Trinity and outrageously fun for all of us."

"Request accepted and thank you for your compliment," Bradsher said as he shifted his eyes and pointed in the direction of William Finger.

"They call me 'Baggy, the Chemist' because of my love of science. If you need any fireworks made for any special occasions, such as our initiation ceremony, I'm the man to see." The room broke out in laughter. "I'm also in the KA fraternity, 9019 Honorary Society, and was a marshal for this year's commencement. I play on the class baseball team. I feel the Tombs should be active in organizing pep rallies for athletic events. You can count me in to help with this."

"Excellent!" Bradsher enthusiastically responded.

William had a question for Bradsher and began by saying, "We're a real mixed bag of nuts sitting around the circle tonight. What're the qualifications a candidate should have to be asked to join the Tombs?"

"Good question, William," Bradsher responded.

"First, I propose the invitee be a junior at Trinity. That would give the inductee two years to participate in the order of the Tombs. The invited members shall participate or have a love for athletics and a strong commitment for the sports programs' betterment at Trinity.

"One of our main objectives is to improve team sportsmanship and student school spirit in athletics on campus. We want the Tombs to lay the groundwork for firmly cementing the relations between Trinity and other schools in the field of sports."

Bradsher continued, "One question that Dr. Kilgo asked is, 'Where do you see this organization in twenty years?'

"I told him that I felt the athletic programs are going to grow faster than weeds in your mother's garden, and that we'll be the strongest and most influential organization on campus."

"I'm Arthur Elliot and I've enjoyed playing on the baseball team with you for the past two years. I'm also in the KA fraternity, a member of 9019, and TBK. I made the track team this year and was a marshal at commencement ceremonies. Bradsher, I would like to see us liven up this place a little bit. Let's get some gals to visit our campus for a party. We can sponsor a spring dance a few weeks before baseball and track seasons begin."

Elliot continued, "We could invite some of the girls from Trinity Park, St. Mary's, and other nearby girls' school. Maybe we get the Kappa Alpha, Alpha Tau Omega, and Kappa Sigma fraternities to co-sponsor the event."

Bradsher complimented him, "That's a great suggestion, Arthur. We could hold a pep rally kicking off the track and baseball seasons and announce the spring dance at the same time.

"Lemuel Hardy Gibbons, you're next. Lem, what do you have for us today?"

"Good afternoon, fellows. I begin by saying that I'm honored to be chosen in the starting lineup for the order of the Tombs."

"Lem, tell us of your involvements in athletics and campus life," Bradsher said.

"I'm a member of the Kappa Sigma Fraternity. Some of my classmates call me 'Cap.' Last September, the executive committee named me captain of the track team. I have enjoyed standing beside Brad as an assistant manager on the baseball team.

"This year, I had the honor of being the treasurer to the athletic department and would love to help with the budget and finances of the Tombs."

"Request accepted," Brad responded with a smile. "Just promise me you'll keep the books balanced."

William Loudermilk stood up, took a step towards Bradsher, and shook his hand. "I appreciate the invitation to join. I love a great debate and the opportunity to speak at the YMCA. I'm an Intersociety debater and am the Columbian Society's secretary. I have recently been appointed as historian for the junior class. I'm sure I'll record some interesting stories about the antics of the Tombs over the next two years."

"Thank you, William. Glad to have you join us."

Bradsher pointed his finger at the next man in the circle.

"I'm Edwin Hoover and I'm the man that whipped Billy Crabtree. Men, when we've got more time, I'll tell you about that tall tale. I'm in the 9010, clerk for the Tribunal and on the executive committee for the Columbian Society. "I love being a part of the Glee Club. Somewhere along the line, this group will need a song to sing, probably at our initiation next March. I'll help write it and coach our team on performing that song."

"Clem, you're next up," Bradsher said.

"I hail from the small town of Roxboro. I'm an ATO, in the 9019 Society, and have a great love for baseball. I am captain for the class baseball team. I've won an orator's medal and was secretary and am now on the executive committee for Columbian."

"Any fresh ideas for the Tombs, Clem?" Bradsher asked.

Clem smiled. "Brad, you're the most famous athlete to ever attend Trinity College. The fans revere you. Let's use this to our advantage and have you give a talk at the YMCA on the merits of athletics in college life. You always have an overflow crowd when you speak. This would be a very effective way to get the message and purpose of the Tombs across to the student body."

"Great idea, Clem. You should speak also," Brad replied.

The last to offer his opinion was a shy young man. He stood a mere five-feet-five-inches tall. He had jet-black eyes and parted his hair down the middle. He wore a bowtie. "My name is John Bailey

Walker Junior. Many people call me Little John. I do not have a lot to say about myself. I'm a member of the Columbian Society and I enjoy the debate process. I love baseball and am on the class baseball team," he said, shuffling his feet.

"Quite frankly, I don't know why I've been asked to join this group of highly accomplished students. I will work hard to serve this organization if I am invited. I have a few suggestions about our initiation."

"Tell us your thoughts, John Bailey," Bradsher said.

"I think we should have an outrageous initiation in March. We, the founding members of the Tombs, should be dressed in pajamas, carrying water buckets, paddles, clocks, and cigars. We have bells around our ankles. Let's make this an initiation to remember with the fireworks. The more ridiculous the better!"

He continued, "We will sit on the chapel stairs on initiation day with twenty-foot-long bamboo fishing poles and pails. Baggy's idea is a good one. Nothing gets someone's attention like fireworks exploding everywhere. We cavort on the library or the chapel stairs until we've gotten the attention of the whole college."

Their team leader let out a hearty laugh and said, "For a little man, you sure do have a big imagination. You're my wild card, John. I've got a feeling you're going to make some interesting contributions to the Tombs."

Arthur Bradsher walked to the middle of the circle and with a loud voice asked, "Who's in, gentlemen?"

All the nine men raised their hands and shouted with joy, "Long live the Tombs! Long live the Tombs!"

Twenty-one

PLAYING THE PROS

I will always treat you with respect. However, please understand when I cross the white lines that from the initial pitch of the first inning to the last pitch of the game, I am not your friend.
~ Arthur Bradsher

B Y MAY 1903, EVERY TEAM WANTED TO KNOCK OFF THE Trinity Nine and every player was gunning for the tar heel sensation, Arthur Bradsher. Every opponent that faced the southpaw hurler deemed it the most important game of the season. If a ball club played a doubleheader against Trinity, they had always led with their ace in the first game. Bradsher always faced the best the opposition had to offer.

The Charlotte professional team was a member of the Carolina Baseball Association. It was made up of star ex-college players and players from various league teams. They were a very strong team and came into the contest against Trinity undefeated. They had two wins against Davidson, and one each from Horner and McAdenville.

The Charlotte Hornets wanted to put another notch in their belt by beating the best pitcher in the South, Arthur Bradsher.

The crafty southpaw from Durham was having a phenomenal junior season. After the first five games, the Trinity Twirler had faced 155 batters and struck out forty-three, allowed twenty-five hits, and walked only two men. His average for the five games was eight strikeouts and five hits per game.

In his only loss of the young season, Bradsher yielded only five hits. Cornell prevailed, five to one. All five of Cornell's runs were unearned, as Trinity made ten errors. Trinity's sloppy defense proved fatal for any chances of winning.

Chadwick, without Bradsher being present, gave his team a tongue-thrashing after the game for their uninspired efforts. "Fellows, this type of sloppy play and lack of hustle are unacceptable in my book," he barked at his teammates. "I expect a significant effort from you guys against South Carolina and Charlotte." He slammed the door behind him when he left.

~

THE DAY BEFORE THE GAME, Chadwick and Bradsher talked about a game plan against Charlotte. "Jesse Oldham is their biggest gun," Chadwick advised. "I've studied his career because he's a catcher. He played college ball with the University of North Carolina in 1891. He even coached the team in 1895.

"Many say he's the best college catcher ever to play in the South. He's played on eight minor league clubs since leaving Carolina." The Trinity catcher added. "Unfortunately, I don't have any more information on the rest of Carolina professional squad."

He continued in a serious tone, "Jesse Oldham's bat and arm need to be respected. His throws are quick and accurate. His bat has always been one of the best in the South. He's a left-handed hitter that loves to jerk the ball." Chadwick displayed a mock swing of his own.

"Oldham bats cleanup spot and in many games," Chadwick continued, "he does just that! He clears the bases driving in runners with his frozen rope line drives and dingers sailing over the fences. Baserunners fear him because his rocket throws usually arrive at the bag before they do.

"Be very careful with Jesse Oldham," the outspoken backstop added. "Throw your pitches to paint the corners of the plate. If you throw anything down the middle, it'll cost you. Don't be afraid of walking Oldham, if you must. Pitch him a couple of inches outside of the strike zone. If he doesn't take the bait, that's fine. You may be better served by giving him a free pass than him driving the ball over the fence."

~

THE CHARLOTTE CAPTAIN has a big bat. He also has a big mouth. The outspoken Charlotte catcher bragged to a reporter the afternoon before the big game with Trinity. He confidently predicted victory.

"We expect to win the game with Trinity tomorrow," Oldham began with an uppity tone in his voice. "They have a good pitcher, but we have very good hitters, who successfully have faced the South's best pitchers. Bradsher will be no match for us."

Catcher Oldham, a cocky talker, could not stop there. "Our men play a better game in the field than probably any team in the South. Our three outfielders are stars and can be counted on for every chance, while the infielders will take care of anything that comes their way."

When Bradsher read Oldham's comments in the morning paper, he thought he would play his game without a lot of trash talk. He'd let his strong arm, nasty curveballs, bat, glove, and his speed on the bases do all the talking for his team and himself. Oldham's cocksure talk motivated Bradsher.

~

IT WAS FIFTEEN MINUTES BEFORE the start of the game. Chadwick had a ritual. He loved to show off his talents. He crouched behind the plate and when he received pitches from his batterymate, he fired off throws to second base and third base. He loved to show off the strength and accuracy of his arm. He did this on five or six pitches. In between his strikes to the bag, he looked over at the opposition, especially Oldham.

Bradsher viewed his strong-armed catcher as an insurance policy against the steal and bunt. Every look over to the Charlotte bench was to serve as a reminder that Bradsher's policy was in full effect and he was fully protected on this sunny spring day.

Oldham yelled out to him, "Why don't you go have a seat, hotdog?"

Coach Stocksdale stood behind him and rolled three balls seven feet in front of the plate. The flamboyant catcher pounced on the mock bunt and fired a bullet to first base. He proceeded to make two hard and accurate throws to each of the other bases.

As he walked towards the bench, he again looked over and pointed his finger at the Charlotte bench.

His look and actions seemed to say, *Go ahead and try to bunt or steal off me, and I'll show you who's boss!*

It was game time!

Twenty-two

PLAY BALL

Baseball is a man maker.
~ Al Spalding - 1875

UMPIRE BROWN SCREAMED, "PLAY BALL!" THE CONTEST would feature the pros against the Trinity College amateurs. It is 1903.

It was a crummy start for Bradsher. Roberson beat out a bunt, and he walked Oldham. The Trinity hurler caught the next hitter, Brown, off balance. He swung at a curveball and sent a can of corn flyball to center fielder Wooten for the first out in the inning.

Great! Now strike out the next two hitters and get out of this inning.

It didn't happen. The cleanup hitter, Springs, drilled a low fastball down the line that kicked up the chalk dust. When the white powder settled, Springs had tripled.

Frustration pumped through Bradsher's veins. He smiled and tried to display calmness. The Trinity Blue were down by a score of two to nothing.

Bradsher grimaced. *Holy Cow! This is getting ugly. It's time to stop the bleeding.*

Springs smiled and clapped his hands as he stood on third base and pointed his finger at the Trinity ace. "We've got your number today, Bradsher!" He was only ninety feet from home plate, with the third potential run. The Trinity strikeout king knew what he must do.

Punch out the next two batters.

Bradsher started Aiken with a high and tight fastball. He was overpowered by the pitch and swung late. The Trinity southpaw came inside with a sharp breaking curveball that froze him for strike two. It was time to waste a pitch to muddy up Aiken's thinking. Bradsher climbed the ladder with a high fastball a foot outside of the strike zone.

The Charlotte second baseman will remember that high ball.

He came back with a twelve-six drop ball that started at the letters. Aikens started his swing high in the zone and he missed it by a foot and a half, as the pitch dropped off the table down below the knees.

"Strike three!" screamed umpire Brown.

Bradsher brought the Trinity faithful to their feet and they started to ring their cowbells, clap, and stomp. He was back in his normal good rhythm.

It is time to knockout Maffit.

He led off the Charlotte shortstop with a couple of fastballs for strikes. He delivered one on the knees and the next on the outside corner at the letters. He finished him off with an inside sweeping curveball that caught him looking for the final out.

The umpire leaped forward and threw a mock knockout punch. "Strike three! You're outta here!"

Puryear led off Trinity's first inning and wasted no time in getting things started. He greeted Smith with a loud crack of the bat as the hard leather ball met the finely-honed piece of timber. He laced a scorching 'seeing-eye single' just beyond the reach of the shortstop. The Trinity nine were off to the races.

The next batter for the boys from Durham was the third sacker, Elliot.

Runs are going to be tough to come by in this contest. Good time to sacrifice bunt to move the runner in scoring position, Bradsher thought.

Coach Stocksdale never gave the bunt signal and Elliot popped up weakly for the first out. The next batter, all-star center fielder

Wooten, had no thoughts about bunting.

Bam!

He launched a mammoth drive over the shallow playing outfielder's head on the fat fastball delivered by Smith. It was belt-high and right down the heart of the plate. He got the barrel out front and the ball hit right on its sweet spot.

Wooten was off with the crack of the bat and had a home run on his mind as he left the batter's box. The fans stomped the bleachers and shouted, "Go, Woot, go!" as he began to circle the bases and the center fielder was on his horse trying to chase down the ball.

"I can do this! Inside-the-parker, here we come!" The fans in the stands heard Wooten yelling at himself.

Halfway to second base, he glanced to his left at his third base coach, who was frantically waving his arms and yelling, "Come on!" As he neared the third base bag, his coach raised both arms to the sky with his palms facing the jolting Wooten. It was a signal to stop. "Hold up! Hold up!" the coach screamed. The baserunner never broke stride as he rounded the base. He was in a full-speed gallop, heading for home.

Pitcher Smith, catcher Oldham and first baseman Springs yelled to their center fielder, "Home! He is going home."

The second baseman, Aiken, scurried towards Roberson deep into the outfield grass and screamed, "Hit the cutoff man!"

The instant shortstop, Maffit, saw the ball sailing over his center fielder's head. He broke toward him and stopped halfway to his teammate. He screamed repeatedly to his center fielder, "Hit me! hit me!"

The ball rolled forever. Roberson bare-handed it at the base of the outfield fence. He wheeled around quickly and threw a bullet towards his strong-armed shortstop, whose back was facing home plate.

As the ball neared his glove, Maffit thought of his next move. Like a ballet dancer doing a pirouette, he rotated his hips to begin a spin move for his throw to his catcher. He heard the snap of the leather when the ball hit his glove. He was ready to cut down the runner trying to score. As his left foot came back down on the solid ground, he cocked his strong arm and planted the cleats of his right foot deeply into the outfield grass. He delivered the straightest, fastest, most accurate throw that anyone in Laffit Stadium had ever witnessed. It was a beautiful and fluid one-piece, catch-and-throw movement. The fans stared in total wonder.

Charlotte's catcher saw the throw coming into the green of the infield and he positioned himself to block the plate. He placed his left foot on the front left edge to keep Wooten's foot from ever reaching the corner. The ball from Maffit hit the infield perfectly, a few feet off the mound and bounded to Oldham. He was wide-eyed as he reached for it.

The turf took a bite out of the speed of the ball coming to the plate. Time froze. The perfect one-bounce throw appeared to get to Oldham prior to the speedy Wooten's arrival.

The advantage shifted to the Charlotte receiver. He caught the perfect strike from his outfielder and gripped the ball firmly. He set up to protect the plate. The muscles in his upper body bulged and he expected an ugly chest-high collision with the charging Wooten.

The fans looked on in horror. Would the collision end the catcher's career?

Oldham and all the screaming fans on both sides were shocked by what happened next.

Twenty-three

THE PLAY AT THE PLATE

Life is a daring adventure, or it is nothing at all.
~ Helen Keller

JESSE OLDHAM WAS PREPARED FOR A BRUTAL COLLISION AT THE plate and his muscles were flexed. He didn't get what he expected.

At the last moment, Wooten bailed out to the right side of the dish with an incredible hook slide. Oldham reached in vain to put the tag on him but missed him by six inches. Umpire Brown went down on one knee and spread his arms out from his body. He screamed at the top of his lungs, "Safe!"

The Charlotte fans were booing the call loudly and the Trinity fans were screaming with sheer delight at Wooten's miraculous slide. The scorekeeper slowly climbed the rickety ladder and hung the crooked number two up on the old wooden scoreboard. Oldham was fuming. He gave the ump a dirty look and kicked dirt onto home plate. He knew it was a tag he should have made. The score was deadlocked at two-two with only one out in the inning.

Howard rubbed the tar rag on the bat handle and then discarded it. Next, he spit a mouthful of nasty black tobacco juice into the palms of his hands and ground the sticky substance onto the bat handle. He wiped his filthy hands across his jersey.

Oldham chattered on every pitch, "Batter, batter, no batter. No-hitter, no-hitter."

Howard choked up two inches on the bat handle. Smith delivered a fastball and he hit a seeing-eye grounder up the middle just beyond the reach of both the shortstop and the second baseman. Bradsher walked past Chadwick on the bench on the way to hit next. They slapped hands, and his catcher screamed, "Hammer it, Brad!"

He stepped into the batter's box hitting in the fifth spot. He had pounded the ball in the first six games of the season and sported a .340 average. He uncoiled his hips and smashed a blue-darter line drive down the right-field line. His lighting speed got him to third base for a triple. Howard crossed the plate giving Trinity a three-two lead. The visiting fans were hollering, "Bradsher, B-r-a-d-s-h-e-r, Bradsher!"

Chadwick followed his buddy to the plate. Brad hollered to him, "Bring me home, Walter!" He drilled a worm-burner that hugged the ground between the first and second basemen. Smith got Webb to pop out and Roper to ground out, finalizing the inning of misery.

Bradsher had two more batters to face in the second inning to complete his first look and evaluate the starting nine for the Hornets.

Chasner led off with a swinging bunt to Elliot at third base. He kicked it. Smith followed with a dying quail bloop hit to shallow right field. Roberson popped up weakly for the first out.

The Carolina hopefuls were slamming their feet against the wooden bleachers and screaming, "Jesse, Jesse." The fans were hungry for another Oldham home run that he was famous for. They were singing, "Home run Jesse, home run Jesse, hit one for Bessie, hit one for Bessie!"

Before stepping into the batter's box, he spit a mouthful of brown tobacco juice into the palm of his hand. He rubbed the nasty sticky substance on the handle of his bat. He reached down and grabbed a handful of brick dust and ground it into the sticky bat handle.

The umpire urged Oldham, "Let's go, Jesse, batter up."

The last thing I'm going to let happen is to let Oldham hit a dinger out of the park.

Bradsher delivered a high brushback pitch that came in dangerously close and about four inches under Oldham's chin. He bailed out and ended up in the red brick dust on his back. The ugly pitch brought out a chorus of boos from the irate Carolina fans.

Chadwick screamed out, "That a boy, Brad, keep him guessing!"

It's time to mix it up and keep Oldham off balance.

He adjusted his fingers on the ball and changed from a fastball to a twelve-six drop ball grip. Bradsher delivered a nasty bender that Oldham's mighty swing missed by a foot. The pitch had him off balance and swinging like a drunk man. The crafty southpaw came back with the same pitch which ended up in the dirt, and the Charlotte catcher laid off it. This brought the count to two and one.

Bradsher thought, *One of the biggest mistakes a pitcher could make against Oldham was to leave a pitch out over the plate, giving him the opportunity to drive it deep. That isn't happening today.*

He jammed him on the next pitch that was just out of the strike zone on the inside corner. This was a battle of the toughest of warriors.

The veteran catcher ran the count full as he fouled off two straight pitches. The seventh pitch delivered was a drop ball that looked like a strike, and Oldham started to swing but held up. He had a good eye.

The pitch was perfect. Bradsher raised his fist into the air in celebration. He looked for the umpire to ring Oldham up with a called strike-three punch-out.

Umpire Brown made a late call. "Ball four," he called out. The bases were now loaded.

The Trinity fans booed, and one disturbing fan screamed out, "The ump is a bum!"

The inning got worse for the Trinity Twirler when he threw a wild pitch on the first ball thrown. Pitcher Smith hustled home for the third Charlotte run. The frustrated lefthander turned his back to the plate and fired the rosin bag to the ground.

It was time for Chadwick to pay a visit to the mound. The inning was getting messy and Bradsher appeared rattled. There was still only one out, and Charlotte had runners on second and third. "Ump, I need a minute to talk to my boy out there.".

"Make it quick."

"Why're you complicating this?" were the first words that came out of Chadwick's mouth.

"I'm struggling a little bit," he said with a downturned expression.

"Look, Bradsher, life's a struggle," his catcher snapped back. "You're tougher than this. You're the best pitcher in the South. Now pitch like it! Let's punch out the next two hitters and get the hell out of here!" he said with his authority. "I ask for only two things. Let me call the pitches and for you to be totally confident in every ball you throw." Chadwick gave a slap of confidence on his sidekick's chest. He turned to head back to the plate and yelled without looking back to the mound, "Let's do this!"

Bradsher got back on track. He struck out Brown on five pitches. When Springs stepped into the batter's box, Chadwick screamed out, "This guy couldn't hit his mother if she was pitching." He was disposed of with six very different looking deliveries.

The Trinity Twirler shut out the professionals for the next seven innings and held them to just three more hits the rest of the contest. He settled down after the second frame with near perfect control, walking only one batter.

The Trinity team had given him good support at the plate, and they added another run in the fourth inning and scored their last run in the sixth.

In nine frames, Puryear went three for five, driving in two runs and scoring three times. Bradsher continued to smack the ball getting three hits in his four at-bats and scoring a run. He had four runs batted in for the afternoon. Wooten hit the thrilling inside-the-park home run and Chadwick went two for four with a stolen base.

Jesse Oldham's biggest mistake for the day was underestimating Arthur Bradsher and the gritty Trinity ball club. The boys from Durham had out-pitched Charlotte and dominated them at the plate. Trinity made two errors, as compared to Charlotte's four.

The crafty southpaw found himself in total control with two outs in the ninth inning against pitcher Smith. He was having his way with him for the day and had already struck him out twice. He was going for a trifecta and his eleventh punch-out of the afternoon.

Chadwick was hollering, "You're the one, you're the hon," on every pitch.

He started Smith with a sweeping curveball strike that came in and jammed him on the hands. His next pitch was a perfectly placed fastball on the outside corner at the knees. He was unable to catch up with it. He climbed the ladder with a high and tight rising fastball that had Smith bailing out of the batter's box. With the ball hidden behind his back, Bradsher changed his grip on the seams of the ball for his knockout pitch.

He reared back, cocked his arm, uncoiled his hips, and delivered. "Swing batter," the feisty catcher yelled! Smith missed the ball by a foot and a half, and it was over. The Trinity ace had struck out the side.

"Ball game!" the umpire shouted out and turned to leave the field.

~

AFTER HE DID a short interview with the local reporter, Bradsher walked over to Jesse Oldham. They walked out to the mound and talked for about fifteen minutes. From across the field, Chadwick observed their body language and mannerisms with their hands. They walked to home plate and again returned to the mound.

What were they talking about? he wondered. A disheartened Chadwick was upset that he wasn't included in the conversation. He turned to walk to the train station.

Later, on the train to Durham, Chadwick asked Bradsher, "What did you and Oldham talk about?"

"We spoke about you, Walter. Jesse feels you have the potential to develop into the best catcher in the South like he was fifteen years ago.

Twenty-four

CAPTAIN AND
CHADWICK
TAKE CHARGE

Defense to me is the key to playing baseball
~ Willie Mays

THE RESULTS THEY HAD ACHIEVED WERE INCREDIBLE AND well earned. Two months prior to the start of the season, Bradsher, Chadwick, Wooten, and Coach Scotsdale had met to discuss goals for the 1904 campaign. Bradsher began by saying, "I will accept for nothing less this season than the SIAA championship. I expect every player, coach, and manager to do whatever it takes to make that happen."

"I need more support from the infield this year, the team captain exclaimed. If we are going to win the championship, we must double up on our infield practice. We need to take ground ball after ground ball until we can't see straight."

Bradsher gave Stocksdale a cold stare. "To accomplish what will be necessary for us to be successful, let's add a couple of assistants to hit ground balls, take throws, and help our team work on the basics."

The Trinity curveball artist slapped his hand on the table and held up two fingers. "In my only two losses last year, we made ten errors in each game. As a team, we committed fifty-seven errors in the nine-complete games I pitched. Coach, that's an average of over six miscues committed per contest. This won't cut it if we expect to win the SIAA this year."

All-Stars Chadwick, bat boy, Bradsher, and Wooten.
~ Courtesy of Duke University Library and Archives

"I feel the same way," Wooten agreed. "I know it's up to us to lead the charge in bringing the champion's trophy to Trinity. No one has had a better view on how last year's team played on defense than me looking in from centerfield. Sometimes, I watched in horror of the sloppy defensive play of our team. We can do much better than our 1903 efforts, but it is going to take demanding work.

"Last year, we played three players at third base, and we committed thirteen errors at that position. I would stick with Webb and Bradsher at third the whole season when they aren't pitching. Let me make it clear to you, Coach, Webb needs to work his ass off to improve his defensive play against the bunt."

It was Chadwick's turn and he faced Coach Stocksdale. There was not the usual smile on the catcher's face. The veins protruded on the back of his neck. He stood rigid and his fists were clenched. The room was quiet, and you could feel the tension that surrounded the coach and his star players.

He cleared his throat, took a deep breath, and said to Stocksdale, "Coach, we need to make some drastic moves."

"Tell me what changes would help the team, and let's talk them out, here and now."

"Coach, the first thing this team needs is a good kick in the butt, and a strong talk on the players making a commitment to excellence for this season," Chadwick said.

The feisty backstop elevated his voice, and his commanding tone became more forceful. He stood so close to Stocksdale, the coach could feel his catcher's breath on his face when he talked. "Let me give you an example of what you should be expecting from our team. Yesterday, Wooten, Bradsher, and I completed a two-month training program to improve our skills. We discussed other matters on how to be better leaders for our team. We talked about ways we can help our men live up to their potential.

"Teams try to beat Brad by playing bunt-and-steal baseball. We've spent months on fielding the bunt and how to pitch around a batter, improving his pickoff moves, and when to pitch out to cut down a baserunner."

Bradsher thought, *Boy, Chadwick would make a fantastic baseball manager.*

"If we can get the other members of this team to share half the fire and determination that Bradsher, Wooten, and I have running through our veins, we'll be on our way to a championship season.

"Coach, it's going to take some changes from doing things the way we've done them in the past two years," the Trinity catcher continued. "It would benefit the team if we started to practice a month earlier. If we have days too cold outside, we need to go inside the gym to practice. We can improve our fielding, bunting and base-running skills, and take extra batting practice every day.

"It needs to be all-in, with no one cutting practices and no exceptions to the team rules." Bradsher thought, *It's obvious that Chadwick had taken over and was leading the meeting.* He knew when it was best to step back and shut up. "What do you think, Coach?" Chadwick asked in a calmer voice.

"I'm willing to commit to upping my game as manager," the coach replied. "I am ready to lead us to the title. You three are great ballplayers and strong leaders. I urge you to help me along the way. I agree we could use some assistance at our practices. Wooten, why don't you and Chadwick put some notices on the bulletin board, and Bradsher, you talk to your two Tombs members that play on the class baseball team. I'll speak to Dr. Kilgo to make sure he makes it a worthwhile experience for the men that join us."

Chadwick responded, "Coach, you need to call a meeting and lay down the law. We'll help you enforce it."

~

IN THE NEXT six weeks, Stocksdale got the support he needed from his three all-star players, and the Trinity baseball team worked their tails off on every aspect of their game, right up to the first game of the season. As they huddled before the first pitch, they put their hands together and yelled, "Team Trinity!"

In his first outing of the year, a warm-up against Trinity Park, Bradsher faced twenty-eight batters and didn't allow a hit or a run. The outcome was a nine-zero shutout. The arduous work and extra practice prior to the beginning of the season had paid off. Trinity College didn't commit a single error in the nine-inning contest, and Webb dazzled handling bunts at third base.

The results in the second game of the young season were even more impressive. Against a much stronger Oakridge team, The Trinity ace again had pinpoint control and gave up one base on balls in a nine-inning, no-hit shutout. The lefty struck out the side in two of the innings. His curveball was sharp-breaking and nasty. He sent one failed batter after another back to the bench cussing, shaking his head, and kicking the dirt.

The Trinity fans screamed at the top of their lungs, blew whistles, rang cowbells, and stomped the wooden stands unmercifully. "Go, Bradsher! Go Bradsher!" they hollered.

The team made only one error. The extra hour of infield

practice at each team meeting was paying off. Chadwick and the infielders were chattering to each other on every pitch. They shouted out: "Batter-batter. No-batter. You're the one! You're the hon!" and "Swing batter, swing!" The atmosphere on the ball field had been electrified.

Bradsher was happy. He flashed his smile often to the batters who were cocky and expectant.

The no-hitter against Oakridge was the third of his college career. The North Carolina wonder walked only one batter in the first two games. He was one of the few lefthanders in the history of the college game that had near perfect control.

Bradsher and Chadwick were on the same page on every pitch. Word spread across the Trinity campus: This team was the real deal. The fans started to come in large numbers to see Trinity and Bradsher perform, and hundreds boarded trains to follow their team across the state of North Carolina.

Next stop was Guilford College. Was there another no-hitter in the Trinity sensation's bag of tricks?

They could smell a championship

Twenty-five

NO HITS

Old-timers at Duke will tell you that back in the early 1900s
when Arthur Bradsher and Bob Gantt were hurling no-hitters,
they were as common as fleas on a hound dog.
~ Ted Mann, Duke publicist

CHADWICK HEARD HIMSELF YELLING AT HIS BEST FRIEND, Arthur Bradsher, and saying, "Are you crazy? You can't quit now." His tone was high pitched, and he was extremely excited in the way he was talking to his teammate. A few minutes passed, and Chadwick realized he was lying in a pool of sweat. He was experiencing one of the worst nightmares of his lifetime.

Earlier that day Trinity College had beaten Guilford College in what seemed to be a boring, lopsided game by a score of sixteen to two with Bradsher pitching in the box for the victors. The press summarized the outcome, as Guilford scored two runs on four hits in the ninth inning. Had Bradsher run out of gas at the end?

What the baseball world didn't understand was the amazing feat that had unfolded on the playing field that day.

After only three games, the direction and momentum of Trinity's baseball successes were being revealed in grand fashion. They had exploded out of the gate like a prize racehorse at Churchill Downs expecting nothing but victory in the race for the roses. Trinity was beginning to flex its muscles in pursuit of the Southern Intercollegiate Athletic Association championship.

~

IN THE PRECEDING SIX WEEKS, Stocksdale got the support he needed from his three-star players, and the Trinity baseball team worked their fannies off on every aspect of their game. As they huddled for the first pitch of the season, they put their hands together in an inner circle and roared, "Team Trinity."

In his first outing of the year, a warm-up game against Trinity Park, Bradsher faced twenty-eight batters and didn't allow a hit in the nine-zero shutout. The hard work and extra practice prior to the beginning of the season made the difference. Trinity did not commit a single error in the entire nine-inning contest.

The results in the second game of the young season were even more impressive. Against a stronger Oakridge team, Bradsher had pinpoint control and did not walk a single batter in a nine-inning, no-hit shutout. His curveball was as nasty, sending one failed batter back to the bench after another. The team made only one error. The fans were starting to come in large numbers to see Trinity and Bradsher perform, and they could sense they were watching a team marching to a championship.

In game three of the season, it happened. All eyes on campus were focused on the game with Guilford College and the Hobbs brothers. Bradsher and Chadwick had spent two hours the day before the big game going through the lineup, discussing their strengths and weaknesses.

In the walk to Hanes Athletic Park, Bradsher had stopped and turned to look Chadwick square in the eye. "You're going to see something today that many may never see again in college baseball."

"What does that mean?" Walter asked.

"Don't ask questions, Walter. Let's go out and win another game," he snapped back at his catcher.

Bradsher stood on the mound in the first inning against Guilford College. Before he threw his first pitch to the leadoff hitter, Chadwick raised his hand to get the attention of the umpire. "Ump, I need to talk to my pitcher for a minute."

"Make it quick, Chadwick, let's get this show on the road," the umpire growled.

He stood directly in front of Bradsher and said, "I want you to nibble on the black edges of the plate on every pitch today. Do not go to the middle ever."

It became evident after the first two innings this was shaping up to be a very special day. The two batterymates were in perfect unison on every pitch. They were like two dancers in perfect harmony with each step. They could read each other's mind.

The score was deadlocked, zip for both teams, after two innings. Even though the Trinity team had not scored yet, they were making great solid contact at the plate. The time the team had spent taking extra batting practice was showing results.

The game remained scoreless for both sides after the third inning. Bradsher had the Guilford team totally puzzled, and frustration was setting in with their hitters. The cunning southpaw's curveballs and drop balls had Guilford totally off balance. They looked like blind men swinging in the dark.

In the bottom fourth inning, Trinity rallied for four runs as balls exploded off their bats. The loyal fans jumped out of their seats and were dancing with joy and excitement.

As Chadwick walked out to catch Bradsher in the bottom of the fifth, the stark realization of what was happening slapped him in the face. Would it be possible for his best friend, the greatest pitcher in the South, to pitch three consecutive no-hitters?

After five complete innings, the fans were starting to whisper between themselves the words no-hitter and no-no. It was at this point of the game, the first signs of tension could be seen. Some fans sat with fists clenched and others seemed frozen, only staring directly at Bradsher. Some of the smiles had disappeared on some of the fans' faces, and some of the fans were feeling tight-chested. Bradsher seemed to be enjoying himself as he struck out the side in the top of the fifth inning.

I'm on my way to pitch three consecutive no-no-hitters and do so without allowing a single walk? Bradsher thought as he walked to the mound.

It had now become apparent that a possible third no-hitter in less than two weeks pitched by Bradsher was more than halfway becoming a reality. No one on the bench said a word aloud about it. His teammates only thought about it and hoped for it.

In the bottom of the sixth inning, not a player on the Trinity team said a word to Bradsher. Most players were so unnerved they wouldn't even look him in the eye. Bradsher sat alone at the end of the sixth inning.

Trinity still led, four-zip. Chadwick cornered Bradsher before they took the field in the bottom of the sixth.

"Buddy, how are you feeling?"

"I am feeling fine, but I got a problem with a blister forming on my throwing hand index finger. After taking a quick look at the finger, Chadwick responded, "I think you'll be fine. Remember nothing down the middle of the plate and put everything on the corners. Let's put these boys to sleep."

Bradsher walked out to the mound to begin the sixth inning He was greeted by the delirious cheers and deafening applause of the fans. The Southern folk hero had captured the hearts and spirit of his admirers. They chanted, "Bradsher … Bradsher … Bradsher," and they knew they were witnessing baseball history.

This had become a love relationship with their beloved star. All the fans on both sides of the field were now pulling for the southpaw pitcher. He flashed his confident grin that was a mix of warmth and sarcasm.

Bradsher retired the side, three up, three down, in the sixth inning. Trinity scored six runs in the bottom of the inning. He was now only nine outs from his third consecutive no-hitter in three games. Bradsher walked to the mound with a swagger in his stride to begin the seventh inning. Nine female students and their friends held up K-cards.

He made the leadoff hitter look foolish on a two-strike drop ball that he swung at and missed by a foot. The next batter was completely confused by Bradsher's selection of pitches. After being caught looking for a third strike, Doak returned to the bench scratching his head and wondering what just happened.

The next batter, "Lucky Lindsey," had designs to break up the Trinity no-hit artist's bid.

Bradsher had other plans for the notorious clutch hitter for Guilford. Lindsey missed the first two pitches, swinging wildly at Bradsher's wicked drop balls and not coming close to connecting. Bradsher had felt pain in his damaged index finger the entire inning. He looked into his glove. The baseball was covered with blood. When he gripped the ball, pain shot through his finger, and he could feel it throb.

The Trinity southpaw needed one more pitch to get him out of the inning.

Make this pitch perfect. I'm not letting 'Lucky Lindsey' break up my no-hitter and ruin my day.

He reared back and delivered a pitch that Lindsey never expected and had never seen from Bradsher before. When he first saw the pitch coming, his eyes got as big as saucers. He was so anxious to hit this deliciously slow-moving seventy-mph changeup ball that seemed to be floating to the plate. He swung early so hard and was so off balance he tumbled to the ground after badly missing the pitch.

The Trinity cyclone had made Lindsey look foolish. It was not going to be his lucky day. He walked back to the dugout with a disgusted look. The fans cheered non-stop after the strikeout. Bradsher walked off the field after completing seven no-hit innings. The Trinity fans and players thought, Only six more outs to go.

Chadwick and Bradsher were due up as the fourth and fifth hitters in the inning. Bradsher approached his catcher and said, "We need to talk." The two walked fifty yards down the right field line. The fans could hear raised voices. The first batter for Trinity in the inning, Smith, sent a screaming double down the left field line, but all eyes in the stands were fixed on Bradsher and Chadwick. The two seemed to be in an intense argument. It looked like they were about to come to blows.

What would happen next was shocking.

Twenty-six

TWO INNINGS FROM HISTORY

If a team is to reach its potential, each player must be willing to subordinate his personal goals to the good of the team.
~ Bud Wilkinson

AND THEN IT HAPPENED. CHADWICK SHOVED HIS BEST FRIEND and his best friend shoved back. Chadwick's loud shouting could be heard all the way to the team benches and the stands. "You're walking away from a record that'll never be duplicated in the game of college baseball. You can't quit now, Bradsher," he cried. "All you need are six easy outs. You've just struck out one of their best hitters to end the seventh inning."

When Coach Stocksdale saw the shoving match begin, he sprinted down the first base line to get between Bradsher and Chadwick.

"What's going on fellows?" The Trinity coach asked in a surprisingly calm manner. "It looks like you two are having your first lovers' quarrel. Why don't you tell me what's got you so upset?

"Bradsher, I'll let you begin as we've been able to hear Chadwick's rants all the way to the bench," Stocksdale finished, sounding a little irritated.

"Coach, I'm taking myself out, and you need to get Wooten to start warming up to come in to pitch in the eighth inning."

"What's wrong?" Stocksdale asked in a concerned voice.

"A blister started forming on my thumb in the fifth inning. I cut my index finger on my throwing hand in the sixth inning sliding into second base. I caught it on the metal buckle holding the bag in place."

He continued, "I'm concerned that if I continue, this may turn into a significant injury. I don't want it to affect me from pitching against Lafayette and Syracuse." Bradsher looked straight into Chadwick's eyes. "This game isn't about my glory, Walter, it's about the team's success in winning the SIAA championship. This game is a laugher. It's time for me to sit the rest of the game on the bench."

Chadwick thought, *What an unselfish son of a bitch!*

"Let's see the hand," his coach demanded in a serious tone. Bradsher held up his left hand.

"Holy crap," Chadwick exclaimed. The index finger was covered with blood, swollen and throbbing. There was a one-inch gash on the finger. The thumb had a dime-sized blister full of fluid.

"You made the right choice, Bradsher. Now, let's all go back to the bench," Stocksdale said. He turned to walk back to make the necessary coaching changes.

Not a word was said between Chadwick and Bradsher while they walked back to join the team.

"Arthur, let me make the changes to the lineup and then I'll get back with you," the coach said to his star pitcher. "Take a seat on the bench. I am going to substitute Justus to pinch-hit for you this inning. You pitched a magnificent game, but you're through for the day."

The Trinity hurler sat on the end of the bench with his hand soaking in ice water and salt. Trinity scored five more runs in the top of the eighth to take a sixteen-to-zero lead. A doctor was sitting in the stands when he noticed Bradsher wasn't going out to the field in the eighth inning. He brought his bag and walked over to check on the southpaw.

"Arthur, are you okay?" Dr. Meadows asked.

"I believe so," he responded, a little disheartened. He then repeated the scenario that he had given to Stocksdale a few minutes earlier.

"Let's do this, Arthur," Dr. Meadows began. "Walk over with me to the spigot and let's get your hand cleaned up. First, I'm going to pop the blister." He took a needle out of his bag and he pricked the blister. He pressed it with his thumb, and the water squirted out. Meadows continued, "I'm going to put a good bit of iodine on the two damaged fingers and then dress them. It doesn't look like you need stitches, so I'm going to put a butterfly on the cut to pull it together.

"Come see me first thing in the morning and let's take another look at the finger and thumb. There will be no charge for your visit."

"Thank you, Dr. Meadows," Arthur gratefully exclaimed. "I'll see you in the morning."

The no-hitter was now shaping up to be a combined no-hitter between Bradsher and Wooten. Trinity's star outfielder got Guilford out one, two, three in the eighth inning.

The no-hit bid ended in the ninth inning as Wooten was battered hard, giving up four hits and two runs before getting the final out to end the game.

He was the best center fielder in the South, but his performance on the mound was a sharp contrast to the ever-present effectiveness of Bradsher.

The large crowd quieted in the ninth with the no-hit artist out of the game. They were in full gear to be a part of another one of their star southpaw's no-hitters up to the eighth inning. The Trinity fans, known for their raucous behavior, had been brought down to a somber level. His departure had taken the wind out of their sails.

As soon as the game ended, Bradsher was approached by fans, the Guilford college players, and members of the press. He downplayed the injury. He saw Chadwick walking off. "I thank each of you for your concern, but I need to get with my catcher. We've had quite a day. Please excuse me, fellows, but I've got to go."

"Walter, wait for me!" Bradsher shouted. He sprinted off to be with his friend to catch the trolley back home.

As they climbed the stairs and entered the trolley, the conductor warmly greeted them.

"Hop on, fellows, for the smoothest ride in Durham." They all laughed.

"Did you boys win?"

"Yes, sir, we won sixteen to two, against Guilford College," said Bradsher.

"Congratulations, this ride is on me. No charge." Chadwick saw the conductor's name on his badge and said as they were going to their seats.

"Thank you, Harold Fields."

The two ballplayers walked past the six riders of the streetcar who were all sitting at the front. They choose to sit at the rear, so they could talk and not be interrupted.

They sat in the leather-bound double seat. The trolley car was first put into use in 1902. The fare to ride was a nickel. The two had traversed across the city from the age of seven predominately by foot, by bicycle, by horse, and occasionally by horse and buggy.

They had traveled for almost four street blocks and not a word had been exchanged. Both had been affected by the shoving match on the ballfield.

Chadwick finally turned to his sidekick and said, "Buddy, I'm sorry to blow up on you and for shoving you."

"Tell me what you're thinking?" Brad asked.

His catcher responded, "I just wanted so badly for you to get your third straight no-hitter to start the season. It would have been a record that probably would have never been matched in a hundred-year period in college ball.

"I saw quickly this was a once in a lifetime opportunity that you or any pitcher in the country would ever see. I was trying hard to make you understand that. And selfishly, maybe I just wanted to be recognized as part of one of the greatest feats in college baseball history."

Walter continued, "Brad, you're the star that always sits at center stage. You usually get the glory and you deserve it. You're the All-America pitcher, the hero to the fans, and the guy that always gets the girl in the movies. Maybe I just wanted to be part of the big show. I wanted to be part of a record that would stand forever, and years later I could look back and see my name in the record books also."

Bradsher looked at his friend and said, "Oh hell, Walter, I'm more disappointed than I am showing. I certainly never would have gotten to where I'm in my career without you. You've been my best friend and an incredible mentor over the past three years. Also, over that period you have been the key player that has turned the Trinity team around. I appreciate all you've done, Walter."

He continued, "I'm certainly smart enough to understand I was in one of the most unique situations in baseball historical past, present, and future. Before I made my decision, I knew if you and I had gone through the final six batters, we would have set them down in order without allowing a hit.

"Walter, my hand was aching, and I was scared that I was going to screw up the rest of the season if I didn't take myself out. I have never quit anything in my life. I felt like my heart was being ripped out to tell you that I was pulling myself out of the game. It hurt like hell."

Chadwick looked at Bradsher and finally understood. He was the consummate team player and put the team before his own fame.

"Well, Brad," he said, "It's been a hell of a start to the season. Do you know what you've accomplished in the first three games this season?"

"It's been a pretty good start." Bradsher smiled.

"Oh my God," Chadwick blurted out and continued. "I know you're the smartest person I've ever known, but sometimes I feel you think like a moron.

"Here is what we've accomplished in the first three games of the season. It's staggering. You have pitched twenty-five no-hit, scoreless innings in the first three games and haven't walked a single batter.

"I guess we'll have to ask ourselves the question: Are the Trinity Blue, and its star southpaw, as good as the first three games of the season seem to indicate?" Chadwick wrapped it up with this sentiment. "The next four contests will reveal the real character and strength of this team. Brad, three northern powerhouses are coming to Durham. In the next ten days, we will face Lafayette, Syracuse twice, and Gettysburg.

"It is time for you, my friend, to prove you're the best pitcher in the South against three of the best teams from the North."

Twenty-seven

LEARNING TO FISH

Many men go fishing all their lives without knowing
that it is not the fish that they are after.
~ Henry David Thoreau

WALTER CHADWICK NOT ONLY TAUGHT ARTHUR Bradsher to pitch a baseball, but he also was instrumental in showing him how to handle a fishing rod. Having been born and raised on the coast in Beaufort, North Carolina, he had a fishing rod in his hands before his fourth birthday.

He loved to share his fishing stories with his best friend, Bradsher. The two had numerous conversations about fishing on the way to baseball practice the first year they had teamed up in 1902. Chadwick was one of the best at spinning a tale, and his stories about growing up on the North Carolina coast were always filled with great adventure.

"My friends and I loved to surfcast in the early morning's ankle-deep in the Atlantic Ocean. We're in search for pompano and bluefish," he explained. "We'd catch a half dozen pompano and take them back to the house. We gutted the fish and filleted the pompano. Mom pan-fried them in the heavy iron skillet with hash brown potatoes. It was one of the best lunches you'd ever eat." Chadwick smiled and licked his lips.

"In the cooler early evenings, we fished off the Beaufort pier that extended out into the deeper waters of the Atlantic," he said.

"It's an opportunity to catch a variety of fish."

"Tell me more," Arthur said.

"The wonderful thing about pier fishing is that you don't have to cast out into uncertain waters. You simply drop your baited line down next to the pillars and wait for a bite. If you don't find an interested fish at first, you just work your way down the next set of columns until you catch one."

Chadwick continued, "One way to spot where the fish are is to watch the birds. Seagulls and other types of birds that hang around the piers will lead you to where the fish may be. They seem to know the local fish swimming patterns and movements at specific times of the day."

"What are some of your other fishing tips?"

"Also, look for cloudy water," he noted. "You'll usually find fish where cloudy water meets clear water."

"You sure know a lot about fishing," Arthur exclaimed.

"I sure ought to," he shot back. "I've had my feet in the water with a fishing rod since I was four years old!"

He continued with his fishing lesson. "Pier fishing opens the door catching many more varieties of fish than surfcasting because you're able to reach depths of the water not possible by fishing off the shore. We caught grey sea trout, Spanish mackerel, bluefish, black sea bass, and once a thirty-pound black drum off the hundred-year-old, forty-foot-wide wooden platform that extended one hundred and fifty feet out into the ocean."

He had Bradsher's attention. "What's the biggest fish you've ever caught?"

Chadwick began with one of his stories. "One afternoon, to me and everyone's great surprise, I hooked a five-foot bull shark. It was mean as the devil. I started shouting, 'I got one, I've got a really big one!' Before I knew it, there were fifteen people standing around me watching me struggle to bring the shark in.

"The damn thing fought like hell and almost snapped my rod. When I got it within five feet of the pier, the crowd and the foreman convinced me to cut my line. I did so with reservation, and the bull shark swam to the deep water."

"Boy, that's quite a story," Arthur said.

~

TWO DAYS BEFORE THEIR SHOWDOWN with Wake Forest, Chadwick showed up for their walk to the ball field with a fishing rod.

"What's with the fishing rod?" Bradsher asked.

"Isn't it a beauty?" he said with great excitement in his voice. "It's a Shakespeare. I bought it at Roach Sporting Goods store."

Walter began to describe his new prize rod and reel. "This is the newest version of the Shakespeare reel. It's handmade out of German nickel with no compromise to the highest standards of quality. The reel level winding mechanism is state of the art, is dependable, and always functions smoothly. Each reel is individually and beautifully engraved 'Shakespeare' on its head plate."

As Chadwick talked, Bradsher thought, *Walter is a natural born salesman. I bet he could even sell ice to an Eskimo.*

He continued with his exciting description of his new Shakespeare rod and reel. "The rod is a is five-feet-seven-inches long and made from bamboo.

"The bamboo has been aged, taking it from green to a light amber color. I think it's handsome," Walter said proudly. "Brad, the rod and reel cost me twenty-five dollars. I had to cut lawns and wash windows for six months of Saturdays to pay for it.

"Brad, I'm going to open your world by teaching you to fish. One day we'll go fishing in the ocean together," Chadwick said assuredly. "You wouldn't believe how the smell of the saltwater, the early morning sunrises and sunsets over the ocean refresh your soul.

"Every fisherman has a distinctive style," he continued. "Your style would be that of the classic English fisherman, the straight-up-and-down cast with the elbow tight against your chest."

Chadwick stopped at a house that had a vacant lot next to it. "Hand me the Shakespeare." He then pointed to a five-foot-in-diameter bare spot in the grass, some fifteen yards away.

"Watch this." Within seconds he brought the rod back and sent it shooting forward. He released the fishing line and sent it flying towards the small circle. The reel made a strong and loud clicking sound as the fishing line came off it, the silver lure directly in the middle of the target. "Yes!" Walter screamed with delight. "You're learning from a master angler," he said proudly.

He gave out the fishing rod to Bradsher. "You try. First, let me give you a quick lesson. You're very smart, my friend, and a quick learner. You can get this," he began. "Hold the rod out in front of you facing your target like you'd do if you would on the pitcher's mound, getting ready to deliver a pitch.

"Next, you need to perfect your grip like you would when you throw a baseball." He held up his thumb and index for his friend to see. "You'll use the thumb to push the release button for the line, and at the same time put your index finger on the spool of line keeping it from coming unraveled. Then bring the rod back, as I demonstrated earlier, and then quickly snap the rod forward."

"Wow, this is like learning to throw my first curveball," the fishing novice said.

"At the exact moment and position, you'd let go of a baseball when you're pitching, you release your finger off the spool. When you raise your finger off the spool and line, it allows the reel to release the line and fly to your target. It's all about technique and timing."

Chadwick finished by saying, "Are you ready for your first cast?"

"I'm ready." Bradsher was feeling uncomfortable and anxious. He looked around him for any obstacles that might interfere with his first cast. He glanced behind to where he was standing, to his left, and then turned back to look forward.

"Quit worrying," Chadwick shouted out to him. "Just focus on hitting the bare spot on the grass. Smooth and easy, just like you're delivering a pitch to home plate. Hit the mitt big fellow."

Bradsher hit the release button on the spool and placed his index finger on the line on the reel. He brought the rod back and, in a fluid motion, brought it swiftly forward. He released the line and let it fly. His first cast did not arch forward as planned. It went straight up into the air and in the limbs of an old oak tree directly above him.

"Wild pitch," Chadwick called out. He had keeled over onto the ground and was laughing so hard he almost peed in his pants. "We're going to work on this some more after practice today," Chadwick said with a wide grin on his face. He cut the fishing line with his pocket knife.

"Let's get to the ballpark," said Chadwick. "We've got work to do. We have Wake Forest for two games and Guilford sandwiched in between in the next eight days. This could be the turning point of our season."

Adams, Henry Bethune, Jr. ("My Dear B. P., the Absent-Minded Man"), Monroe, N. C.—Prepared for College at Monroe High School; member Columbian Literary Society; President, '04; Orator's Medal, '04; Secretary and Treasurer Y. M. C. A., '04; Secretary and Treasurer Historical Society; Glee Club, '03 and '04; Leader Mandolin Club, '03 and '04; Assistant Librarian, '04.

Beachboard, Zachary Pearl, ("Beach," the College Financier), Bell Buckle, Tenn.—Prepared at Webb School; Columbian; Corresponding Secretary, '02; Chairman Executive Committee, '04; Business Manager Archive, '04; Manager "The Inn;" College Electrician, '03 and '04; member Science Club; Glee Club, '03 and '04; Manager Trinity Business Agency; Class Baseball Team.

Bradsher, Arthur Brown; ("Brad., the King of the Southern Diamond"), Durham, N. C.—Prepared at Durham High School.—Columbian; Marshal for Intersociety Debate, '02 and '03; Member Executive Committee Athletic Association; Pitcher on Baseball Team, '01-'04; Captain Baseball Team, '03-'04; Alpha Tau Omega Fraternity; member "Tombs," a Junior Class secret society; member "9019," a local patriotic society. T. B. K.

Budd, Walter Pemberton, ("My Dear T. G., the Busy Man"), Durham, N. C.; Prepared at Durham High School.—Columbian; Recording Secretary, '01; Corresponding Secretary, '02; President, '04; Marshal Trinity-Wake Forest Debate, '01; Prize Winner Sophomore Debate, '02; Intersociety Debate, '03; Marshal for Commencement '02; Chief Marshal Commencement, '03; Vice-President of Class; Freshman Honors, '01; Sophomore Honors, '02; Glee Club, '03 and '04; Manager Glee and Mandolin Clubs, '04; Member "College Quartet;" Editor-in-Chief of Archive, '04; Pitcher on Class Baseball Team. T. B. K.

Bynum, Frederick Williamson, ("Toot," the Newspaper Fiend), Pittsboro, N. C.—Prepared at Oak Ridge; University of N. C., '00 and '01; Trinity, '03 and '04; Columbian; Chairman Executive Committee, '04; Baseball Team, '03 and '04.

Eaker, Victor Columbus, ("Old Pat,") Delight, N. C.—Prepared at Trinity Park School; Columbian; Marshal, '01; Treasurer, '02 and '03; Track Team, '02 and '03; "9019."

[2]

Arthur Bradsher's 1904 yearbook page.
~ Courtesy of Duke University Library and Archives

Trinity Methodist Church looking forward to the Altar.
Seating capacity is approximately 900 persons.

Clockwise from above: Alter looking
back to the Mural of Ascension;
125 ft. Steeple; and, Estey Organ.

Base Ball Mitts.

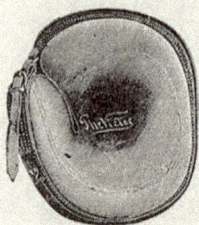

No. 15L. Front View. No. 15L. Back View. Nos. 16S and 7C.

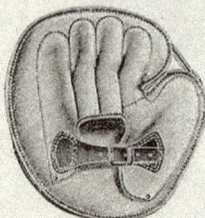

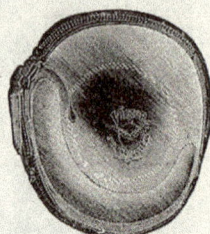

Catchers' Mitts.

Each.

No. 15L—Professional. Best French Calf Skin. Sewed with Extra Heavy Waxed Thread. Double Front. Patent Lace and Thumb Attachment. Strap and Buckle............................$8.00 ....

No. 16S—High Grade Drab Calf Skin, trimmed with Russia Calf. Double Stitched Palm. Patent Lace and Thumb Attachment. Strap and Buckle... 6.00 ....

No. 7C—Selected Brown Calf Skin. Heel Ridge and Double Stitched Palm. Patent Lace and Thumb Attachment. Strap and Buckle... 4.50 ....

Catcher's Mitts 1901-1905. Shown in Reach sports catalogue.

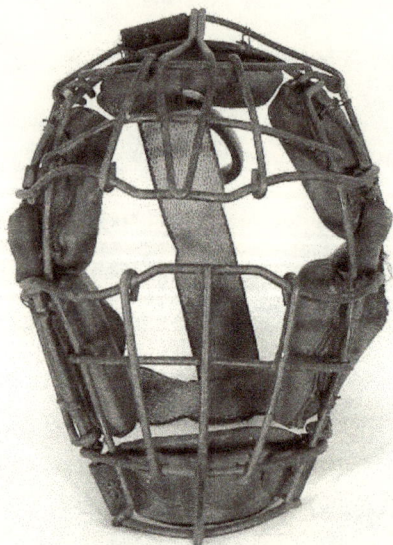

Catcher's Mask in 1901.

Harvard Star, William Reid's Catcher's Mitt in 1901. ~ Courtesy of Brett Mills Photography, New York City

~ Unless noted, all Photos Courtesy of Antique Athletic, Orwigsburg PA

156

Vintage 1901 Fielder's Glove.

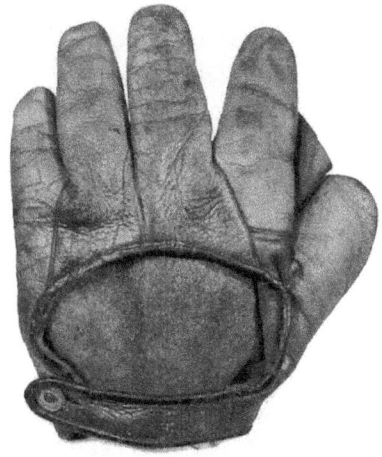

1901 Inflatable Catcher's Chest Protector.

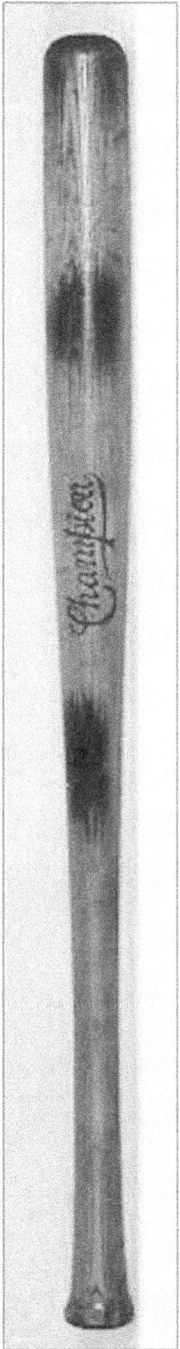

Burnished 1901 Baseball Bat.

Leather High-Top 1901 Baseball Shoes.

The Neuse River today.
~ Courtesy of the N.C. Wildlife Resources Commission

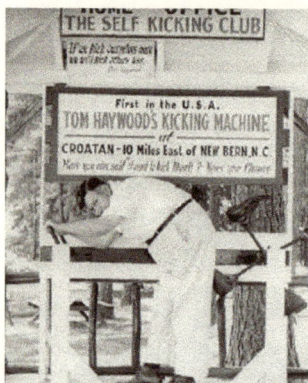

Tom Haywood's Country Store kicking machine.

~ Photos courtesy of the Bradsher Family

The Bradsher Family vacation at the Neuse River.

Ocean map leading to the Neuse River.
~ Courtesy of *Sail Magazine*

Name *Muse, Lizzie C.*		Class			
FRESHMAN YEAR.	SUBJECTS	HOURS.	FALL	SPRING	REM.
1901-02	German	3	89	90	
	Latin	3	95	96	
	English	3	94	92	
	History	3	90	81	
	Math.	3	90	90	
	Bible	1			
	TOTAL	16			
SOPHOMORE YEAR 1902-03	Latin II	3	95	93	
	English II	3	90	88	
	French I	3	90	85	
	German II	3	88	90	
	Bible	1	90		
	Mathematics II	3	85		No Report
	Chemistry I	3	90	80	
	TOTAL	19			
JUNIOR YEAR.					

Lizzie Muse original Trinity transcript 1901-1902.
She recieved a full scholarship for her second year.
~ Courtesy of Duke University Library and Archives

Lizzie with her   *Early years of the Bradsher Family*
Mother and Sisters   *Mary (5), Lizzie (30), Charles (3).*
~ Courtesy of the Bradsher Family

1903 Trinity Team.
~ Courtesy of Duke University Library and Archives

Hanes Field in 1907. One of the most popular college baseball venues to play at the turn of the twentieth century.
~ Courtesy of Duke University Library and Archives

Fans in the stands, 1901.
~ Courtesy of Eastern Washington State University

Trinity Library, built in 1903.

Trinity College Entrance in 1903.

Trinity Campus in 1901.

Washington Duke building used for classrooms, residence, and administrative offices, built in 1892.

~ All photos courtesy of Wilson Library (UNC)

Twenty-eight

THE FURMAN GAME
AND BILLY LAVAL

Few that ever competed against him
ever looked down on Billy Laval.
Nor did they call him any name except one out of respect.
~ The Greenville Times - 1904

BILLY LAVAL STOOD FIVE-FEET-EIGHT INCHES. HE WEIGHED about 135 pounds. He was known as "The Fox." Despite his size, few who ever competed against him ever looked down on Laval. Nor did they call him any name except one out of respect.

The newspapers heralded it as the battle of the North versus the South. The championship team, Furman, representing the state of South Carolina, lined up to face the projected champion of North Carolina, Trinity College.

Reporters from five Southern states had swarmed to Greenville to cover this epic battle featuring two cunning southpaws taking the mound.

The game had been promoted like a heavyweight boxing match. The two fighting pitchers both had an arsenal that could take them the distance.

Laval was undefeated coming into the contest. The pitcher was effective because of superb control over an assortment of curves and spitballs.

Bradsher, after winning his first nine games, had lost a 5-4 decision against A&M. He had certainly pitched well enough to win, but Trinity committed six errors, and only two of the opponent's runs were earned.

Pep rallies had been held on both campuses in the week preceding the showdown. Hundreds of students attended the high-energy rallies. Baseball was king on both campuses, and about 700 fans were expected to witness the game.

Approximately 250 loyal Trinity fans traveled by train from Durham to Greenville to see their folk hero pitch. Ticket prices had been set at fifty cents per student and twenty-five cents for ladies. The weather for the game was perfect with sunny and mild conditions and no threat of rain.

The day before traveling to Greenville, Bradsher and Chadwick met at Murphy's for a sandwich and to discuss the Furman line-up. Not a full minute had passed when Chadwick started in with Bradsher.

"Don't get careless with Laval. He's a great pitcher but also a smart hitter. Just keep him off balance and close him out with your drop ball." He shifted to the next key hitter in the Furman lineup. Shavel is their home-run hitter. He is a fence buster. With one swing of the bat, this power hitter can ruin a beautiful day's work and send you straight to Loserville. Bam!" Chadwick exclaimed as he slapped the wooden table.

"Brad, you've done a magnificent job helping Stocksdale coach this team. It's amazing that the fundamentals we have worked on have produced a championship team. We will do fine tomorrow. I predict another win," he said confidently. The two best friends finished their sandwiches then headed back to the dormitory.

~

GAME TIME WAS AT THREE-THIRTY. The Trinity team boarded the train the next morning at the Durham terminal at ten-thirty. It would be a three-and-a-half-hour train ride on the Southern 317 to Greenville.

Also boarding the train to Greenville was Lizzie Muse. She had never seen Arthur Bradsher throw one single pitch.

Her girlfriends had tried their best to convince Lizzie to experience one of his pitching performances that everyone in the state was talking about. "Lizzie, he's an honor roll student, Captain of the team, a very humble man, a devout Christian, and to top that off, he's gorgeous," her girlfriend said.

Her friends had finally talked her into joining them for the trip to Greenville. Lizzie had to babysit to earn the money to buy her train ticket.

It was a perfect day for baseball with blue skies, temperatures in the mid-seventies, and a slight breeze blowing in from the outfield. Patterson Field was manicured to perfection. The fans were buzzing about what they expected from this very special ball game.

Both teams' fans were ready for a day filled with great pitching, excitement and the unexpected. Reporters had come from all over the South to cover the action, and it was time for the game to begin. The vendors were hawking their bags of peanuts and freshly made popcorn. Both sold for a nickel.

Trinity was up first to face southpaw Billy Laval, and he didn't disappoint his adoring fans. He retired the first three batters in the contest.

As Bradsher walked to the mound, the loud chorus of cheers began. He'd won the hearts of the fans with his pitching perfection, calm, and respectful demeanor.

Bradsher got the leadoff batter, Bowen, to line out to the third baseman for the first out. The next batter, Middlebrook, after working him to a full count, singled to center field. Next up was Shaver, a hulk of a man, standing six-feet-and-two inches and weighing 215 pounds.

Chadwick had warned his batterymate about Shaver's ability to go deep. He would need to mix up his pitches to keep the power hitter off balance. He started off cautiously with a curveball and then a fastball just outside the strike zone. The count was a dangerous 2-0. The next delivery would be a hitter's pitch.

The cocky catcher screamed at his pitcher, "Let's give this big sissy something he can't see. Throw him the dark ball ... throw him the dark ball!"

The Trinity sensation delivered a slow-moving changeup. Shaver couldn't lay off it, swinging way ahead of the floater for a strike. The big man slammed his bat to the ground in disgust. You could almost feel the ground shake.

On the next pitch, Furman's Middlebrook took off running to second base. With a perfect hook slide, he avoided Smith's tag. The fast-moving ump was right on top of the play, and hollered, "You're safe!" The hometown fans were delighted.

On the next pitch, a passed ball by the catcher, Chadwick, allowed the baserunner to reach third base. There was still one out and the dangerous slugger, Shaver, staring into Bradsher's eyes. The strikeout king stepped off the mound and took a long deep breath.

It looks like the only thing that is going to get me out of this mess will be a couple of strikeouts. It's time for a couple of visits from Uncle Charles.

His next throw was an inside fastball on the hands that froze Shaver. The umpire screamed, strike two. Shaver didn't like the call and started mouthing off to umpire.

"What do you mean, strike?" he snarled.

The umpire, Mr. Thomas, was a big man equal to the stature of Shaver. He circled to the front of the plate and bent over to brush it off. As he stood up erect, he looked the Furman slugger eye to eye, and growled, "This isn't going to be a day for arguing. You keep it up, you're going to find your ass sitting on the bench for the rest of the game."

He is in a place of frustration and off-balance. This is exactly where I like the hitter to take himself.

The Trinity lefty smiled at Shaver and seemed to irritate him.

With two strikes, he reared back, cocked his arm, and delivered a nasty drop ball that started at the letters and ended up at the knees.

Shaver was so fooled that he never got his bat off his shoulder. The ump lunged forward and punched his fist forward, symbolizing a called strike knockout punch from the curveball artist. "You're out," he said to the delight of the Trinity fans. Bradsher had ignited the cheering fans.

Pitcher and team Captain Laval was up next and batting cleanup. With a man anxious to score from third base, the Trinity ace realized this may be one of the most important outs in the game. He sent a sweeping curveball Laval's way for a called strike. On the next pitch, he overpowered him on a high and tight fastball on the hands. The pitch handcuffed Laval and he popped up weakly to end the inning.

He kept the Furman team guessing like a master magician in the second and third innings. He fanned three in a row in the third to retire the side in short order. The fans broke out their K-cards and by the end of the third inning, he had posted five strikeouts.

Base hits by Wren, Howard, and a fumbled ball hit by Wooten brought in two runs in the bottom of the third to make the score two to zero. Both teams put up nothing but goose eggs until the sixth inning when Smith, for Trinity, led off with a two-bagger to centerfield. Howard put runners on the corners with a hit to right field.

As Bradsher came to the plate, the fans were in a frenzy with shouts of "Bradsher, Bradsher." They're ringing cowbells, blowing whistles, and pounding the wooden grandstands with their feet. On the first pitch, Bradsher scorched a blue darter over the third base bag and Jones, fully extending his body, made a miraculous stop. But the throw from his knees to home was late and Trinity had their third run of the game.

It was a day where the southpaw sensation had his way with the Furman batters. Going into the ninth inning, he had allowed just two singles. The Trinity hurler started off the inning with a strikeout of Bowen.

Chadwick was chattering non-stop, "Batter, batter, no batter, and you are the one, you are the hon." When the Furman hitter stepped into the batter's box, the brilliant catcher asked, "How's your mother?" The rebel backstop would do anything to distract the hitter.

The next Furman batter, Middlebrook, hit a "can of corn"

fly out to center fielder Flowers. The lazy fly ball floated directly above the center fielder and parachuted straight down. He didn't have to move to make the catch for the second out of the inning. The fans were holding up the K cards numbering thirteen in a row. Due up next in the order was power hitter Shaver, who had already struck out twice.

Chadwick's words from the previous day's conversation entered Bradsher's head.

Don't get careless with Shaver. One swing from the big man can ruin your day.

Trinity's star pitcher started Shaver off with a twelve-six drop ball that he swung violently at and missed. Bradsher wasted the next pitch high and tight on Shaver to back him off the plate.

The pitch came dangerously close to hitting Shaver, and the Furman fans sent out a chorus of boos. His catcher signaled for a curveball on the inside corner at the knees, and the shrewd southpaw delivered the perfect pitch for a called second strike.

Bradsher turned to look at the old wooden scoreboard out in right field. There was not a crooked number on Furman's side of the scoreboard. There were eight goose eggs that hung proudly on the board, and the North Carolina hurler intended to have a ninth join them.

God, I want this shutout.

The Trinity lefty was one strike away from pitching another shutout for the record books. He thought about throwing another curveball to the Furman slugger but changed his mind. Shaver stood coiled like a cobra. The veins on his forearms were showing because of his tight grip on the bat. He delivered a fastball two inches off on the outside corner of the plate, at the knees.

As the pitch traveled its first sixty feet, six inches and crossed the first few inches of the plate, it looked perfect to Bradsher.

I've got him, I've got him. He will never hit a fastball low and two inches outside the strike zone, Bradsher imagined.

He could taste another shutout and game-ending punchout. He delivered to the "big man."

The decisive moment had arrived, but Shaver murdered the

ball for a 350-foot drive over the fence in right field. He celebrated his massive home run and gleefully danced around the bases. The hometown fans finally had something to cheer about. They went crazy.

Boy, this hurts to be one pitch from a shutout, and have it taken away with one swing. I should have thrown him a bender.

Bradsher kept his cool and gave a broad smile to the Furman fans.

The next batter, Laval, hit a weak comebacker to the Trinity pitcher and the ball game was over, Trinity winning, 3-1.

He walked off the mound to congratulate his opponents and meet the press.

He wondered how Shaver had connected with his perfectly placed pitch.

Twenty-nine

MEETING LIZZIE MUSE

The world needs more love at first sight.
~ Maggie Stiefvater

L IZZIE MUSE HAD WATCHED ARTHUR VERY CLOSELY THAT
afternoon at Patterson Field. She noticed traits perhaps
only a woman would have an intuition for. She observed and noted
many things about his demeanor and appearance. He was good
looking, well-built, cool, and confident.

As she watched him perform that day, she saw how calm he
remained in the tightest of situations. He seemed to be in total
control of his emotions as well as his repertoire of the pitches.

He seemed to be having fun with every ball he threw past the
hitters. She couldn't believe how composed he was when Shaver
stole a shutout from the record books by hitting a home run with
two out and two strikes on him in the ninth inning.

She also perceived his giving spirit when he walked
immediately after the last out to the Furman team to shake hands
and congratulate every player on a well-played contest.

Wow! I have not even met him, and I am already attracted, she
thought.

"Brad," a deep voice rang out. He turned to see the muscular
Eddie Shaver standing in front of him. The Furman clean-up hitter
extended his bear-sized hand and shook the Trinity hurler's hand.

"That was a brilliantly pitched game, my friend."

"I thought I had you again in the ninth inning," Bradsher said to the big man Shaver. "How'd you hit that pitch?" he asked. "I thought I located the pitch perfectly."

"It was perfect, Brad, perfect for me. I guessed on the pitch and guessed you would throw it in that exact spot on the knees. You did, and I hammered it over the fence." They both laughed.

Billy Laval tapped Bradsher on the shoulder. "Great work, Brad. You were magnificent today."

"Thanks, Billy, you pitched great today, also. You deserved more support than your team gave you today."

The Furman Captain added, "I just wanted to say it's been a pleasure playing against you. I have a lot of respect for you, as do the rest of the players on my team. Good luck to you next year, and I hope our paths will cross in the future."

"Me, too, Billy. Take care."

The two locked eyes then departed after a firm handshake. He turned to head over to answer a few questions from the reporters.

After talking to the press, Bradsher walked back to the stands where the fans were still celebrating. Chadwick greeted him. "Come on, I want to introduce you to someone."

He strode with his all-star catcher to greet the appreciative fans. Fifteen yards from the bleachers, he noticed one girl who stood out. She was one of the prettiest girls he had ever seen. He was awestruck at how natural she looked with her hair pulled back. Her beautiful skin glowed and her smile was captivating.

Chadwick began his introduction, "Arthur Brown Bradsher, I'd like to introduce you to my cousin, Lizzie Chadwick Muse."

All five-feet-two inches of Lizzie stepped forward to meet Arthur. She was clearly fit and looked to be around a hundred pounds. He noticed she had perfect teeth and hypnotic eyes. Her hair was thick, full, and honey golden-brown.

"I must say you put on quite a performance today, Mr. Bradsher. I've never been a fan of college baseball, and I can see that after today, maybe I should start following the sport."

"First, Miss Muse, I thank you for your compliments. Please, call me Arthur or Brad. Whatever you are most comfortable with suits me just fine. What's that you have, Lizzie?" he asked.

"It is my K-card. I held it up when you struck out Shaver in the sixth inning for your tenth strikeout of the day. It was the second time you had punched him out. I thought you had him again in the ninth inning."

Boy, she's drop-dead gorgeous, and I'll bet smart, too.

"I thought I had him too."

Coach Stocksdale came over to the bleachers and announced, "The train will be leaving for Durham in thirty minutes. It's time for all of us to get over to the depot."

Arthur looked into Lizzie's dark-brown eyes. "It's been a real pleasure meeting you, Lizzie." Her beautiful smile was captivating.

She grasped his hand. "Me, too, Arthur." Lizzie felt light-headed from his touch.

She and her two best friends started walking towards the depot. After they had walked twenty-five yards, they heard him hollering. "Lizzie, please stop for a moment. I have something to ask you. Could we speak in private?"

"Sure."

They walked a few yards away. As he stood in front her, he said, "I know we have just met, and I don't want to be forward with you. I'd like you to accompany me to the ATO Gala Bash in three weeks at the Hotel Carrolina."

"I'd be thrilled and honored to attend the gala with you, Arthur," she responded with a gleam in her eye.

Boy, I would love to kiss her right now, he thought.

As Lizzie and her girlfriends headed for the train depot, he watched their every step. Suddenly, she stopped and looked back over her shoulder towards Arthur and waved. He had gotten his first look back from Lizzie.

"Bradsher, are you going to stand there gawking at your new girlfriend, or are you coming with us to catch the train?" Stocksdale asked. "It's time to skidoo."

"Yes, Coach." He watched her disappear from his sight. He was already missing her.

He boarded the Southern 317 and sat next to his best friend. "Well, what's on your mind Mr. Bradsher, as Miss Lizzie called you?" He laughed and slapped his thigh.

"Why'd you wait so long to introduce me to your cousin?"

Chadwick answered, "The first reason is that her mother didn't want her to date until she turned eighteen years of age. She just celebrated her eighteenth birthday. The second reason is, I didn't think you're ready to have her in life, with everything you've got going on.

"She is one of the most special people I've known in my lifetime. Lizzie is a girl of great physical beauty, but most importantly, she is kind and generous.

"My cousin is one of the three women accepted to Trinity in 1901. You two probably never crossed paths because she kept mainly to her herself studying for her teaching degree. She left Trinity after her sophomore year to teach in the high school system in Durham.

"Brad she is the oldest of eight children and is very responsible. I would suggest if you want to get close to her, you need to gain the respect of her parents and be close to them. They're great people."

"Thanks, buddy, for catching such a great game today and introducing me to your cousin. I'll be forever grateful for giving us the opportunity to meet." He shifted over to another seat, so he could spread out and get some shuteye.

As he drifted to sleep, he thought about the lovely and smart Lizzie Muse.

He dreamed, *What would be the possibilities that might occur between him and her in the future?*

Thirty

FIRST DATE AT THE GALA BALL

Where there is kindness there is goodness and
where there is goodness there is magic.
~ Cinderella

L IZZIE SPRINTED FROM THE TRAIN STATION TO HER HOME ON
Morris Street. She could not wait to share the big news
with her mother and the excitement of meeting Arthur at the
Furman game.

She ran through the parlor of the Muse home, shouting with
more joy her mother had ever heard her express. "Mother, Mother,
I have a date for the ball!"

"Settle down, dear, take a deep breath and relax. Tell me what
you're so excited about."

After her mother had calmed her down, she explained she'd
been invited to the Alpha Tau Omega yearly celebration at the
Hotel Carrolina, just a few blocks away from their residence on
Morris Street. The celebration was to take place in three weeks.

At age fifteen, Lizzie had blossomed into a beautiful young
woman. She entered Trinity College the next year at sixteen. Many
of her friends, neighbors, and students at Trinity, and the Durham
town people said Lizzie was the prettiest young girl in the city.

She was the first-born child in a family of eight children. She
had been discouraged from dating until she was entrenched in

her college studies and had made decisions about her vocational passions. Her mother did not want her to date until she turned eighteen.

"Who is this young man that has asked you out?" her mother asked. This was a big step for her inexperienced daughter and a mother that was concerned about her first date.

"He's a baseball player and a great one at that. He pitches for Trinity, and they call him the 'King of the Southern Diamond,'" she began in an excited voice.

"Mom, we talked for fifteen minutes after the game, and he's very soft-spoken and attentive. The girls I went with to the game say he's a leader on the campus and a devout Christian."

"Interesting observations, Lizzie, anything else?"

"Yes, Mother, he's the most handsome man that I've ever met."

"Well, my dear child, I need to meet your knight in shining armor. If you're going to the gala event, we are going to have to sew you a dress, and you're going to have to pay for the material. We will go down to Cochran's tomorrow and see what he can do to help us.

"Let's see if he needs some part-time help for the next couple of weeks to help you pay for it," her mother said with great affection for her daughter.

"Thank you, Mother. I love you dearly." She reached out and squeezed her hand.

~

THE NEXT MORNING, Lizzie and her mother stood before Mr. Cochran in his little clothing boutique on Main Street. "Mrs. Muse, to make the dress from the pattern you've shown me would call for about three and a half yards of silk or twenty-seven inches wide, with a yard of silk for the embroidery for the collar and deep cuffs.

"I have about four yards of stunning blue silk I'll give you for a fair price. This color would look magnificent on Lizzie. I would be honored to have her work for me for a week or so until the material is paid for. I'll give you the fabrics to take home today, so you can start sewing the gown for what sounds like a very special night," he generously offered.

"Oh, Mother, I love you so," Mr. Cochran could hear her saying as they began their walk back to their home on Morris Street.

~

ARTHUR WANTED TO MAKE the ATO gala event a night to remember for Lizzie. He rented a horse and buggy. The carriage driver, Billy Weems, was a friend from school and had secured him a very good price for its use for the ride to the Hotel Carrolina. Arthur dressed in a tuxedo that had belonged to his father. He looked extremely handsome and was anxious to see Lizzie.

His stomach was filled with butterflies. He was nervous because he really wanted to please her. He felt like he always did before he pitched a big game.

They arrived at seven-thirty in front of the Muse home. He hopped down from the carriage and proceeded to the front door. When the front swung open, the entire family was waiting to meet him. Seven of the eight Muse children and their parents were lined up in the parlor. One by one they greeted Arthur.

Gosh, it looks like the whole family wants to check me out and make sure I pass inspection.

Lizzie's mother first approached him. "Good evening, Arthur." She offered her hand to him. "Good evening, Mrs. Muse. It's certainly a pleasure to meet all of you." He heard footsteps from the top of the stairs and gazed in awe of Lizzie coming down.

She's the most elegant and breathtaking creature I have ever laid my eyes on.

"You look stunning, Lizzie," Arthur said.

She blushed.

"Thank you, Arthur, you must pay some of the compliments to my talented seamstress." She looked over at her mother and gave her a wink.

It was a busy night in downtown Durham with a large group attending the Alpha Tau Omega event at the Hotel Carrolina, and another large contingency attending the Kappa Alpha banquet at the Epworth Inn. Main Street was crowded with horses and horse-drawn vehicles. There were hitching posts in front of the stores, hotel, and theater, and water fountains here and there for thirsty horses. With school being out, the movie theater was bustling with business.

Arthur shouted to his friend who was driving the carriage, "Billy, can we circle the block and bring us to the Hotel Carrolina by coming through downtown up Main Street?"

"I'll be glad to," he answered. "It will be exciting to see all the people hustling about on such a busy night."

"It's the gaslight age and it's always fun to watch the lamplighter in front of Murphy's with the long pole making his rounds at sundown to light up the lamps," Brad said. Murphy's Bar was packed.

The streets were filled with people and full of fashion on this special night. Women wore tightly corseted long gowns or dresses. Many of the dresses had a high collar and ribbons and lace. Most of the women wore broad sweeping hats, many adorned with feathers. They had full "Gibson Girl" hairstyles and appeared very lady-like.

"Arthur, I want to thank you for the carriage ride. This is very exciting for me. It may sound strange to you, but I've never been downtown at night."

Almost every man that evening was wearing a hat. Coming out of Murphy's, a more casual establishment, most of the men had on straw-hat boaters with a two-inch band. The attire became more formal as they pulled up to the Hotel Carrolina.

"This is Durham's first luxury hotel and was built by industrialist Julian Carr in 1898," Arthur explained. "The large, ornate Queen Anne Victorian building is stunning. It houses seventy-three rooms. No attention to the finest detail has been spared in this grand structure. It has eight fireplaces and twenty-two crystal chandeliers. The six verandas offer scenic views of downtown Durham and the surrounding neighborhoods. I love the rounded porches with the turrets and ballesteros railing posts. Its architecture is magnificent!"

"Oh, Arthur, I can't express how special this is to me. I have walked by this grand hotel a hundred times since I was a young girl and fantasized, I would someday get an opportunity to have dinner and dance the night away here. Now that dream is coming true with my Prince Charming."

Hotel Carrolina, Durham's first luxury hotel
~ Courtesy of Wilson Library (UNC)

Arthur thought, *I have already fallen in love.*

Arthur and Lizzie had a few more minutes to observe as they were now the third carriage in line waiting to pull up to the front door. The men strolled by in their tuxedos, dinner jackets, formal tails, and perfectly polished shoes. Most sported either a bowler or a six-inch top hat.

The women's gowns were exquisite as they walked by. "I've seen enough ladies passing by us in the last ten minutes to say you're the most breathtaking belle of the ball this evening," Arthur said. "When God created beauty, he molded it after you."

She squeezed his hand upon receiving the compliment and whispered to him, "Arthur, you're the most handsome man I have ever met. You are a true gentleman."

They exited the carriage to enjoy a night they would never forget.

Thirty-one

DINNER WITH
THE GOVERNOR

Beauty begins the moment you decide to be yourself.
~ Coco Chanel

THE FIRST MINUTE ARTHUR AND LIZZIE ENTERED THE HOTEL Carrolina, all eyes shifted on them. Heads turned, and people glared in their direction as they walked through the lobby to the ballroom. The room buzzed with a sudden chatter. On this delightful summer night, the usual center of attention that was often bestowed on the famous and handsome baseball star had shifted to his date, the young and radiant Lizzie Muse. It was the first time they were seen together.

The gown her mother made was a pattern from a French magazine. It was as magnificent as her natural glowing beauty. The floor-length gown was heaven blue in color and created from silk, without a train. Lizzie chose not to wear a hat for the evening. Her full and wavy golden-brown hair was one of her best features.

Walking through the parlor of the hotel to the grand dining hall, fraternity brothers and teammates Flowers, Ogburn, and Howard greeted Arthur. He introduced them and their dates to Lizzie. Each girl complimented her on her striking gown.

"Thank you for your compliments." Lizzie blushed. "The three of you look splendid tonight."

"Where's Chadwick?" Arthur asked.
"Over at the bar," Howard answered.

A likeness of the gown Lizzie wore to the ATO Gala event in 1905.
~ Courtesy of the Bradsher Family

~

THE DINING ROOM WAS A VERITABLE FAIRYLAND decorated with light blue and gold streamers, wrapping the four large columns from the ceiling to the floor. There were bowers palms and ferns decorated with miniature colored lights. The dining room table was arranged to form a Maltese cross, the emblem of the ATO fraternity.

The central chandelier was draped with hanging amaranths and gracefully festooned with dozens of daisies and carnations. Freshly cut and colorful flowers were placed everywhere. American Beauty roses and carnations created a magnificent centerpiece to the banquet table.

The heavy-set silver candelabras cast a soft, warm light over the already enchanting scene for the guests sitting at the table.

The gourmet dinner was a six-course meal, prepared by the fabled Raleigh chef and caterer, Dughi. He had placed sixty dainty engraved menu cards next to the dinner plates.

Lizzie looked into his eyes and smiled. "I must say, Mr. Bradsher, when you boys throw a party, you spare no expense. Will you dance with me?"

The classical musical selections were rendered by the First Regiment Band. The two danced fluidly together and became one on the dance floor. Lizzie trembled during the first waltz. She closed her eyes and melted in his embrace.

Dinner was ready to be served and everyone was asked to be seated. It would be an unforgettable six-course meal, and five of the active ATO members were asked to give a toast. Arthur's was entitled, "My College."

Lizzie was greeted by a deep voice as she took her seat. "Good evening, young lady, I'm Governor C.B. Aycock. You look very lovely in your gown. I look forward to sharing a conversation with you during dinner."

The governor turned to Lizzie and said, "I understand you're the youngest student to ever attend Trinity College and managed to make straight A's your first year. They tell me you were awarded a scholarship for your sophomore year."

"I won't ask where you get your information, Governor, but you are correct."

Governor Aycock looked at Arthur. "You must be Bradsher, the no-hit and strikeout king that led Trinity to the SIAA championship this year. Congratulations on a great season, champ. Is it true that John Heisman named you the 'King of Southern the Diamond?' I also understand that you graduated cum laude."

"Yes, sir, all of those assertions are correct," he courteously answered him.

As he enjoyed the first course, a shrimp cocktail, he thought, *I can clearly see how C.B. Aycock has been elected governor. He is a master of the compliment. He is on top of things.*

Arthur looked over at Lizzie and gave a smile and a slight wink. He reached down and squeezed her right hand. He already had feelings for her. He was thrilled and proud to be with her.

Between the second and third course, the toastmaster rang his bell. "I understand we have Arthur Bradsher to give the first toast of the evening, and it is entitled, 'My College.'"

He stood proudly and addressed the awaiting guests. "Ladies and gentlemen, please raise your glasses as I toast Trinity College. As some of you know, my father passed away when I was four. We have been plagued with too many of my family dying at an early age.

"Trinity has become my family for the past five years. I have been mentored and comforted and led to excel by my coaches, friends, team players, Cap Card, and President Kilgo. I will always be loyal to Trinity. The friendships that I've formed in this fraternity, in the classroom, and on the baseball field will be in my heart for the rest of my life."

Applause filled the room for over a minute. Sixty guests clinked their glasses. They shouted, "Hear ye, hear ye!"

Dinner was concluded with the choice of a plump crème puff or crème Brule. The waiters brought coffee, and the band played in the background.

"Let's steal one dance before we eat our dessert," Arthur said with a twinkle in his eye. They had the floor to themselves. The orchestra was playing "The Blue Danube" waltz and Lizzie felt like she was melting in Arthur's arms as they glided around the floor. His hand flexed on her back and he pulled her closer.

"Thank you for this very dear time, Arthur. I hope we will always remember it as a special night for us."

He tenderly smoothed the hair from her face and ran his thumb over her eyebrow. "You are a beautiful child of God," he said. He kissed her softly on her forehead. Her hair smelled like lavender.

After dessert, they said their adieus to Gov. Aycock and the hosts and prepared to leave. "Lizzie, help me find Walter before we leave. I haven't spoken to him all night."

"There he is." She pointed to him across the room.

Bradsher hustled over to him. He gave Walter a big hug and slapped his back.

"We're getting ready to leave and I just wanted to see if you wanted to get together tomorrow and talk about next year."

He acted distantly and was hesitant and nervous when he spoke. This wasn't like his usually confident sidekick.

"Are you all right, Walter?" Arthur asked.

He shuffled his feet and didn't answer the question. "Okay, I'll meet you at Hanes Field tomorrow at eleven." He changed the subject. "Do you promise to always take care of my cousin?"

Arthur looked over at his new sweetheart and squeezed her hand. "I'll always treat her with love and respect. You can count on that."

Arthur and Lizzie turned to leave. They held hands as they walked through the hotel to leave for home. They made a beautiful couple.

It was a splendid night for a stroll up Morris Street.

ALPHA TAU OMEGA.

Prof. R. L. Flowers, A. B. Bradsher, A. B. Duke, L. P. Howard, H. C. Satterfield, A. G. Odell, G. B. Cooper, J. W. Hutchison, "Billy," W. W. Chadwick.

ATO Fraternity at Duke University, 1904.
~ Courtesy of Duke University Library and Archives

Thirty-two

THE FIRST KISS

Our first kiss will always make me smile.
~ Lizzie Muse

ARTHUR AND LIZZIE LEFT THE GALA CELEBRATION JUST PAST midnight.

"Let's talk," he said as they walked toward her parents' house on Morris Street. He pointed to the glorious midnight sky and said, "Is this not the most stunning array of stars you've ever seen? Isn't God's creation splendid?"

"Yes, it truly is," she responded. They stopped and gazed up at the thousands of stars. She stood in front of Arthur; his arms were wrapped around her waist. She could feel his warm breath on her neck and became lost in the stars and his embrace.

"Let's continue, Lizzie." He reached his hand to hers. She grasped it tightly. He felt her warmth flow into him. His touch sent trembles through her. She suddenly stumbled, and Arthur quickly steadied her. "Are you all right?"

"I think I'm okay. Just a little lightheaded from the excitement of the night."

As they approached her parents' house, he said, "I don't want this night to end. Can we sit over here on the bench and talk and get to know each other better?"

"I'd like that. Let me check in with my mom first. She worries herself to death about me. If it is okay, I'm going to run upstairs and change out of this gown. Give me ten minutes, and I'll join you."

~

THE TWO TALKED for almost four hours about family, college, God, and baseball. It was a conversation that found a lot of common ground between the two.

Arthur told about selling tobacco for the American Tobacco Company during the summer as an eighteen-year-old. Lizzie talked about the six-week Sunday School training course she had taken the proceeding summer in Wilmington, North Carolina.

Lizzie sighed. "What a special time, studying the word of the Lord by the magnificence of the ocean," she said. They both talked about their families, and their stories were very different.

She even wanted to talk about baseball and looked directly into Arthur's eyes, asking him, "How does it feel to walk out to the mound to pitch the first inning of a game?" Lizzie wanted to understand some of the emotions that roamed through Arthur's heart when he did what he loved best.

"A bolt of energy runs through my veins before I begin a game. There's a feeling of some tension and anxiety. The first thing I do is turn around and look well beyond the center fielder and even farther beyond the outfield fence. Then I say a short prayer.

"It might go like this: 'Lord, there is no one on this ballfield better prepared for victory than me. Help me have fun in this contest and be respectable in my play. Please help me and my teammates perform to our best abilities.' After I've turned it over to my Savior, my tension disappears."

"Wow, that's a powerful thought. It makes perfect sense to turn it over to God to see it through," Lizzie exclaimed.

Arthur reached for her hand. "Tell me about your experiences at Trinity."

"I've had so much good bestowed on me in my life. God has blessed me with a large family and very loving parents. I've been raised to take advantage of the education offered to me and to excel in my classes. Whatever I didn't learn within the walls of the public school, my mother taught me at home.

"As I mentioned earlier, I enrolled at Trinity at sixteen and succeeded in making the honor roll my freshman year. I was one of the seven honor students who was offered scholarships for the sophomore year. There were only two women, Alice Craft and myself."

Arthur smiled. *She is not only gorgeous, but she's also brilliant, too.*

"In the two years I studied at Trinity, I received enough training to get what is deemed the equivalent of a teaching degree. This allowed me to teach in the Durham high school system. Some of my students were older than I. Let me say, leaving Trinity was a very tough decision, and I was flooded with conflicting emotions. I felt that there were others that needed my help."

"What drew you to teaching?"

"The less fortunate. I wanted to provide the poorest and most neglected students the opportunity to learn and be taught by someone who really cared about them. I realized I was carrying them in my heart."

"That's so good of you, Lizzie." He paused. "May I be honest with you?" He looked deeply into her inviting eyes. "I'm having that feeling that I experience just before I pitch an important game. My heart is starting to race, and I feel a little anxious about what's next."

"Are you okay?"

"Lizzie, may I kiss you?" he said softly. Not a word was exchanged for the next minute as Arthur and Lizzie leaned into each other and shared their slow, warm kiss. She quivered when their lips met. It was her first kiss.

"There you've gone and done it, Arthur!" Her eyes fluttered, and she seemed out of breath. "If you keep this up much longer, I may find myself falling in love with you." They held hands and talked for another hour until the break of day.

"Lizzie, this has been one of the best nights of my life." His voice was very soothing. "Now it's five-forty-five. The sun is about to rise from its sleep. Listen to the chorus of birds singing. We've seen the stars and now the start of the rising sun, all in one glorious night together."

"This is a time in my life I shall never forget and will cherish forever," she responded. She stepped toward him, put her arms around his neck, stood on her tiptoes, and kissed him again. The soft kiss sent chills down his spine.

"Let me walk you to the door," Arthur offered. As she was about to enter the house with her hand on the doorknob, she turned back to Arthur and embraced him strongly and kissed him.

Never had he seen a face so pure.

She let herself into the house.

Arthur turned to run back to campus. He had a wide smile on his face, and the sun was rising over Hanes Field.

Thirty-three

THE SEDUCTION OF
THE NEUSE RIVER

The Neuse River could be
as calm and seductive as a beautiful woman.
But if storms rushed in,
it could be as ugly as a jealous husband.
~ Bradsher

COME WITH ME, CHADWICK, AND HAVE SOME FUN," BRAD called out to his best friend. "Let's celebrate our championship season by going fishing in the Neuse River. You have heard me talk about Dr. Wilson. He's been like a father to me since my father died when I was four. He has a farm overlooking the river that's only four hundred yards from the steel Neuse River bridge.

"It was constructed in 1898 and is phenomenal, as it spans a mile across the Neuse. Fishing around its support columns offers great opportunities to land red drum, speckled trout, and an occasional striped bass. There's a train leaving next Friday night at ten and arriving at New Bern at five.

"Dr. Wilson or his son will pick us up the terminal; we should be on the river fishing by six-fifteen. If we want to stay for a couple of days, Dr. Wilson said he would accommodate us with camping gear, bait, firewood, and any other essentials we might need."

"I'm in."

The day before their trip, the weather report threatened storms, but they decided to continue with their plans for the fishing expedition.

Dr. Wilson and Bradsher discussed plans for the fishing trip to New Bern. "There's a flat area at the lower part of my farm that I used to camp with my son when he was young. The view of the river is breathtaking. It's only a couple hundred yards from the bridge, which's a great spot to fish."

"Thanks for your generosity, Doc," Arthur responded.

"I haven't seen Walter since your no-hitter against Wake Forest two years ago. It will be fun to sit down with him and talk baseball. You boys should be arriving at the depot in the morning at five fifteen. I will be there with a horse and buggy to pick you up."

~

THE DAY HAD COME for their trip to New Bern. Bradsher walked to the Durham train depot with two fishing rods, a small suitcase, and a lunch pail. He wore his Trinity baseball cap. During his walk, he thought about Walter.

Something was wrong.

He wanted to talk about the upcoming 1905 season, but Chadwick seemed to be holding something back. He asked his sidekick of four years, "What's wrong, Walter?"

Bradsher and Chadwick nervously paced back and forth in the train car for two hours. The usual smiles shared by the two for the last three years were not present. They discussed Chadwick's serious dilemma and whether he had a future at Trinity College. "Oh my God, Walter, why didn't you tell me about this earlier."

All of a sudden, Walter stumbled and collapsed off the train's leather bench. He never raised his eyes and he stared at the floor. He answered Bradsher, "I'm so ashamed."

The two of them had not come up with no real solutions. "Let's talk in the morning. It's great to be with you, Walter. Let's get some sleep. We've got a big day tomorrow." As he drifted away in sleep, his thoughts were of Lizzie.

~

THE THREE BLASTS of the train horn woke up Bradsher and
Chadwick as the 317 Southern came to a slow stop in New Bern.
Dr. Wilson was waiting for the Trinity batterymates. "Good day,
fellows. Let's get you two to the house for some fresh coffee and
breakfast. Max is cooking for all of us."

The three men walked into the kitchen enveloped with
beautiful aromas. They smelled the fried bacon and sausage. Max
had prepared a breakfast of scrambled eggs, sausage, bacon,
pancakes, and homemade biscuits for his guests. The coffee was
black and full-bodied.

"Max, do you want to fish with us this morning?" Arthur
asked.

"I'm disappointed I won't be able to join you. I've got some
business I need to take care of in town."

Dr. Wilson chimed in, "Fellows, out on the front porch you
will find some fresh bait and a couple of my favorite lures. I will
walk down to the river with you. We are about to see one stunning
sunrise."

Four kerosene lanterns approached the water's edge. The
sun hadn't woken yet from its dark abyss. As they reached the
shoreline, the sun began making its magnificent ascent over the
water. The first orange hued rays of the sunrise began to peak from
the vast horizon stretching from what seemed forever along the
Neuse River. As the assentation became stronger, it seemed to blush
and turned the sky and clouds a pinkish color.

"Gentlemen, this sunrise is simply too beautiful for words.
It's undeniable that only God could have created something this
breathtaking."

Dr. Wilson and Max walked over to the flat area he had
suggested they camp. "We've already brought you down a dozen
logs and some kindling for a fire tonight. You'll find some sleeping
bags and a two-man tent in the garage."

Their host pointed in the direction of the Neuse River Bridge.
"Around those pillars, you'll find the stripers and trout. They feed

off the plankton and small river life that is attached to the piers just under the waterline."

He turned to head back to the house. "Fellows, we'll come down and check on you around noon. Come up and join us for lunch. Walter, Brad assures me you've some good baseball stories for me." He turned and walked up to the house with Max, patting his son on his back as they climbed the hill.

The Neuse River Bridge - Built in 1898. Torn Down in 1950
~ Courtesy of Wilson Library UNC

The Neuse River was a welcoming and generous host for their fishing adventure on this crisp fall day. They found the fish were in a feeding frenzy. First, it was striped bass that had struck one of Dr. Wilson's favorite lures, the Jenny. Bradsher screamed, "I've hooked another one!" He tugged back on his rod and a twelve-inch striped bass leaped into the air. The green and silver lure looked like a small minnow and had three sets of double hooks attached to its belly. The trout and bass couldn't resist its sparkling movement.

A speckled trout was the next fish caught. It attacked Chadwick's hook loaded with a plump live worm. They had brought in twenty-two fish; they threw back a dozen.

Ten remaining fish squirmed in the five-gallon bucket. Brad

said to his best friend, "Let's gut and clean whatever we catch today and cook some of it for dinner tonight. We'll give the rest to the Doc and Max for being such good hosts."

They had a full morning of fishing down in the river. Chadwick shouted out to Bradsher, "It looks like the bridge keeper has left. Let's go up and fish off the bridge. It'll be fun."

In the first minutes after stepping onto the mile-long, state-of-the-art steel bridge, Bradsher noticed a change in temperature and a sudden increase in the wind. He looked to the north, up the river, and found himself looking directly in the face of a blackening sky. Bradsher knew how quickly the weather could change on the Neuse River; the conditions could move from a calm morning of fishing to a scene up on the bridge where the storm would raise its ugly head.

~

BRADSHER HEARD CHADWICK shouting from somewhere up above and was shocked to see him tight walking up above at the top of the bridge. "Hey, Brad, watch me go!" The wind suddenly changed, and the downbursts shifted. Bradsher watched in horror as Chadwick was having trouble keeping his balance. He looked shaky.

How can such a brilliant ballplayer act like such an idiot?

He screamed at his crazy friend, "Walter come down from up there before you kill yourself. There's a storm about to blow through here and you're going to get hurt."

He did not have to look back far up the river to see a wall of rain coming towards the bridge. The sky had completely darkened, and lighting and thunder could be heard up the river. The sudden change in temperature created a hailstorm Bradsher had never seen. Nickel-sized hail was bouncing everywhere onto the metal bridge. The wind was howling.

This time he commanded Chadwick to get down from the railing. "Climb down now before I come up there and yank your sorry ass down."

"Okay, Brad, help me down." No sooner had the words came

out of Chadwick's mouth is when it happened. Boom! A lightning bolt struck the bridge with such force that the bridge shook. Bradsher was five feet from reaching him when he saw his best friend slip from the railing and plummet towards the river.

Expecting a safer fall, Bradsher was shocked as Chadwick landed on a log that had dislodged itself from the riverbank. His best friend was already forty yards down the river and screaming, "Help me, Bradsher, help me! I think I've broken my back!" Blood was spurting from his shoulder area. "Help me, I'm bleeding to death! Please save me. I'm scared I am going to drown," he screamed in horror.

Bradsher ran to the middle of the bridge, climbed up on the railing, and jumped.

Thirty-four

THE FALL

You call it a near death experience, I call it a near life experience!
~ L.J. Vanier

AFTER A THIRTY-FOOT DROP, BRADSHER HIT THE NEUSE RIVER, swimming desperately toward his best friend. Chadwick had traveled forty yards from the Neuse River bridge. Bradsher rode the swift current of the river from the center of her girth. Chadwick traveled slower, being out of the fast-flowing current, as he was closer to the shore.

He shouted, "Damn it, help me, Bradsher! I'm hurt bad!"

Scared that he was going to lose Walter, he pounded his arms into the water, stroke after stroke, to reach him. His efforts were working. He was gaining and now was only fifteen yards away.

Chadwick was howling aloud as the pain was shooting through his shoulder, back, and hip. He continued to scream. "Help me please, God! Please help me!" He was dizzy, and his vision was starting to blur. The normal sharpness of the leaves became fuzzy as he passed the trees lining the shoreline.

In of the corner of his eye, Bradsher saw Dr. Wilson and Max scrambling down the hill. They had heard the terrifying screams. Brad swam harder to get to Walter and finally reached him. He collared him around the neck and kicked to reach the shoreline. The bloody mess and the disfigurement of his shoulder shocked him.

He screamed to Doc Wilson, "Tell Max to go get the stretcher, old towels, and your medical bag. Tell him to hurry!"

Max took off running up the hill to the house.

Knowing that Walter was about to go into shock, Dr. Wilson yelled, "Bring a blanket!"

Dr. Wilson looked at Bradsher struggling to bring Chadwick to the shore. He jumped in the river to help. When he reached them, he took charge.

"Arthur, listen to me. I want you to make every effort to keep Walter alert. Keep talking to him and make sure he stays awake. Max will be here in a few minutes, and we'll load him on the stretcher and take him to the hospital."

"Yes, sir. I will do whatever it takes to help my friend."

"Tell me where you are hurting, Walter," Dr. Wilson said.

He moaned, "Jesus, uh. Oh my God. I think I have broken my shoulder and maybe my hip."

The doctor pressed his hand on his neck, shoulder, back, and hip. "Tell me what you feel as I press with my hand, Walter?"

"Uh. Oh my God. That hurts."

"Can you feel your legs?" Dr. Wilson asked. Walter was barely coherent because of excessive blood loss.

"Yes, I can feel my legs," he weakly answered.

"Is there anything else that's hurt you?"

"Hell yes! There's a bone sticking through my shirt, and I'm scared."

Bradsher felt Chadwick squeezing his hand in response.

Max arrived with the stretcher and laid it at the edge of the river. They slowly lifted him out of the river and laid him on it.

Dr. Wilson raised his voice to his son, "Max, go up and get the horse and wagon ready to head to the hospital. Go into the house and get three pillows and put them in the wagon. Call the hospital to tell them that we will be there in thirty minutes and tell them to be ready to give him a blood transfusion. Explain his condition to the nurse or doctor. Also, grab Walter's wallet and identification that's in his bag in the kitchen."

"I got this, Dad," Max told him. "I'll be ready for you when you get the stretcher up to the house."

"Do you know your blood type?" Dr. Wilson asked.

"Yes, Doc, it's A-negative," he said, slurring his words.

Dr. Wilson, as he was giving instructions, had been working on Chadwick. First, he needed to stop the bleeding, and second, try to assess his injuries. The collarbone had snapped when he had fallen on top of the log that broke through the skin at the top of his shoulder. The collarbone, and possibly the shoulder, would need surgery.

Hospital X-rays would tell the seriousness of his hip injury. One of Dr. Wilson's first concerns with an open wound was the risk of infection.

He opened his doctor's bag and pulled out a flask of whiskey. He asked Arthur, "Do you want a swig?"

"I probably need one, but no thank you, I don't drink."

"Well, I guess this is as good a time as ever to start," he said with a chuckle. He then lifted the flask to his lips and took a long swig.

He poured the whiskey over the open wound. Chadwick yelled, "It burns! It burns!" Next, the doctor took a quart water bottle out of his bag and poured the water over the wound two or three times.

While working on dressing the wound, he said to Bradsher, "While I wrap the wound, I want you to go get your fishing rods and pour the fish back in the river. Make it quick!"

The doctor proceeded to tape gauze at the spot of the wound and kept wrapping the gauze over the shoulder and under the armpit. Chadwick screamed in pain when the wound was being dressed. Dr. Wilson continued until the wrapping was tight and compressed enough to stabilize the shoulder and stop most of the bleeding. He kept talking and repeating, "Hold on, Walter, hold on. We're heading to the hospital."

Bradsher could hear his best friend crying in pain as he headed back from the bridge with the fishing gear.

"Arthur, put the fishing rods next to Walter and let's carry the stretcher and our friend up the hill."

He was barely conscious and had gone into shock. He was moaning about the pain in his shoulder and in his hip. He had lost a dangerous amount of blood. When they reached the top of the hill, they found the wagon hitched to one of Dr. Wilson's favorite horses, Big Red. Max had saddled his horse, Pretty Boy, for the ride to the hospital.

"Max, I want you to ride ahead to the hospital and have the doctors and attending nurses ready for Chadwick when we arrive. Tell them how serious Chadwick's condition is with the broken collarbone and shoulder wounds, and a large amount of blood he lost.

"He'll need an immediate blood transfusion and X-rays performed. Inform them to have two pints of A-negative blood ready for him and that there may be hip injuries, and his blood pressure has skyrocketed to two hundred over one twenty-five with a pulse rate of one forty-five. Now, go! We will be fifteen minutes behind you. Also, start filling out the appropriate paperwork."

"Yes, sir," he answered. Max galloped off in a cloud of dust.

Bradsher and the doctor lifted Chadwick and the stretcher and set him in the wagon on top of the pillows, securing him with some rope from the barn. Dr. Wilson said, "I want you to ride back here with Walter. Keep talking to him and make sure he stays awake."

The three started their journey to the hospital down the long bumpy driveway of the Wilson farm. Bradsher hoped they would get to the hospital in time to save his friend's life.

Twenty minutes later they arrived at the New Bern Memorial Hospital. The staff waited at the front door to give Chadwick immediate care. They lifted the stretcher upon a transportation dolly and wheeled him quickly to the emergency room. The nurse immediately took his blood pressure. It had edged up and was still dangerously high at 220/120.

The attending doctor, a Dr. Franklin, gave the first order, "Let's get him out of these wet and dirty clothes and clean him up." He turned to Bradsher and said, "Son, I'm going to ask you to sit outside. We have a lot of work to do here. We'll keep you informed on the condition of your friend."

Dr. Franklin urgently gave his instructions to a nurse named Phillips. "Go ahead and hook the patient up for the blood transfusion. Dr. Wilson, I am shorthanded and need you to assist. Cut his shorts off with surgical scissors." They started the sponge bath on him, and within ten minutes they had him clean and in a hospital gown.

An hour and a half passed without a word from the medical team. Bradsher worried whether Walter would make it or not. He decided it was out of his hands, and it was time to let go and put it in the hands of God. He knew the Lord already had a plan for Walter. Arthur got down on his knees and started praying. "Help my dear friend, my Lord ..."

~

AFTER THREE AND A HALF HOURS, the door opened from the emergency room and Dr. Wilson appeared. He was dressed in operating scrubs, which were covered with blood. As he approached Bradsher, he looked down at the floor.

"Arthur, I'm sorry to have to tell you this," he began. "Your friend has had a tough go at it," he said in a shallow voice. "Walter won't be with the Trinity team next season."

Your best friend has died. These were the words that he thought he would hear next.

Then Dr. Wilson looked up and stared deeply in Bradsher's eyes. A broken Bradsher didn't expect Dr. Wilson's next words.

"I think we've saved his life. With time, he will heal."

Thirty-five

WINNERS NEVER QUIT

If you believe in yourself and have dedication and pride
- and never quit, you'll be a winner.
The price of victory is high but so are the rewards.
~ Coach Paul "Bear" Bryant

WOO-WOO, WOO-WOO, THE HORN ON THE OLD STEAM locomotive sounded as it barreled down the track towards Greenville, South Carolina. O. Maxwell Gardner was aboard the Southern Railway 317 that was now pulling into the W. Washington Street Depot, built in 1850. The train's engine let go of the steam that was trapped in its iron lungs. The sound heard was a long drawn out "shshshshshshsh," as it released the hot, smoky steam. Max Gardner stepped off the train and was greeted by John Heisman.

The 1905 baseball season had one more week of play left, and the two good friends had decided to go trout fishing. "The horse and buggy are tied up over there," the Tech coach said. "Wilson Johns, one of the players from this year's Furman baseball team will drive us to our campsite on the Chattooga River." Both men loved the outdoors and to camp and fish.

"Good afternoon, gentlemen," Wilson said to the two as they boarded the carriage. "I put a couple of Coca-Colas in a bucket of ice on the floorboard. Help yourself. I laid the opener on top."

"Thank you, Wilson," Heisman responded. "Tell us what you have planned?"

"First of all, we are heading for the river, where you will find some of the best trout fishing in the South. You should expect to catch a variety of trout, brown, speckled, and rainbow. In the back of the wagon, I have loaded for you fly rods, waders, a couple of sleeping bags, some firewood, and a freshly baked apple pie my mother made."

"The pie smells great!"

"I also brought you a fish holder, to cook your trout over the fire tonight, a coffee pot, a small fry pan, and some freshly ground coffee. Mom put a quarter pound of bacon and a half-dozen eggs in the cooler."

"Sounds like the first-rate service. Your mother is a dear woman. How long is the ride to our spot on the river?"

"It will take us about thirty minutes to get to the mouth of the river." He turned and handed Heisman a couple of cigars. "Coach, I understand you like this brand. Gentlemen, relax, light up and enjoy the scenic ride."

This is a smart and thoughtful young man, Heisman reflected.

The three men traded stories along the way to the fishing spot. "I understand you played for the Furman baseball team this year, and that you faced Arthur Bradsher of Trinity College," Gardner said.

"Yes, sir, we sure did," Wilson answered. "He pitched a no-hitter against us. There is no tougher pitcher in the South. His control was perfect, and his benders were impossible to hit. I was batting three hundred going into the game and went o for four. He didn't walk a batter and stuck out sixteen. They won, seven to nothing."

Heisman winked at Gardner. Twenty minutes had passed and both men had smoked their cigars to the end.

Wilson shouted out, "As we leave the main road and head down this trail to the river, it is going to get a little rough, so hold on tight. I ought to have you fellows fly fishing in the wild and scenic Chattooga in the next thirty minutes."

~

"I DON'T KNOW HOW Bradsher stayed in the saddle," Gardner said. "With two of Trinity's all-star players not returning for their senior year, the 1905 season was a really rough ride. I do not think Bradsher would have lost a single game with Wooten and Chadwick in the lineup. He could have quit or thrown up his hands in frustration after those first seven games." Both men were knee-deep in their waders in the cool and clear Chattooga River.

Heisman answered him as he cast his line. "Bradsher is not the type to ever quit. When the going got tough, he would always raise the level of his game to meet the challenge. His six straight wins going into the final game of his college career against Wake Forest had made most people forget what a tough first half of the season it had been. Max, did you bring the stats?"

Max cast his line in a different direction. "John, his numbers for the first seven games of the season were off the charts. In seven games, he gave up just three hits per game and walked eight batters. I will remind you, four of those walks were against you."

"You don't need to remind me, Max, I remember every one."

"He suffered another heartbreaker at Clemson after he left Atlanta. I cannot imagine how he felt after losing to the Tigers giving up an unearned run in the tenth inning after striking out sixteen batters.

"He allowed only six earned runs in his first seven games of the 1905 season. Those numbers are crazy, as was his record of two-four-and-one. He pitched brilliantly, but his record didn't reflect it. He delivered from the mound as well as any college baseball player to start off the first half of the season."

"Wow! I got one," Heisman shouted.

"Me, too!" Max screamed out in joy.

The sportsmen worked their lines for the next ten minutes. Both fishes fought hard and dirty. Each broke the water a dozen times and several times jumped out of the water to a height of eighteen inches. They were skilled fishermen and worked patiently to land their prized catch. Max snagged a large speckled trout and

John hooked in a smaller rainbow trout.

"These will make a great dinner."

Heisman agreed with him. "Let's clean and gut the fish while we've got some light, build a campfire, lay out the sleeping bags, and gather some more kindling."

"I can't believe Wilson supplied us these feathers down pillows," Max said as he sipped his Coca-Cola and stared into the fire. "This is pretty darn nice."

Heisman reached into his coat and pulled out a silver flask. "Care for a little whiskey?"

"Sure."

The two enjoyed their bourbon and cokes and listened to the freshly caught trout crackle and sizzle over the fire.

"This fish holder is very effective," Max marveled as he turned it over to cook the other side of the aromatic fish. They had put four small purple potatoes in a piece of foil and laid them on the coals over an hour ago. He mashed the potatoes with his index finger, and they were soft.

John raised his cup and proposed a toast. "Max may your joys be as deep as the ocean, and your sorrows as light as it's foam. Here's to many years of good health and a lasting friendship between the two of us."

Hardly a word was said during the first ten minutes the men ate their dinner. They were hungry, and the grilled fish and the potatoes were tasty. Max spoke first. "You know with everything we have accomplished today; I haven't yet congratulated you and Georgia Tech for winning the SIAA championship this year. Fantastic job, Coach."

"Thank you, Max. We had to go through Bradsher and Trinity College to get to the championship." Heisman laughed. "They called it 'the greatest game ever played in Dixieland,' and I truly believe it was. The title could have gone to them or us. It was the key game of the year and winner take all. We had a little luck along the way. I actually feel for the Trinity Twirler a little bit."

Boy, the fierce Heisman had a heart and a real humility sometimes, Max thought.

"Bradsher has won six straight games to take him up to the last game he'd ever play at Trinity. If his team can get him a run or two against Wake next week, he will finish with seven straight wins!" Max said.

Heisman unzipped his sleeping bag and crawled in. "Let's get some sleep."

"Goodnight, Coach."

~

THE EARLY MORNING DARKNESS escaped into a glorious sunrise over the Chattooga.

The sound of the cool water cascading over the river rock is one that I yearn for as it brings a unique energy to my body, Heisman thought.

He continued to feed the hungry fire with bone dry kindling and the seasoned maple wood that Wilson had supplied them. The fire popped and emitted a crackling sound with each newly added piece of wood, showing off bright orange and red flames.

John heard Max stirring. "Good morning, my friend. Are you ready to catch a couple of trout and have them for breakfast? There is some coffee at the edge of the fire. Help yourself."

Now that's the Heisman I know, Max thought.

He got up and rolled up his sleeping bag with the pillow in it and tied it off. Heisman did the same.

Fifteen minutes later, they were in the river making their first casts. It was eight o'clock. They walked down the river to a spot that was very calm and mirror-like. Heisman spoke first as they both cast their lines. "This is a perfect time to fish. The morning sun warms the shallows, creating more comfortable water temperatures for fish to feed. As we get into late spring and early summer, trout bite most during this hour of feeding time, when mosquitos and bugs are most active.

"Strike!" he shouted. "I got one and this is a really big one!" He worked the fish for the next ten minutes until he brought him within three feet from where he stood.

"Let me help you," Max said as he moved over to the large fish that still had a lot of fight left. He scooped him up in his fishing net and raised it up above his head. "What a beauty."

"Max let's fish for another hour then gut the fish and cook breakfast. Maybe afterward we could take a hike." He pointed up the mountain.

"Sounds like a great plan," Max said as they both entered the river and cast their lines with a quick snap of their fly rods.

They stood side by side and John said to his friend, "Max, you have had an impressive football career at State and Carolina. You were Captain of both football teams. You have also become an accomplished journalist. What are your plans?"

"I'm about to start in the field of law. Years down the road, I see myself spending a lifetime in politics."

"Am I looking at the future governor of North Carolina?"

"You might very well be, John."

~

TROUT MADE a magnificent breakfast.

After their hike, the two friends packed up and waited for Wilson Johns to pick them up and take them to the train depot. Within minutes, they heard the horse and wagon creaking down the trail.

"Good afternoon, gentlemen, how was everything?"

"Perfect. Thanks to you, Wilson."

~

THE TWO MEN STOOD before each other at the steps of the train. "John, it's been a real pleasure. Let's talk soon."

"I am still troubled about this Bradsher issue of him getting the proper recognition for the extraordinary year he had, even though his record didn't indicate it," Heisman said.

"If anyone has the power to give credit where it is due, John, you have those resources. I am sure you will come up with the proper solution."

"Let's stay in touch."

Max Gardner boarded the train for Raleigh.

Thirty-six

THE FINAL GAME

It ain't over till it's over.
~ Yogi Berra

I
T WAS THE FINAL GAME FOR THE KING OF THE SOUTHERN DIAMOND. His superbly orchestrated career was culminating in the most anticipated game in Southern college baseball history. Trinity and Bradsher were on a six-game winning streak. Eight days earlier, Trinity won in a one-to-zero shutout against this same Wake Forest squad. The Trinity southpaw had missed his sixth college no-hitter by one single hit in the ninth inning of the game.

The season finale had been postponed due to the death of Washington Duke on the original day the game was scheduled to be played, May 7th. It was rescheduled twice in the next eight days due to miserable weather in Raleigh. Record rainfalls had made the ballfield unplayable, and the severe thunderstorms had everyone's thoughts on personal safety and not baseball. Today's weather was glorious. The sky above was heaven blue, and the green grass on the diamond's outfield had been freshly cut and manicured.

The hometown newspaper, *The Morning Post,* described the scene. "Two redoubtable pitchers were set to face each other. Bradsher for Trinity and Edwards for Wake Forest. The Trinity Twirler, a southpaw cyclone, and the Wake Forest pitcher, a right-handed tornado."

Bradsher and the Trinity nine had been extremely successful against Wake Forest between the years 1901 and 1905. Bradsher had shut out Wake six times in that five-year period, two of those during this current season. His record was seven to one against the Baptists. He knew all too well that this would motivate the Wake team to play harder to win in this game of redemption. He also hadn't pitched in fourteen days.

As was the usual case when the Trinity legend pitched, his fans had followed him to Raleigh to see him perform. The loyal devotees had scheduled a special train from Durham to bring a huge contingency to Raleigh to root for their hero of the past five years. It was his last college game and his supporters wanted to see him lead his team to victory one last time. Over a hundred fans flocked to the bullpen prior to the game's start to watch their beloved star warm up.

One of the most popular girls in North Carolina had come to the game with her friends on the train from Durham. Lizzie Muse, Bradsher's special girl, had a front-row seat on Trinity's bleachers. She wore a yellow summer dress and had her beautiful hair pulled back in French braids. Her sparkling blue eyes searched the field for her beau, Bradsher.

Vendors circled the stands and shouted, "Get your salty soft pretzel, crispy grilled hot dog, roasted peanuts, and cold Coca-Cola—right here—only a nickel." Buddy, the most aggressive of all the concessionaires, jingled as he hustled hawking his wares with all the five-cent pieces in his pockets.

The excited ticket scalper waived a handful of tickets in the air. He screamed, "Only four tickets left for you to see the *King of the Southern Diamond* pitch his final game!"

He was approached by an anxious young fan immediately. "I would like to purchase your four remaining tickets—how much?"

"That will be a dollar a ticket," the portly ticket seller exclaimed.

"You must be kidding, the price for the last game was twenty-five cents. This is highway robbery."

```
─────────────────────────────────────

ADMIT ONE
─────────────

TRINITY VS. WAKE FOREST COLLEGE
MONDAY, MAY 8, 1905

HALF TICKET 25 CENTS

─────────────────────────────────────
```

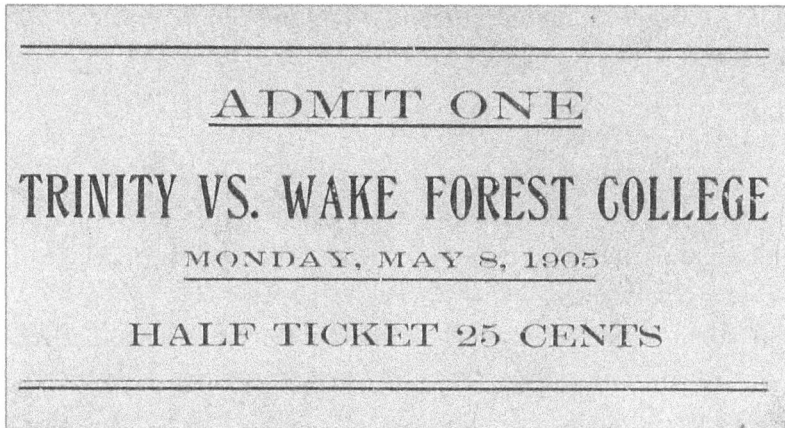

Original ticket for the last game Arthur Bradsher pitched in.
The game was actually played on May 17, 1905.
~ Courtesy of Brad Hayes

"Look, bud, I'm not going to argue with you. You either want to see the King pitch his last game or you don't. Take it or leave it."

The young student reached into his coat and retrieved four dollars and handed it over to the scalper. He turned and took off in a mad sprint to the ballfield, shouting along the way, "I got the tickets, I got them!"

~

DURING THE TRAIN RIDE to Raleigh, Bradsher visualized the game in his thoughts. He knew the strengths and weaknesses of the Wake Forest team player for player. He had faced Wake Forest eight days back in Durham and completely shut them down. The Trinity southpaw had allowed Wake only one hit. On that day, Bradsher kept piling on the misery by piling on the strikeouts. At game's end, he struck out eighteen disheartened Wake batters. It was the southpaw sensation's fifteenth shutout of his Trinity career.

One of his team's shortcomings was their weak hitting. Trinity's team batting average for the 1905 season was a dismal .196. He had realistic expectations of what it was going to take to win. He felt he was going to have to pitch his sixteenth career shutout for the Trinity Blue to win this game. He was excited to get started.

Both clubs were ready for the battle royal to begin at the Raleigh Fairgrounds. An overflow crowd of over seven hundred fans was packed closely together on both sides of the diamond. Ticket prices had been raised, and one of the largest crowds for a college game ever played in the South showed up. The price of a ticket on the grandstand was fifty cents; on the "bleacher" seats, thirty-five cents; and general admission, twenty-five cents. The air was buzzing with excitement as the smell of freshly made popcorn drifted by.

The News and Observer would report, "Pretty girls were there, all smiles and feminine graces, not to mention stunning summer costumes. The old rooters, the middle-aged rooters, the young college rooters, a class unto themselves apart, were all in evidence to the good, and when tense moments came there was bedlam."

For eight innings, not a runner had gotten beyond second base. Bradsher and Edwards were matching each other pitch-for-pitch like two champion prizefighters exchanging punches in a heated twelve-rounder. Batters were falling before the fans like the trees had fallen in last week's turbulent thunderstorms.

Inning after inning, the scorekeeper would climb his old rickety ladder to hang another zero on the scoreboard. Every time a zero would go up, the crowd would roar. In the eighth inning, he brought the raucous crowd to their feet with loud cheers and laughter when he missed a step on the ladder and fell to the ground.

When Bradsher made his way out to the mound to start the ninth, he looked at the seventeen goose eggs on the scoreboard and was confident there would be one more zero added on the board soon. The Trinity team had left ten men on base in a scoring position in their nine innings of plate appearances. The Trinity southpaw stepped on the mound and smiled as reality had set in. *My boys are the worst hitting team in the South.* Bradsher was due up first if he could bring his team into the tenth inning. *God, bring me through this ninth inning and give me an opportunity to help us win in the next stanza.*

Fifty feet in front of the outfield fence, Flowers, his very capable center fielder, was grazing his territory like an anxious bobcat and deciding where he was going to position himself for the next batter coming up in the inning.

Flowers had excellent reflexes, was known for a good glove, and had a strong arm. His play was pale in comparison to the 1904 all-star season Wooten had, but Flowers had worked hard and had a respectable year.

By the ninth inning, the fans were delirious. On every pitch, there were gasps, yells, moans, boos, cheers, and the pounding of the bleachers with their feet. As the Trinity team took the field in the last half of the ninth inning, the fans on the Trinity side were cheering, "Bradsher! Bradsher! Bradsher!"

When the Wake fans had failed to shout down the Trinity fans, they decided to join in on the fun and became part of the Bradsher chant.

The Trinity sensation had only allowed two hits and struck out nine as the leadoff batter approached the plate. Bradsher wiped the sweat from his brow and scratched the dirt with his cleats just below the rubber. Crouched catcher Wren gave a one-finer signal and tapped the inside of his right leg.

Fastball on the corner at the knees, Bradsher thought. *This one's gonna be a doozy.* He reared back and delivered the pitch.

Turner laid down a perfect bunt, hustling down the first baseline, beating catcher Wren's throw by a hair. Next up, Edwards made a sacrifice bunt, pitcher to first. Upon fielding the ball, the Trinity southpaw declined to throw out the lead runner at second, who was already sliding into second, so he wisely threw out the runner at first.

Morgan was the third batter to bunt in the inning and he sacrificed, advancing Turner to third.

Holy cow, these guys are bunting me to death!

The fans on both sides were going crazy pounding the bleachers with their feet. The deafening noise sounded like a train rumbling down the tracks.

Bradsher raised his left arm in the air, pointed to the sky with two fingers, and shouted to his team, "Two in the well." He looked beyond his center fielder Flowers to the distant horizon and suddenly, the game became frozen in time. He was not conscious of the cheers and screaming surrounding him.

His mind was in a quiet place and he thought these words: *Thank you, Lord, for what you have given me.*

He turned and faced the batter with steely-eyed determination. It was time to end this inning right here and now. On the first pitch to Goodwyn, the ball sailed high and tight and almost hit him. As the umpire called, "Ball one," the Trinity fans were booing, and the Wake fans were cheering him on loudly. His next pitch, a sweeping curveball on the outside corner on the knees was a thing of beauty. "Strike!" He climbed the ladder with a high and outside fastball that Goodwyn couldn't catch up with. The ump barked out, "Strike two." He was one pitch away from pulling another shutout inning out of his bag of tricks.

The Trinity ace had been in this strikeout situation 576 previous times in his college career, and he knew exactly where he was going with his next pitch. He had set Goldwyn up perfectly by going inside with the brushback pitch, then outside corner with the curve and outside again with the fastball. He perfectly visualized his strikeout pitch. He could see it hitting the catcher's mitt low below the knees, just outside the strike zone.

The decisive moment had arrived and Bradsher reared back, rotated his hips, cocked his arm, pushed off the rubber, and brought his body forward as he delivered his sweeping curveball. His planned pitch would be outside the strike zone by a couple of inches where a batter would chase it and whiff at it. A pitch is so delicious in the eyes of the batter, it was nearly impossible to lay off.

As his curveball bent along its way to within fourteen inches of the catcher's mitt, it looked ideal.

Bradsher could visual the dust exploding out of the catcher's mitt as soon as the ball hit it and hear the umpire's strike call—but the sound heard was a weak thump.

Goldwyn had stolen the pitch from catcher Wren's mitt at the last split second and dropped a weak sinking liner, a dying quail, a blooper, surely to drop into center field for the winning hit. Bradsher started to walk to the bench. To Bradsher's astonishment, and that of the other players and fans, Flowers, his center fielder, was charging towards the ball like a raging bull. He looked down and at the last possible second and dove with his body fully extended for the ball. Did he catch it? Flowers was rolled over upside down and everyone on the field was running towards him.

The umpire got there first to see if Flowers had made the impossible catch and held onto the ball. The ump quickly bent down on one knee and started pounding the ground with his fist. He waved out his arms from either side of his body and announced, "Safe!"

The season was over.

~

BRADSHER BARELY REMEMBERED walking over to congratulate the Wake Forest team and shake the hand of each player and coach. He told his counterpart, pitcher Edwards, "I have become a better man because of this day." He thanked him for the tough battle.

Lizzie walked over to where the team was congregated before heading to the station to take the train back to Durham. He gave her a long embrace. She looked deeply into Arthur's eyes and said warmly, "I am always so proud of you."

He thanked her for being at his last game and kissed her. She was such a comfort in his life.

It would be a long train ride back to Durham. He was tired. His baseball thoughts soon drifted over to thoughts about the beautiful Lizzie and his future with her. The pros were calling. He was worried about how things were going to work out.

~

BRADSHER WALKED OUT of his apartment a week later to find a note from Cap Card, Trinity's athletic director, who had been his friend and mentor from the first days he came on the job in the fall of 1902. In the short, handwritten note, he thanked Arthur for everything he had done for Trinity in his career and invited him to grab lunch at the end of the week. "And by the way, I thought you might want to see what the press had to say about you."

~

"IT IS SUCH PLAYERS that Trinity has on her team which lends countenance to baseball. Their pitcher, Mr. Bradsher, during his career at Trinity has made a reputation throughout the South as a college pitcher, both in his ability as a ballplayer and a gentleman of rare qualifications. No man can bring an unfair charge against him of doing an unfair act on the diamond. Despite the fact, he is one of the best pitchers Wake Forest has ever had to encounter during the last four years, it regrets to see him leave. May he make the success in life that he did on the diamond."

The News and Observer - May 18, 1905.

~

Arthur Bradsher Pitching Statistics 1901-1905

YEAR	WON	LOST	ERA	ER	IP	RUNS	SO	CG	SHO	BB	Hits
1901	6	4	3.76	29	77	46	70	9	1	11	59
1902	8	3	1.89	18	95	30	67	11	4	11	45
1903	7	2	1.93	17	83	34	99	9	0	8	49
1904	13	1	1.29	16	124	24	171	13	5	4	47
1905	8	5	0.746	10	134	17	169	14	5	11	44
TOTAL	42	15	1.75	90	513	151	576	56	15	45	244

Bradsher pitched in 2 other games that resulted in ties. He pitched 16 innings against Mercer in 2 games, not allowing a hit or a run. He didn't walk a batter in either contest.

YEAR	GS	WHIP	H/9 innings	SO/9 innings	BB/9 Innings	K/BB
1901	10	0.897	6.89	8.07	1.269	6.36
1902	11	0.589	4.26	5.58	1.04	5.36
1903	9	0.686	5.31	10.73	0.86	12.37
1904	14	0.411	2.47	12.41	0.29	42.75
1905	14	0.41	2.34	11.35	0.73	15.36
TOTAL	58	0.56	4.28	9.96	0.79	12.62

During his career at Trinity College/Duke Arthur Bradsher pitched 5 complete game no-hitters, 15 shutouts and struck out 15 or more batters on 10 occasions. In the 1904 championship season, Bradsher compiled a 13-1 record, struck out 171, and walked only 4 hitters the entire season. Bradsher Captained the Trinity baseball team for three consecutive years.

Thirty-seven

THE INTERVIEW

Talent is cheaper than table salt.
What separates the talented individual
from the successful one is a lot of hard work.
~ Stephen King

O. MAXWELL GARDNER PULLED A BOTTLE OF TWELVE YEAR
bourbon and a box of Cuban cigars from the drawer of
his old mahogany desk. He handed his best reporter, Billy Meyers,
the telephone. "Fellows, we're going to be here awhile. Billy, call
your girlfriend and, Walter, call your wife. Tell them you will be
home around midnight.

"Gentlemen, I'm meeting John Heisman tomorrow in Durham.
He wants us to come up with a list of questions and a format
for his and my interview with the famed Trinity pitcher, Arthur
Bradsher," Gardner said, instructing his newspaper crew.

He passed a couple of Cohiba cigars to his two reporters and
poured three drinks cowboy style in fancy highball glasses.

Billy Meyers's face winched as took the first sip of the straight
bourbon.

"Heisman is picking his all-star team for the 1905 season
and will be writing an article next month on his final picks. He is
also working on a piece for a major publication. The story will be
entitled, 'Making a pitch for the best pitcher in college baseball

history,'" he finished saying as he lit his cigar.

Gardner took a long draw of his rich-flavored Cuban and exhaled with a smile on his face. He handed a yellow pad and a couple of freshly sharpened No. 2 pencils to his assistants. "Men, let's get busy."

~

At five p.m. the next day, Gardner stood on the platform in the Durham train terminal waiting for John Heisman to arrive from Atlanta. They were to meet Arthur Bradsher at the Hotel Carrolina.

Heisman stepped off the train and approached Gardner. He was impeccably dressed in a three-piece Brooks Brothers suit, his shoes were shined, and he sported fashionable horn-rimmed glasses. "Good to see you, Max. Are we ready to meet with my favorite college baseball player in the South?" He greeted Gardner with a firm handshake and a pat on his back.

"We're on go, John. My boys did an excellent job last night preparing for the interview. We arrived at six questions of his baseball career and his personal life for the basis of the interview."

"Thanks for your due diligence, Max, I appreciate it," he said. They hustled up the steps of the Grand Hotel Carrolina, Durham's first luxury hotel.

Arthur greeted Heisman and Gardner with a broad smile and a strong grip. "Welcome to Durham, gentlemen, I hope you had a good trip. I reserved this table over in the corner. I've also confirmed your reservations are set for your stay at the Hotel Carrolina. Here are your room keys. I understand they serve an excellent breakfast. They start serving at seven."

The waiter approached the table to take their drink orders. The three men took their seats. "What'll you have gentlemen," he asked in a cheerful tone.

Heisman ordered first. "Bring me a twelve-year-old bourbon on the rocks."

"I'll have a draft beer," Max requested.

"Please bring me an iced tea," Arthur said.

As the waiter finished with the order, Heisman asked, "Son, could you bring us a bowl of nuts, also?"

The drinks were brought to the table, and Max took a sip of his ice-cold beer. He led off with the first question. "Trinity gave you the opportunity to play baseball and receive an excellent education. What'd you give back to your college?"

"That's a great question," Arthur began. "First, I'll always be grateful for my many experiences at Trinity. Being able to compete on such an important level on the baseball diamond will have a resounding effect, whether I play pro ball or not, and how I approach the rest of my life.

"The education I received during the four years of undergraduate school, and my fifth year getting my Master's degree, taught me to be consistent in my studies and always be hungry for new knowledge."

He continued, "I've given my all during my five years there.

"On the ball field, I have represented the college with integrity. I competed in a manner that the SIAA wanted to see in its athletes—to be clean and sportsmanlike and play with high character. Dr. Kilgo told me that I brought a lot of positive attention to our school."

"Your accomplishments and good character shed a very positive light on Trinity," Heisman agreed.

"I've modeled my behavior after one of my sports heroes, Christy Mathewson. He was a true gentleman and a devout Christian, but when he crossed the white lines was a fierce competitor. He accepted the outcome in each game he pitched, win or lose, in an honorable way. Mathewson is a star player who manages to stay extremely humble."

"Arthur, I witnessed that firsthand in our game in Atlanta. I have never seen a player keep his composure as well as you did under such tough circumstances," Heisman commented.

"Thanks, Coach, that was a tough loss."

"Max, I was extremely fortunate in the five years I pitched for Trinity. In the fifty-eight contests I pitched, I only had four or five bad games. One of those disappointing games was against Tech in my sophomore year. We were heavily favored to win. I had four straight wins and I felt and looked unstoppable.

"Unexpected to me, I was called to pitch relief in the Mercer game. I pitched six perfect innings, striking out twelve batters. The game was called because of darkness after the twelfth inning with the game ending in a four-four tie."

"Arthur, I remember the day I read the article about that game in *The Atlanta Constitution*. It was a remarkable performance and the first time it really sunk in that you were an incredible pitcher and a strikeout artist." Heisman tapped the table with his thumb. "Absolutely amazing."

"I was tired after that," Bradsher continued. "It's the only game of my college career that I pitched in relief. Then along came Tech. They would be the fifth opponent that I faced in eleven days. We were heavily favored.

"One newspaper said, 'Don't bet against Bradsher and Trinity in this one.'

"Granted, we made ten errors and Chadwick didn't play that day, but Tech read my pitches like a book. I was flat as a pancake, with no zip. They pounded me for ten hits and ten runs. I really stunk." He laughed and pinched his nose.

"Holy cow! That's a lot of innings to pitch in eleven days," the Tech coach said.

"*The Atlanta Constitution* reported, and I quote, 'Bradsher smiled grimly, and took his medicine with grace. It's a new experience for him, but not once did he get rattled.'

"I feel I represented Trinity in an honorable fashion that day."

"How was your experience as Captain of the team for most of your career at Trinity?" Heisman asked

"I was Captain for three years and it was a very fulfilling experience. Walter Chadwick and I helped with some of the coaching duties when Stocksdale became shorthanded. When we saw areas of play that needed to be improved, Walter and I acted on them.

"As far as giving back to Trinity off the field, I tried to participate as often as possible. One reporter wrote, 'Bradsher always led a worthy cause.' I was asked numerous times to speak at the YMCA.

"I spoke on topics such as living a toned life in college and the merits of participating in athletics in college.

"I was also asked to speak on the merits of the SIAA and how it was helping in keeping the integrity in college sports. I participated as a marshal in the Trinity debates and am a member of the ATO fraternity.

"In 1903, I was the principal founder of an honorary athletic society called the Order of the Tombs. It's been one of the strongest organizations for the last three years and I'm extremely proud of my work here. It'll be very important to the college as the athletic programs grow and flourish."

"How were your grades at Trinity?" Gardner asked.

"Academically, I was one of the four students selected cum laude in the graduating class of 1904. In 1905, I received my master's degree and at commencement presented my twenty-one-page thesis entitled, 'The manufacturing of tobacco in North Carolina.'"

Gardner jumped in and asked, "Do you feel you're going to pursue a career in the tobacco industry, or do you think you're going to play professional baseball?"

Gardner and Heisman leaned in towards Bradsher.

Thirty-eight

THE ANSWER

You never really understand a person
until you consider things from his point of view
... until you climb inside of his skin and walk around in it.
~ Harper Lee

THE TRINITY ALL-STAR BEGAN, "YOU ASK, WILL IT BE TOBACCO or baseball?"

It's the question every baseball fan in the country is anxious to get an answer to," John Heisman said as he tapped his spoon on his coffee cup.

Bradsher reacted. "I've been contacted by several of the baseball bosses who feel I could start directly in the pros next year. I agree with them and would love to pitch in the big leagues. Men, I have an unbridled passion for the game of baseball."

Bradsher shook his head. "Max and Mr. Heisman, I hate to disappoint you, but I can't give you an answer today. After Lizzie and I have thoroughly looked at the pros and the cons of baseball versus the tobacco business, I will have an answer. She knows my deep love for the game. We want to have a large family and be involved with the church."

"Arthur, you may not be able to have all of that and play pro ball too," the Tech coach pointed out.

"I hate to get personal, Arthur," Max confessed, "but have you proposed to your girl?"

"Not yet, but I'm almost there. I will let you know. Fellows, let's take a minute and eat some of this fine prime beef."

After a few minutes of enjoying their meal, Heisman asked Brad, "Can we continue?"

"Sure, Coach. Ask away."

"How do you think the season would have played out with Walter Chadwick behind the plate?"

"Great question," Bradsher said as he tapped the table with the palm of his hand. "Boy, did we miss him in 1905! Walter was a great defensive catcher, a clutch .340 lifetime hitter, team leader, and a real difference maker. Our record as batterymates was twenty-eight wins against only three losses in the games he caught me between 1902 and 1904. Walter and I were opposites in almost every way imaginable, but we were an unbeatable pair on the diamond.

"Teams wouldn't bunt or steal on him because of his quickness out of the box and arm strength. He made only two errors in 1904, and but four errors in 1903. Wren and Roper had a combined twelve errors in 1905," Bradsher explained. "Wren cost us the game against you, Coach. He had two wild throws when Tech stole and two passed balls. Also, their combined batting average for the 1905 season was a dismal .170."

"That was half of Chadwick's batting average for the 1904 season," Gardner pointed out.

"He'd pounce on the bunted ball like a cat on a mouse. We were beaten by the bunt and steal in 1905. It wouldn't have happened if Walter had been behind the plate!" Bradsher said, with a steely-eyed look at Heisman.

"In 1904, Walter batted .338 and had twenty-two hits, seven stolen bases, and scored thirteen runs," Bradsher began by rattling off statistics. "He and I went thirteen and one."

"What was most difficult about 1905?" Heisman asked.

"I didn't have Chadwick," Bradsher blurted out. "I don't think we would have lost a game with him in our lineup. You cannot imagine what an uphill struggle the 1905 season was without him and Wooten in the lineup. Starting the 1905 campaign with a two-four-and-one record was tough."

"But your stats were the best of any pitcher in the country," Heisman said.

"I appreciate your acknowledging that, Coach. We lost five games and tied one game in 1905 when I pitched. We scored a total of six runs in those six appearances and my ERA was 1.01. Those twenty-two hits by my sidekick would have made an enormous difference in those contests."

"You certainly know your statistics," Max said.

"Stats don't lie. They paint a very real picture of the truth," the Trinity ace replied.

"Let me explain where I'm coming from with some of my answers to your questions," Bradsher offered. "I know I sound a little self-serving, but I'm being counseled by Cap Card on how to speak with confidence and be effective in negotiations with the pro bosses that are contacting me.

"I've lived a humble and reserved life during my five years at Trinity. My cocky catcher always said I was boring because I was so soft-spoken. He called me a square."

"I certainly wouldn't call you boring, Arthur," Gardner said. "You brought more excitement to the game of college baseball than fans have ever witnessed. I will give you credit for your humility."

"Let's get back to Chadwick for a minute," Heisman said. "What other ways did he support you?"

"I was more effective at the plate with Chadwick batting directly behind me. Pitchers feared him. Consequently, they gave me better pitches to hit with him in the lineup, batting behind me. In the 1903 season when Coach Stocksdale batted me third and Walter fourth, I lead the team in hitting with a .352 average. My catcher was a team leader during his time on the baseball team. At five feet and seven inches and a hundred-fifty pounds, he wasn't afraid of anyone or anything. He led the team like a tough little field general. He was a teacher and encourager. Walter inspired our team in the three years he played.

"He and I were joined at the hip. We seldom disagreed on pitch calls. He was truly a calming force for me in the years we worked together. No one framed a pitch better than my cunning catcher. That stolen pitch gave me an extra strikeout or two and probably saved me a run a game. Umpires can be fooled by a skilled illusionist like Chadwick."

The Trinity southpaw talked with the same emotion he had when he took the game into the seventh inning on his way to another no-hitter. "And finally, he was a great compliment to me because we prepared for each team we played in the manner that you do, Mr. Heisman. We scouted and analyzed every hitter that we would face in the next game and discuss their strengths and weaknesses.

"You know the feeling, Mr., Heisman, sometimes we knew what a hitter was thinking before the thought even crossed his own mind.

"And finally, Walter was a renegade. There was never a boring moment with him on the team. He was the match that lit the firecracker. He was one of a kind."

The three men laughed, raised and clinked their glasses.

Bradsher slapped the table and stood. "I can't tell you how good that feels to get the Chadwick issue off my chest." He sat back down and cut an end piece off his steak. After he swallowed, he looked across the table.

Heisman scratched his chin. "I rated Chadwick as the second or third best catcher in the South. After listening to you Arthur, I may have ranked him number one."

"So, tell me, Mr. Heisman. How would Arthur Bradsher and Trinity have fared if Walter Chadwick had been in the lineup?" The Trinity southpaw drew a big imaginary question mark on the table and tapped his finger for the dot.

He cut a thick slice of his red medium-rare steak. He stuck his fork into the juicy piece of meat and displayed it to Heisman and Gardner. He smiled as he brought the perfectly cooked piece of sirloin to his lips.

He would now have a few minutes to enjoy his meal as John Heisman gave him the answer.

Thirty-nine

BEST PITCHER
IN THE COUNTRY

Walter Clarkson was wild as ribbon clerk at the seashore ...
~ The Washington Times - 1904

JOHN HEISMAN TOOK A SIP OF HIS WHISKEY AND BEGAN,
"Bradsher, the 1905 season would have been as
different as night and day if Chadwick and Wooten
were in the lineup. I know Tech would not have beaten Trinity
if your backstop was fielding the bunts and protecting against the
steal. Wooten was an all-star center fielder that helped your team
win for three years."

O. Max Gardner stepped into the conversation. "John is going
to spend some time discussing Chadwick's importance to your
team, but I will tell you why I picked Wooten as my all-star center
fielder for the 1904 season. He didn't make an error for the entire
year."

"I also think your control would have been better in our game
if you weren't preoccupied with baserunners trying to steal on
every pitch. I'm sorry to have pulled that on you," Heisman said.

"It was a genius move to run on every ball I delivered," he said
to the Tech coach.

"With as well as you pitched in 1905, you may have won all
those five one-run losses if he was in the lineup. If not all five, four

out of five. He'd have won a couple of those games with his bat alone," Heisman concluded.

As the server was taking the plates away, Max Gardner asked, "Who wants coffee and dessert?"

After looking at the menu, Heisman answered first. "I will have a brandy and a piece of carrot cake. How about you, Brad?"

"I'll try the carrot cake and a cup of coffee with cream and sugar, thank you."

Max ordered next. "I'll have a brandy, cup of black coffee and a crème brulee."

After the desserts were served, Heisman took the first bite of the carrot cake. "Good gracious, this is moist." He held up a forkful of a piece of the cake. "Take a look. I hear they embellish the cake with fresh coconut, pecans, and pineapple."

Max offered another question. "Brad, you won thirteen games and lost one in 1904. In 1905, you won eight and lost five. Also, you pitched the Miracle at Mercer and struck out twenty-two batters without allowing a hit. What was your favorite year?"

"Good question, Max.

"The 1904 season was a dream story. As you know I started the season with twenty-one no-hit innings before taking myself out in the eighth inning with two injured fingers. That's when Coach Heisman over there named me the King of the Southern Diamond."

Bradsher slapped his palm on the table. "If I had to do over again, I would've listened to Chadwick. I would have taped my fingers together and gone for the third no-hitter in a row.

"Our 1904 baseball team was running on all cylinders. The work we had done in the months before the start of the season paid huge dividends. Our hitting, fielding, and pitching were great the entire season, as well as the karma between the players. We were having fun all the way to winning the SIAA championship.

"Six significant things happened to me in 1904. I won thirteen out of fourteen games. I struck out a hundred and seventy-one batters. I pitched two no-hitters and five shutouts. Our team won the Southern Intercollegiate Athletic Association championship and

I was picked on the all-conference team."

"That's only five highlights," Gardner pointed out.

"Max, the sixth was not just a highlight, it was a life-changing event," Bradsher said with a gleam in his eye. "My new life began the first day I met the exceptional Lizzie Muse after the Furman game in 1904."

"I thought you were brilliant in the 1905 season with what you had to work with," Heisman offered. "What're your feelings about your last season at Trinity?"

Arthur began, "The 1904 season was fun, and the 1905 season was certainly more challenging. At times, it was an uphill battle.

"After the first seven games of the 1905 season, my record was two wins, four losses and the no-hit tie at Mercer. By contrast, my record for the same time in the 1904 season was nine and zero.

"Sometimes that tough climb to the top can bring out the best in us versus the effortless walk on flat terrain. The 1905 season certainly tested my character and strengthened my resolve to finish strong."

I bounced back to win six straight games leading up to the final game against Wake Forest. During that stretch, I pitched three shutouts and my fourth career no-hitter."

"You finished like a charging bull," Max said, slapping his palm with Bradsher's.

"We lost the final game of the season, one to nothing, in the ninth inning. We left nine men on base, which dearly cost us.

"Mr. Heisman, our main goal in 1905 was to win our second straight SIAA championship, and darn if we didn't almost do it. We sure gave Tech and Mercer a run for their money."

"Arthur, I have one final question for you," the Tech coach began. "Most of the coaches and sportswriters in the country feel that you and Walter Clarkson are the two finest pitchers to come out of college baseball since Christy Mathewson pitched with Bucknell in 1895. How do you compare the two of you, and who's the superior pitcher?"

"Walter Clarkson and I pitched under totally different circumstances. He was a talented ballplayer that pitched his first game for the varsity club at Harvard as a twenty-three-year-old sophomore. He had pitched in organized ball since he was nine years old. I was never an official member of an organized team until I made the Trinity team as a walk-on freshman in 1901.

"He stood five feet and nine inches and weighed a hundred and forty-five pounds. He relied almost totally on his fastball. Some said he overthrew his fastball, often causing problems with his control. I stand six feet, weigh a hundred and seventy-five pounds, and pride myself of having near-perfect control of all my pitches."

Max chimed in, "Yeah, in the game against Georgetown, Clarkson was out of control. One pitch was outside, the next pitch way inside, another ball was a thrown over the catcher's head, and the next pitch is thrown into the dirt. He walked seven batters, threw six wild pitches, and hit one batter," Gardner finished shaking his head in disbelief. "The reporter for *The Washington Times* wrote the next day, 'Walter Clarkson was wild as ribbon clerk at the seashore.' They all laughed. Georgetown won the game by a score of six to zero."

"Well, to your point, Max, he walked nine batters against Princeton, hit a batter, and threw a wild pitch. At times, Clarkson had catastrophic control problems. I personally believe his mechanics suffered when he tried to overthrow his pitches. It's why he was ineffective when it rained. If the skies opened, soaking the mound, he refused to pitch. I wish I would have had that luxury.

"Walter and I are both excellent hitters, fielders, and baserunners." He laughed and smacked his palm on the table. "I hold a record Clarkson could never match. I am the only left-handed player in college baseball history to pitch, play complete games at third base, shortstop, second base, and first base."

Heisman laughed. "I don't think that feat will ever be matched."

"I'll point to the areas that gave Clarkson a superior advantage when he pitched. He pitched for the strongest team in the country between 1901 and 1904. In 1901, Harvard had a record of eighteen wins against only two defeats, and in 1902 their season resulted in twenty-one wins to three defeats.

"Their team was extremely skilled in every aspect of the game. They were very strong defensively and their lineup was packed with power. Harvard's all-star catcher, Big Man Reid, didn't make an error during the 1901 season and hit six homers out of the park.

"Frantz could also sink your ship with one of his deep missiles. He hit four dingers over the fence in 1901. Clarkson, Stillman, Story, and Kernan were also long-ball threats. The four of them hit a combined seven home runs in the 1901 season.

"Our 1905 team hit only one home run and our team season batting average was .193. We had a lot of lost opportunities during the season. In our final game of the season loss to Wake Forest, we left nine men on base. Against Mercer, we stranded seven baserunners. In both games, we failed to score."

"Your offense was terribly weak," Gardner agreed.

"And now to the ten-thousand-dollar question of who's the best pitcher in the country between Clarkson and me. Gentlemen, I will give each of you one vote. Pretend I'm not in the room. Mr. Heisman, who do cast your vote for and why?"

John Heisman cleared his throat and began by saying, "I cast my vote for Bradsher. I feel he's the best college pitcher in the country for three reasons. First, he's mastered the control of his pitches better than any college pitcher I've ever seen. Second, his repertoire of four pitches kept the batter off-balance and fooled ninety-five percent of the time. And third, he's a strong and inspiring leader of men."

Max spoke next. "I'll also give my nod to the Trinity ace. The most important three things a pitcher must have to be highly successful can be summed up in three words: control, control, and control.

"He must have pinpoint control and not walk batters. What concerns me about Clarkson is in his twenty-seven wins he walked three, or more, batters ten times. Bradsher, on the other hand, only walked four batters the entire 1904 championship season.

"A second important measure of control is keeping your cool and not getting disheveled in tough game situations. And the third is being able to control a curveball and drop ball on the outside corners of the plate on almost every pitch. He had the best breaking ball in the history of college baseball and wasn't afraid to throw it on a three-two count. Bradsher did that better than any college pitcher I've ever seen."

Arthur looked troubled, and Max asked him, "Are you okay?"

"Max, I'm not comfortable with you printing your story at this time. I want to honor Lizzie by keeping our lives private right now. We need to talk and make some very tough decisions about our future."

He continued, "Even though the season is over and my career at Trinity is completed, I don't want to dishonor any of my teammates.

"You and I know the answers to the Chadwick question, on how the season might have turned out if he'd been my catcher for the 1905 season. But what we are not certain about is by my answering that question, how much that we might hurt, my catcher, Wren. Also, we really don't know what skeletons and emotions that might be brought out of Chadwick's closet. I would really appreciate the two of you understanding my request. For now, let's just let a dead dog lie."

Heisman responded, "I think I can speak for Max in saying this. We understand your feelings and are glad to honor your request."

Gardner nodded his head in agreement.

Brad extended his hand out and shook hands with Heisman and then Gardner. "Gentlemen, I want to thank you both for dinner and a very enjoyable evening. Let's talk again soon."

He reached into his pocket and pulled out a two-dollar bill and laid it on the table. "Thanks for the offer to buy me dinner, but I'm still an amateur."

The three men smiled, and Bradsher turned to exit the Hotel Carrolina.

Forty

HEISMAN PICKS
THE BEST

*The pitcher is the mud-sill of any team. He should be necessarily a
man of good judgment, with perfect control, with deceptive curves,
and a good man with his stick. There is but one man in the state
who possesses all the above characteristics and that man is
Arthur Bradsher of Trinity.*
~ Maxwell Gardner - *Morning Observer* - 1904

AFTER JOHN HEISMAN'S 1905 SELECTION OF THE SOUTHERN
All-Stars and naming Arthur Bradsher as the top
player in the South, and perhaps in the country, the attention was
being focused on the Trinity ace in an extraordinary way. After
evaluating over 250 players from twenty-three teams in the SIAA,
he decided on Bradsher as his top pic and the Captain of the 1905
All-Star team.

Every day he was receiving a duffle bag of letters and telegrams
from fans, opposing teams' players, and baseball bosses. One
sportswriter wrote, "Every woman in the South wants to marry
him and every baseball boss in the country wants to own him."

The houseboy at Bradsher's dorm, Morrison, greeted as he
entered the hallway. Morrison declared in his thick southern
accent, "Mr. Arthur, you suh, are poplar. The bag is filt with a slew
of letters and telegrams from all over the cuntry. Some of the letters

are even parfumed."

"Thank you, my friend. Let's put them in the corner and I will get to them later." Bradsher grasped the door handle to leave, then let go of it and turned to the houseboy. "You like baseball, don't you Morrison? I've seen you watching us play from up on the hill."

"I surely does."

Bradsher smiled at his friend. Why don't you and I go for a pitch next week. I've got a couple of extra gloves. Let's meet at Hanes Field at noon on Tuesday."

Morrison's face glowed with excitement. "I be there."

Bradsher reached into his pocket and retrieved a couple of two dollar bills and pressed them into Morrison's palm. "I want to thank you for everything you've done for me the last couple of years."

Arthur turned and left.

He first heard about Heisman's selections from a newspaper article that W.W. Card had dropped off at his dormitory. There was a write-up in *The Atlanta Constitution* on his selections. The Tech coach was very detail-oriented in his evaluation of the top players for his all-star lineup. He analyzed four to six players at every position before picking his top starting nine.

The genius coach emphasized in his final selections that this all-star team could compete with the all-star team of the North. He pointed out the Southern teams had many successes against such strong teams as Syracuse, St. John's, Hobart, Lafayette, Washington and Lee, Harvard, Gettysburg, Lehigh, and Cornell.

He named seven pitchers he considered as his top pitcher representing the South. He narrowed it down to Weems of Auburn, Day of Georgia Tech, and picked Bradsher as his starting pitcher and Captain of the team.

The Tech coach's comments on his own pitcher, Day, were as follows: "I choose the last-named, after much deliberation, because in no game has he been knocked out of the box or been heavily hit and he has pitched a great many games this year. Then too, he is a quite reliable batter and very fast on the bases. He has lost but one game this year - that by a score of 1-0."

He made these comments about his top selection. "Easily, the name that shines clearest and brightest in this array of exceptional talent is that of Bradsher. This young man is beyond all questioning the most prominent player of the season. With most extraordinary ability as a pitcher, he combines the advantages of being a good batter and base runner."

He continued to praise the North Carolina wonder in his selection. "Add to these a sunny disposition, a firm determination and words of endurance and you understand why he has been able to place himself head and shoulders above all other pitchers of the year. And I would have him Captain of my team. He has the bearing of a gentleman, the forbearance of a true sportsman, and the ideal temperament of the fighting athlete, ever determined, never dismayed, always strong with a persistent smile to help out. As Captain, he would be a credit and ornament to any team."

The thoroughness of Heisman's description of the players fully demonstrated how deeply he studied each player. This deep knowledge of all the players and their strengths and weaknesses was a major contributing factor in his winning the SIAA championship in 1905.

After reading the newspaper article, Bradsher opened the personalized note from W.W. Card.

"Brad, congratulations on the due credit you are being given from coaches, fans, and sports-writers on your illustrious career. Everyone at our institution is greatly appreciative in the manner you have represented the college and the honor and shining light you have put on Trinity. Let me know if we can have lunch together and discuss some matters in a couple of days. Kindest Regards, Cap."

The Trinity all-star had received telegrams from two of the most powerful bosses in the major leagues. The telegrams stated that they would like to meet him and make him an offer to play professionally. Both telegrams indicated, from their scout reports, Bradsher could start next year in the major leagues, without having to break in with the minor leagues.

Bradsher decided he was going to take a jog over and find

Cap Card, the man that had been his mentor for the past three years. He would be better able to navigate the unfamiliar waters of professional baseball with the mature judgment and help from his trusted confidant.

Bradsher got lucky. He found his friend at his mailbox. "Cap, thank you for dropping Heisman's article by for me. Do you think we could go grab a sandwich and discuss my future? I could really use your help. You've been like a brother to me since we first met."

"Let's walk to Murphy's," Cap suggested, "and see what we can accomplish with your concerns." The two good friends walked down Elm Street to their favorite eating establishment.

The minute the Trinity star walked into Murphy's, patrons were saying hello and congratulating him on his great season. Many in the eatery were reaching out to thank him on how he had represented Trinity and the city of Durham.

Card guided his friend over to the booth in the corner. "Let's sit here so we can talk with some privacy. I didn't expect to hear from you so soon. I thought you might want to soak in the glory for a while. Is there some urgency to our meeting today?"

Bradsher replied, "I have some decisions to make in these upcoming days that may affect the rest of my life."

Card asked, "Tell me what's on your mind?"

Bradsher fidgeted. "I want to play professional baseball next year. Two baseball bosses contacted me and they both feel I could start for their teams next year without spending time in the minors. I've also received telegrams this past week from Boston, New York, and Baltimore."

Card asked, "Tell me more about your thoughts."

Bradsher began, "I feel I will add value to any team in the majors. With the expansion of the league and the addition of the American League, I have been offered ten thousand dollars a year for my services with expectations I would win twenty games a year, draw more fans, and help them win the pennant."

"What does your sweetheart, Lizzie, say about all this?" he asked in a concerned tone.

"We haven't had a serious discussion about this yet."

Cap raised his eyebrows and his forehead wrinkled.

"Well, it is time for you to have that discussion with her. Brad, you obviously have two loves in your life, baseball, and Lizzie. You may find out you can't have both if you play professional baseball," Card said seriously.

The wise athletic director tapped his finger on the table. "The demanding schedule of the major-league season would affect other areas of your life, such as having little time to spend with your family and less involvement with your church. Finally, there is the financial consideration. Whereas, the sum of ten thousand dollars may seem like a lot of money, how would it stack up against if you have a successful career in business? Most people who meet you say you will be a high-ranking executive someday. I agree with them."

"I will finish with this," Card said. "Give some serious thought to what we've discussed and call Lizzie. Tell her you need to have a talk. I'm always here if you need to bounce some ideas off me."

As they reached the dorm, Card shook Arthur's hand. "I hope this works out for you. I would hate to see you lose your love, Lizzie."

Forty-one

TRAIN RIDE
TO NEW BERN

*The best and most beautiful things in the world cannot
be seen or even touched, they must be felt with the heart.*
~ Helen Keller

A SLIGHTLY BUILT WOMAN, CORAH REMARRIED ODAH CARVER
seven years after her husband, Charles Bradsher, died of
tuberculosis. She ran a boarding house after she moved her family
from Roxboro to Durham to earn money for her family and to
educate her son at a fine college like Trinity.

His mother sat across from him at the mahogany table in their
home on Cleveland Street. It had a beautiful inlay along its edge
and was set under a lavish ten-light crystal chandelier. "Arthur, I'm
so proud of everything you have accomplished at Trinity College
on the playing field and, especially, your academic successes.
Graduating cum laude is quite an achievement and one you should
be very proud of, too."

"Thank you, Mother, for all your support along the way."

She continued, "You've set a fine example for the young men
at Trinity and others across the state of North Carolina to follow."

"You know I've always tried to do my best."

She slid a small, purple, velvet drawstring bag across the table
to her son and said, "I want you to have this." He reached in the

velvet bag and pulled out a little box.

"Open it," she said with an endearing smile.

"Oh my God, Mother, I've never seen a ring so impressive."

She was very proud of it, slipping it on her finger. You were too young to remember this ring. Tears welled in her eyes. Your father gave it to me the night he proposed. He worked over a year at the pharmacy, while he was in medical school, to pay for it," she lovingly described it.

"It's a one-and-half-carat, European-cut diamond set in a fourteen-karat, squared-white gold setting. It's flanked by four European cut diamonds on the yellow gold shank."

He was such a sweet and dear man. He said my beauty was deserving of a ring this exquisite."

"I've always been told that he loved you so much, Mother."

"When the day comes to propose to Lizzie, give her this ring and tell her exactly what your father said to me. She is so lovely inside and out, Arthur. You're very blessed to have found each other. She is an exceptional woman that deserves a special ring like this. In the meantime, I want you to take it to the bank and give it to Mr. Spearman to put in the safety deposit box."

He reached across the table and grasped his mother's small, soft hand. "Thank you." He looked into her hazel eyes, now full of tears.

"Mother, this ring is going to mean so much to Lizzie and make her feel part of the family. It will always serve as a remembrance of you."

He hugged her and kissed her on the cheek and turned to leave. After taking a couple of steps towards the door, he stopped and turned to his mother. "I love you more than I will ever be able to express. I'll come to see you when I return from New Bern."

He jumped up on the carriage next to his friend Billy.

"Next stop, the Main Street Bank, and then we'll pick up Lizzie on Morris Street."

Billy responded cheerfully, "Aye-aye, Captain."

As he exited the carriage, he said, "I'll only be a minute." He hustled into the bank to find Mr. Spearman. Billy watched him through the large plate glass window of the bank. He appeared to sign a document, and the two exchanged something.

Arthur left the bank with a big smile on his face and hopped up on the carriage. "Let's go pick up Lizzie."

"Are you going to propose to her?" he suddenly blurted out.

Arthur laughed. "Wow, I never expected that question from you, Billy. I sure do love her. We have a lot to talk about before that decision is made. It's the main reason we are spending a few days together at the river house in New Bern.

"Give me about ten minutes to talk to her and we'll be ready to head to the train station." He jumped down from the carriage.

After several knocks, the front door opened, and the entire Muse family greeted him. There were ten of them. Mr. and Mrs. Muse welcomed Arthur with a handshake and a hug.

"Arthur, you've met most of our children. Going down the line is Little Joel, Amy, Frank, Ben, Helen, Mildred, and William."

"Good afternoon," he said, grinning.

Lizzie stood perfectly still with her leather suitcase set in front of her. Her face was flushed, and she was nervous. It would be a new experience for her to travel with a man.

She looked stunning in a white, puffed sleeve blouse with a silk above-the-neck collar. She wore an ankle-length pleated skirt. Her dress was tucked in at the waist, which accentuated her petite figure.

Arthur caught himself lost in his stare at Lizzie. He couldn't take his eyes off her. Her natural beauty always astonished him. Her hair was braided and pulled back, showing off her angelic face.

"Are you ready?" He reached his hand out to her. She trembled as their hands touched.

All the Muse children broke ranks and circled Arthur and Lizzie. They tugged at both, especially Arthur. "I think we better get going. Here is a copy of our schedule." He handed it to Mr. Muse, who said, "Ben, will you please bring your sister's suitcase out to the carriage?"

Arthur reached out to grasp Lizzie's hand and walked with her from the parlor to the carriage. He helped her to reach the first step and climb aboard.

Billy greeted her. "Good to see you again, Lizzie."

"It's nice to see you, Billy. Thank you for your help."

Billy yanked on the reins and yelled "Heehaw!" Two minutes later they were trotting down Morris Street on the way to the train station. Arthur put his arm around his girlfriend and gave her a gentle embrace.

As they came to a halt in front of the train depot, Arthur handed Billy a folded two-dollar bill and thanked him. "Lizzie will be back on Monday at five-thirty p.m. Could you please pick her up? I'm going to stay a few more days and do some fishing."

Billy responded, "I will be at the depot at five-thirty sharp."

~

LIZZIE AND ARTHUR HELD HANDS as the train chugged down the tracks leaving Durham. They had never traveled together and were not sure what to expect. They both knew this was an important trip for them to get to know each other better.

Very little was said during the first twenty minutes of the train ride. Awkwardness and nervousness surrounded them. Arthur broke the ice. "Lizzie, please open your heart to me. I promise that I'll be open and honest with you."

"Thank you, Arthur," she responded in a soft voice. She reached out to grasp his hand.

"May I kiss you, Lizzie?"

"I would like that very much." Her eyes fluttered as she leaned towards him.

The train rumbled down the tracks to New Bern for fifteen minutes before another word was spoken. "Lizzie, tell me about your year of teaching and about a few of your students."

"One student that I worked with the last half of the school year was a black child whose mother was an alcoholic and the father was in prison. His homeroom teacher told me over lunch he was a troublemaker and hard to manage.

"'He's a bad kid,' she snarled.

"That afternoon, I went to the principal's office and asked if the boy could be transferred into my homeroom. She agreed to send him to me that afternoon. I addressed my class before he showed up. 'Everyone, a young boy named Will Potter will be joining our classroom this afternoon. He comes from a broken family and doesn't have many friends. He is struggling, and I'm going to try and help him. I ask each of you to treat Will with kindness, acceptance, and respect like you would want.'"

"How did it work out with the boy?" Arthur asked.

"It was a demanding situation. Will was angry, frustrated, and could not read. He hardly ever spoke and never smiled. I worked with him every day after school and he made a great deal of progress. For the first time in his life, he felt someone really cared about him. I finally got him to smile. The students helped with this in so many ways.

"He finished his first book just before the school year ended. I have never seen a child so happy and proud of himself. He was grinning ear to ear the last days of school. I gave him a couple of books to take home and read for the summer."

"Lizzie, your heart is so full for others. To leave Trinity to teach speaks volumes about your loving spirit"

"I love you, Arthur, and am grateful that you care enough about me to bring me to New Bern. I'm going to lay my head on your shoulder, close my eyes, and dream about what I hope my future is going to be with you"

~

WHEN LIZZIE WOKE, the train was pulling up to the New Bern depot. "There's Dr. Wilson," Arthur said. He picked up her suitcase and helped her off the train.

Five minutes later, they were trotting down the road to the river house.

Forty-two

SUNSET FROM
THE BRIDGE

The supreme human law is love ...
~ Saint Augustine

L IZZIE, JUST SITTING HERE HOLDING YOUR HAND AND
watching the sunset is calming to me," Arthur said.
"Being with you and looking at God's splendid creation, brings me
to a place of complete peace."

The sun mellowed, a sharp contrast to the bright fireball which
hung over the Neuse River in the early afternoon. The distant
horizon swallowed the glowing sun as the light of day slowly
faded away. The early evening had a cool crispness, typical for
September.

The sky smiled and blushed with colors of pink, red, blue, and
yellow, mirrored by wildflowers in the distant field running along
the river. The last rays of the sun were fading into twilight. Soon
the sky would explode with stars.

~

A T THE EDGE OF THE BLUFF, Dr. Wilson sat next to the blazing
fire pit. The burning embers warmed his body, chilly in the night.
The sappy pine firewood crackled, hissed, and snapped. It spat
sparks.

He thought of his wife, Mary Katherine, whom he'd lost to pneumonia five years earlier.

He missed his Kate. He longed for her bright disposition, their long conversations, warm kisses, her pouts, and her sexy, lithe and supple body. She had a beauty that was present in all seasons.

As the red embers of the fire shot into the darkened sky, he looked upwards. He spoke to her. "My dearest love, I think of you every day. Every time you come into my thoughts."

"I celebrate the wonderful years we shared together. I shake my fist in the air and exclaim, Kate, we had the greatest life together. My love, we had what most people cannot even imagine in a relationship. Every day with you was a beautiful one, even during tough times. I stand steadfast with my love for you, my darling. I know we will be joined together someday in Heaven."

He left his view of the setting sun and turned his gaze to the Neuse River bridge. As the darkness arrived, he could barely make out the silhouette of the two lovebirds sitting in the buggy. Earlier, they had crossed the magnificent mile-long steel structure, turned around and traveled to a stop directly in the middle.

Dr. Wilson was struck by how handsome and in love they seemed to be. He prayed that this weekend would bring them together for a lifetime.

~

LIZZIE TURNED TO ARTHUR, and he gently pulled her close. He slowly kissed her soft lips. Her eyes were shut, and she shivered. He broke off the kiss. "Are you chilled, my love, do you want my jacket?"

"Arthur, sometimes I just don't think you understand, my handsome man." Her face was glowing with happiness as she broke out into a gleaming smile. "It is you that causes me to quiver. You move me deeply every time you kiss me."

They kissed again.

Lizzie broke the embrace and addressed Arthur with a serious look on her face. "You told me on the train to open my heart to you."

"I want you to share your feelings and express your hopes and fears," he responded with gentleness.

Her eyes had become moist. "There has not been an hour in a day since the Furman game last year that I haven't thought of you. I love you more than any woman ever can or ever will. Every time I see you, my heart races."

"Every opportunity I witnessed you pitch, my heart swelled with pride," she said with a slight smile.

"There is no doubt in my mind that you can start in the pros next year. I have never met a man so driven to perfection. I do not think anyone has worked harder to improve his skills and lead a team as you have at Trinity.

"I've done my research, Arthur, and professional baseball is a dirty business. Seldom is a game played without fistfights, obscene language, gambling, and threatening comments. Most of the players drink too much, smoke, chew, cuss their opposition, argue with the umpires, and run with 'girls of the night.' Arthur, I would hate to see you caught in the middle of this much-maligned game and lifestyle.

"The bosses are desperate for a man who will lead and play with your perseverance and calmness of mind. I've watched in awe of how you stir the emotions of everyone that comes to see you pitch."

Her face was now wet with tears. Her voice shook with desperation. "Arthur I am terrified I'm going to lose you to the major leagues and not have the life I have so yearned for. What am I going to do, and what will happen to us if you go pro?" She collapsed on his chest.

He held her tight and not a word was spoken for ten minutes. The only sound heard was the distant raucous hooting of the white owl.

He raised her chin off his chest and fixed his eyes on hers. "We'll get through this Lizzie; we'll get through this." He reached for the reins and yanked them.

Dr. Wilson heard the boards of the Neuse River bridge clap as the horse and buggy rolled over them. He stood and put a couple of logs on the fire.

~

"DR. WILSON, I think I'm going to turn in early. I want to thank you for your hospitality." She stepped forward and gave him a warm hug.

"Sleep well, my darling child. I laid some towels on your bed."

She turned to her love. "You get some sleep. I will see you early in the morning."

Arthur never took his eyes off Lizzie walking back to the river house. Just before she reached the stairs, she turned and waved. The lookback gave him a good feeling and he smiled.

"Come join me for a few minutes, Arthur, before you head to the campsite. Has Lizzie been crying tonight?" he asked

"Yes, sir, she has. I am struggling with the decision of whether or not to play pro baseball. We talked about it for a few minutes and then she cried. She's afraid she is going to lose me to the major leagues. Doc, I'm concerned I may not have her in my life if I join the big leagues next year."

"Maybe you don't know enough about how she sees your future together and what she's willing to commit to. When you hear her side of the matter, you may have a clearer vision of what is best for both of you. What do you want in your life with her? I can tell you in the brief time I've been around her; she would be a fine wife."

"I want to marry Lizzie, have four or five kids, serve my church, and someday own a farm like this. I would like to play pro baseball if that is possible."

"Son, what you may discover on this important journey is the stark realization that you can't have both."

"Doc, I am going to head down to the campsite and get some shuteye. Thanks for your advice."

As he walked down the steep stairs to the river, it hit him that three wise men had now given him the same council.

Sometimes, you cannot have both.

~

IN THE RIVER HOUSE, Lizzie was on her knees praying. She finished her pray with tears in her eyes. After spending time with her Lord and Savior, she felt at peace and climbed into bed for a much-needed sleep.

Forty-three

SUNRISE ON THE RIVER

The soul attracts what it secretly harbors.
~ James Allen

SHE FOLDED BACK THE TENT FLAP. "ARTHUR, WAKE UP, IT'S Lizzie!" Her broad smile and beaming face greeted him. Her beauty is so fresh, he thought. It was five-thirty and the morning was still dark. "Let's build a fire, Arthur, and watch the sun rise over the Neuse River."

He started the fire with the bucket of pine cuttings and aged hardwood logs that Dr. Wilson supplied. The sticky sap was swallowed by the wanting lips of the bursting flames. The fire ignited, crackled and shot embers towards the darkened sky.

Both entered the tent and lay on their stomachs side by side. Without speaking, both looked out into the eyes of the distant horizon, waiting for the sun to show its first smile over the Neuse.

They were embraced by silence until a beautiful birdsong was heard over the gently flowing river. Lizzie ran her hand through his thick hair, kissed him on the forehead, and whispered, "I love you, Arthur."

"Kiss me, Lizzie," he said in a soft voice. He felt her tremble as their lips first touched. They kissed for five minutes without saying a word.

"I love you, my dearest, and always will. You have deeply

touched my heart," she said, exiting the tent. She blushed and smiled. "You make me dizzy, Arthur." She laughed. "Let's go up to the house and join Dr. Wilson for breakfast. I'll cook for you gentlemen."

They climbed the steep staircase to the river house, hand in hand. Lizzie looked back at the river and exclaimed, "Oh, my goodness, look at that sunrise." Darkness had surrendered to the first blush of the rising sun. The pinkness they saw in the early morning sky mirrored itself on the magnificent river below. She squeezed Arthur's hand tightly and kissed him on his cheek.

The kitchen smelled of fried bacon, and strongly brewed coffee greeted them as they stepped through the back door to the kitchen. Dr. Wilson stood over the stove, getting a head start to breakfast. He moved the sizzling and crackling bacon around in the heavy cast-iron frying pan with a fork.

"Everything smells and looks great," Lizzie said, giving Dr. Wilson a hug. "When you finish cooking the eggs and bacon, I'll make some pancakes."

"Good morning. You both look happy," the doctor said cheerfully. "Lizzie, you're up mighty early this morning."

"I wanted Arthur to get up to watch the sunrise," she said. Her face had become a blushed pink. "We have a lot to accomplish and enjoy the next two days."

"What are your plans for today?" he asked the young couple, who were holding hands at the breakfast table.

Arthur responded first. "As soon as I finish breakfast, I'm going down to fly fish. The stripers and trout will be in a feeding frenzy at this time in the morning."

"Son, I've put the fly rod and the spinning reel on the front porch. I've attached a couple of my favorite lures and rustled up some fresh bait."

"Thank you, Doc."

"How about you, young lady? What suits your fancy for this glorious day?"

"I'm going to take a quick bath and then prepare a picnic lunch for Arthur and me to enjoy down by the river. I'm going to put down a blanket and sit by the edge of the river, read some poetry, and watch him fish," she said with a sparkle in her eyes.

"I have a quilt and a basket that Mrs. Wilson and I used on our picnics that you can use. There are some luncheon meats, cheese, and strawberries in the icebox. Help yourself."

"Thank you for your hospitality." She flipped the last batch of pancakes.

Dr. Wilson set the large platter on the kitchen table. Arthur stared hungrily at the bacon, sausage, and scrambled eggs. Lizzie set down a plate of pancakes and a bowl of grits next to the platter. The homemade biscuits and jam were the next to make their way to the table.

As they sat down to eat, Dr. Wilson said, "Let's bless this meal." The three bowed their heads and held hands.

"Dear Heavenly Father, we thank you for all the blessings we receive from you this morning: our good health, our hearts open to love and friendship, our minds that are capable of learning so much and passing that knowledge on to others, and the food you provide to us to feed and nourish our bodies. Lord, let this be a weekend this nice couple can learn more about each other and come together in mind and spirit. In Jesus name, we pray. Amen."

"Let's dig in and enjoy this hearty Southern breakfast. Young lady, please pass me the biscuits. Try the jam. I made it from the apples from the old crabapple tree on the back part of the farm."

"Pretty yummy," she said after she bit into a biscuit smeared with the thick and sticky jam.

Arthur winked at his girlfriend. "What a fine meal this is," he said. "I'm not sure I've eaten better tomatoes. They're deep-red, ripe and delicious."

"Kids, let's get the kitchen clean so you can get on with your day."

~

THIRTY MINUTES LATER, Arthur was knee-deep in the Neuse River, fishing for trout with his fly rod. The crisp September air and the glistening of the calm water lifted his spirits. He looked forward to spending quality time with his love.

With his back to the river, Arthur watched her descend the stairs from the bluff. As she walked towards him, he could not take his eyes off her. Her fresh look was breathtaking. She appeared happy as she approached him, carrying a picnic basket and a patchwork quilt. She spread the quilt out on the ground. He climbed out of the river and took off his waders. "Let's talk," he said, reaching out for her hand.

"I didn't answer your question this morning about how many children I'd like to have." He raised his hand and extended four fingers and thumb.

"Do you think if you play professional baseball, you could have a large family and be an involved father?"

"I don't know, Lizzie." He kissed her on her cheek. He stood up, put on his waders, and entered the river. He moved out into the water about fifty feet.

She did not go back to reading her book of poetry but kept a steady eye on Arthur as he cast his fly line into the water. The river glistened from the reflection of the sun. She was attracted to his tall, muscular body and his ever-present athletic spirit.

Lizzie asked as he made his next cast, "Do you want to play baseball in the big leagues, Arthur?"

"I do," he answered as a large trout violently struck his lure. He fought the trout for several minutes without saying anything to her. The spirited fish leaped twice out of the water about fourteen inches. Arthur fought the raucous two-pound fish for about three minutes before he netted the trout. He finished his statement. "I just don't know if it is possible to play professional baseball, have a large family and a successful marriage."

As he turned to walk back to the shore, he was shocked to see that Lizzie was gone. He looked up to the bluff and saw her running up the stairs.

Tears were streaming down her face.

Dr. Wilson entered the kitchen and heard Lizzie sobbing. Her head was resting on her arms on the table. He placed his hand on her shoulder to comfort her. She raised her head to reveal a tear-soaked face, sobbing and saying, "Oh, Dr. Wilson, I'm losing Arthur to the pros, I'm losing him to the pros!"

Hearing the screen door shut, Lizzie and Dr. Wilson turned to see Arthur standing in the doorway.

He looked frightened. "What's wrong, Lizzie?"

Forty-four

THE PROPOSAL

When souls find comfort in one another, separation is not possible.
~ N.R. Hart

ARTHUR WALKED OVER TO LIZZIE AND EMBRACED HER. "YOU left before I could finish my answer to your question. I finished by saying, 'I'm not sure that I can do both.' Darling, why don't you go rest for a couple of hours while Dr. Wilson and I will set up a place we can picnic by the river." He kissed her on her forehead before she turned to head back to the bedroom.

~

"THIS WILL BE A GOOD PLACE for you to sit and listen to what Lizzie wants in her future with you," Dr. Wilson said. He spread the quilt under a shade tree at the edge of the river. "This patchwork means a lot to me. Kate made it five years before she passed away. We had many romantic picnics on this very quilt. You and Lizzie will enjoy it this afternoon."

"Thank you, Doc, for everything you've done for me," he said, looking down at the ground.

"Is everything okay, Arthur? You seem troubled."

"I'd like to make a proposal to Lizzie that she gives me a year in the majors to see if I make it big," he said awkwardly.

Dr. Wilson looked concerned and spoke. "In suggesting that

to her, aren't you sending a message that you are choosing pro baseball over her? Arthur, listen to her this afternoon and learn more of what fills her heart. Good luck, Arthur; let's head back to the house. Give her another hour of sleep."

~

ARTHUR SAT ON THE EDGE of the bed as she slept. He watched her take short peaceful breaths. He reached out and gently grasped her hand and it caused her to stir. He imagined being with her every night with her cradled in his arms as they drifted off to sleep.

He was enveloped by the quietness of the room, only offset by her gentle breathing. He remembered how much he missed her on the ten days of the Southern tour.

I would love to know your dreams, my love, maybe later you will share them with me. I hope you are dreaming about our life together.

He sat quietly for another fifteen minutes when a gentle voice beckoned him. "Arthur, it's a glorious way to wake up with you by my side. I love you so." He leaned towards his love and gently kissed her.

"I love you with all my heart." He kissed her again.

Suddenly, he stood. "We need to talk. Let's take a walk down to the river. I have prepared a picnic for us. Freshen up and I'll meet you on the porch."

As he left the room, the phone rang in the kitchen, and she heard him answer it. "Yes, sir, this is Arthur Bradsher. Wow, that is a very generous proposal. Yes, sir, I need to call you back in the morning."

~

SHE ENTERED THE KITCHEN and Arthur smiled. She wore a floral ankle-length sundress and no makeup. "My goodness, you look stunning and, as usual, you take my breath away." He reached out for her hand and helped her down the steep stairs to the river.

She sat down on the quilt and reached for Arthur to join her. "I appreciate your thoughtfulness. This is very nice."

"Lizzie, I want you to take a few minutes and tell me what the future holds for us"

"Arthur, I feel very secure that there's a special love between us that runs very deep in both our hearts. I think the success of our future may depend on your decision whether you go into pro baseball. If you join the majors, I doubt we could have the large family we both want."

"You don't think we could have both?" he responded.

"No, I don't Arthur, and being separated from you for half the year would be unbearable for me."

"What if I didn't play pro baseball, and I go into the tobacco business?"

Lizzie revealed the biggest smile he had ever seen on her face. "You would make me the happiest woman in America," she said, beaming. She reached for Arthur and then jumped into his arms. They laughed for ten minutes and then kissed.

She finally said, "We'll pray about it in church, where we will both become heavily involved." She went on for another hour, sharing her sharp vision of their future together.

Arthur knew in his heart where he needed to be. Arthur reached out for Lizzie's hand and said, "let's go for a walk along the river."

~

THEY WALKED for five minutes without speaking. "Are you okay, Arthur?"

In a startled tone, he said, "Did you see that fish jump, Lizzie?"

"I sure did," she responded. When the fish came back down and broke the surface of the river, the impact formed a circle. The size of the expanding circle was a little over five feet in diameter.

Arthur reached into his pleated pocket and pulled out a flat river stone. "Watch this."

He hurled the flat stone towards the circle from about twenty-five yards. The stone started on its flight much to the left of his intended target. She watched in astonishment as the smooth and shiny black stone traveled on a sharply bending path until it reached the circle. Plunk was the sound it made. It landed in the middle of the ripple.

"You're pretty amazing," she said to her dear boyfriend.

When the stone hit the first circle, its impact started another circle to form. As the circle expanded, he reached into his pocket for a second stone. He reared back and threw it in the direction of the newly forming circle.

Once again, his toss started about six feet to the left of the rippling circle. It traveled in an arch, like one of his curveballs, and like the pitch he delivered from the mound, his throw was perfectly accurate.

Like magic, it dropped right in the middle of the circle. Instead of the thump sound when a baseball hits the catcher's mitt, the sound of the stone hitting the water again was plunk.

"I'm very impressed, Mr. Bradsher." She chuckled. "Do you have any other tricks up your sleeve?"

He reached out his left hand to her. He felt her tremble as their hands first touched "Let's walk along the river and talk." It was a sun-drenched day with only a gentle wind coming off the river.

They walked together along the shoreline.

He had made a crucial decision. How would she react?

Arthur looked to the distant sky. He was a little nervous about what he was going to say next.

"Lizzie, a team called me while you were resting. They really want me to join their organization. They offered me an annual salary of $10,000 for my first two years. You know how much I love baseball, and it is a real bundle of money."

She was scared she was going to lose her love to baseball. She was trembling. "What did you tell them, Arthur?"

A fish jumped just as she spoke. Arthur reached into his pocket for another stone. As he was pulling it out of his pocket, he turned to Lizzie and stared deeply into her eyes.

"I said that I would have to talk with my future wife before I made any decisions."

He revealed the stone he was reaching for. It was his mother's engagement ring. Arthur got down on one knee. "Will you marry me, my love?"

Tears were streaming down Lizzie's face. She looked to the heavens and shouted, "Yes, Arthur, Yes! I will marry you!"

Forty-five

THE PETERSBURG YEARS

Love is the most important thing in the world,
but baseball is pretty good, too.
~ Yogi Berra

ARTHUR BRADSHER DROVE WITH THE TOP DOWN AND A WIDE grin on his face. The 1910 Packard Model 30 made him feel like a million bucks.

This automobile is a showstopper.

He wanted a car that was rough-road worthy for short trips, like this trip to the train depot located in Richmond. He also needed a road vehicle that would accommodate his growing family.

Selfishly, he desired an automobile that would impress his tobacco clients.

I never thought I would be driving a luxury car at this stage of my young business career, he thought as pressed his foot down on the accelerator. Export Leaf Tobacco Company bought it at sixty percent of value, out of foreclosure, which made it possible to put Arthur in the driver's seat.

He arrived in Richmond at eleven-forty-five. The trip took about seventy minutes to drive the twenty-one-miles to the destination. He had shown up early and was anxious to reunite with his family.

The Southern 321 chugged into the Main Street Station twenty minutes later. The train slowed and came to a noisy, grinding stop. The station was filled with steam as it hissed from the train's flue.

As soon as he saw Lizzie, holding three-old-Mary Elizabeth, he sprinted toward his two loves. He picked up his delicate wife and daughter six inches off the ground and spun them around. He let little Mary down, and embraced Lizzie, kissing her passionately.

Down below, a little voice said, "What about me, Daddy?"

Arthur dropped down on one knee and looked deeply into Mary's captivating blue-green eyes. There was a short pause until she said, "Daddy, I missed you."

Bradsher hesitated before he responded. He was choked with emotion. "I've missed you more than you'll ever know." He kissed Mary on the forehead and gave her a gentle squeeze.

Lizzie thought, *Arthur is the most handsome and loving man I have ever known.*

He stood and picked up two of the larger suitcases. He signaled to the porter to give him a hand, noticing his nametag. "John, thank you for your assistance. We're the first spot in the parking lot."

There it stood in all its glory. The luxury driving machine had a burnt orange exterior and deep-brown leather bucket seats.

Arthur Bradsher's 1910 Packard
~ Courtesy of the Detroit Public Library

"Oh, my goodness," Lizzie exclaimed, "Am I in a dream? This is smashing!"

Arthur bragged, "It runs like a dream and will be a great family car."

He reached out his hand to his wife. "Don't worry, Lizzie. The Export Leaf Tobacco Company is taking care of most of the costs and expenses of this dreamboat of an automobile.

"Let's head to Petersburg. It's an exceptional city and will be a wonderful place for us to raise a family." It was Lizzie's first day in Petersburg. Arthur had started his job with Export Leaf Tobacco two months earlier and was living in an apartment near his office.

He walked to the front of the car and turned the crank. It started immediately. The engine had a smooth sound to it.

They all took their seats in the Packard. Lizzie turned to Arthur and said, "Any other surprises up your sleeve?"

"Sure, there will be. I'll always have your best interests in mind," he assured her. "Relax, my dearest, today is going to be a wonderful day

~

ARTHUR LOOKED IN THE REARVIEW MIRROR and saw a wide-eyed three-year-old Mary, standing up on the back seat, totally mesmerized by the passing terrain. She had never ridden in a convertible before; her curly hair was blowing in the wind.

"Lizzie, a huge fair is coming to Petersburg in three months. There will be horse races, cattle, and other farm animals. The fair will also featue arts, crafts, and fireworks every night. It should be great family fun."

They passed a farm and she shouted, "Look at the cows, Daddy! Can we stop and pet them?"

Arthur looked at Lizzie, and she nodded yes.

"Mary, we'll stop for a couple of minutes," he said. He turned off the main road and pulled over to the split rail fence at the edge of the pasture.

Lizzie carried Mary to the fence and put her down. Arthur cut a slice of apple with his pocketknife and set it on the rail next to her. Mary grabbed the lower rail of the fence to steady herself as the seven-hundred-pound cow stepped toward her.

The cow snorted, which startled the little girl. She flinched but didn't retreat. Mary could feel the warmth of the cow's breath on her face. She closed her eyes. The next thing she knew, the cow was licking her face.

"Let's go, girls," Arthur said. "We've got plenty to see in Petersburg."

A mile down the road, little Mary exclaimed, "Daddy, can we get a cow someday?"

"I hope so, my sweet child."

It was a day Mary would never forget. Her father's sweetness had created a memory she would hold in her heart for a lifetime.

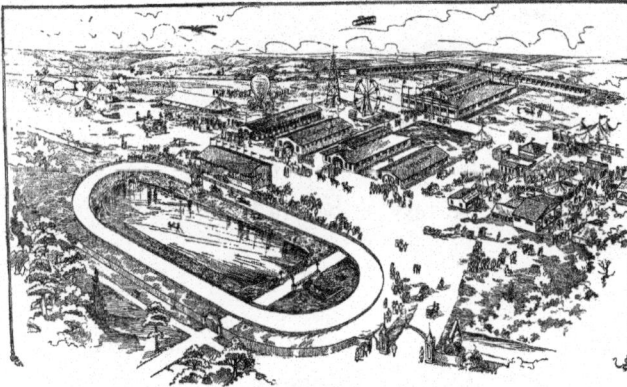

Big Fair at Petersburg
October 17th-21st Inclusive
$12,000 PREMIUMS FOR EXHIBITS AND **$12,000**
RACE PURSES

Great Wild West Show and Other Attractions Give Free Exhibitions Every Day and Night
Thousand Dollar Display of Fireworks Every Night

Auditorium Building will be filled with the most magnificent Arts and Crafts Exhibits. Agricultural Building will contain finest display of Farm Products ever shown in Virginia. Cattle, Sheep, Swine and Poultry Exhibits will equal any in the State. Acres of Farm Machinery Exhibits showing New and up-to-date Tools never before seen in Virginia. This feature alone should attract every farmer in the State.

Every seat in our Magnificent Grandstand commands a view of the entire track, and with 150 entries of the Fastest Horses in this Country, those who enjoy Good Racing will be more than repaid for their trip to the Fair.
Automobiles and Vehicles Admitted Free

Birdseye View of the Fair Buildings and the Most Beautiful Grounds in the State.   Half-Mile Track Surrounding a Natural Lake

Southside Agricultural Fair
Jas. McI. Ruffin, Mgr.   **Petersburg, Va.**

1911 Big Fair in Petersburg
~ Courtesy of the Click Americana

~

THE REVEREND D. T. MERRIT greeted the Bradsher family when they walked through the front door of Market Street Methodist.

"Welcome to our city and our church," he said. "Did Arthur drive you through downtown Petersburg?"

"He sure did," she said with a smile. "Downtown has a lot of hustle and bustle."

"Arthur said you only have a couple of minutes to visit. Let me give you the nickel tour," declared the Reverend with open arms.

SYCAMORE STREET FROM FRANKLIN STREET, PETERSBURG, VA.

Downtown Petersburg
~ Courtesy of the Bradsher Family

~

THE BRADSHER FAMILY stood in the sanctuary and Lizzie thanked the reverend for his hospitality.

"I look forward to serving you and the Lord in this church," she said. "May I say a short prayer?"

"I would like that," D.T Merritt responded.

"Let's hold hands." Little Mary reached up to grasp her mother and father's hands.

"Our Father, we count our blessings on this beautiful day in Petersburg. We love you, Lord, and we will serve you steadfastly for the rest of our days. In Jesus name, we pray. Amen."

~

"One more stop and I'll take you gals to the apartment to freshen up," Arthur said, turning onto South Sycamore Street.

"What a beautiful neighborhood," Lizzie commented.

Arthur pointed. "That's Central Park. It stretches for two blocks. Lizzie, you and Mary close your eyes. No peeking or it'll ruin the surprise." He pulled the car over to the curb and turned off the engine. "Stay seated, and I'll get the door for you."

The three held hands and walked down the sidewalk. Lizzie and Mary still had their eyes shut.

"Do you know where we are, Lizzie?"

"In the park?" she asked.

"We're home, Lizzie. Now open your eyes." Arthur handed Lizzie a note that was pinned on the front door.

It simply read, *Welcome to your new home, Bradsher family. May it bring you as many years of happiness as it bought us.*

Arthur kissed Lizzie on her cheek and turned to open the front door. "Oh, Arthur, this is the home I've dreamed about since I was a little girl. I love the picket fence and the handsome shutters. And we are right across from the park!"

"Lizzie, we are walking distance from the church."

They stepped through the front door and Lizzie gasped. She was greeted by twelve-foot ceilings, a large living room with a fireplace, and a grand central staircase leading up to four bedrooms. Arthur had brought the furniture from the apartment and out of storage from his company's warehouse and smartly arranged it in the home. There were bouquets of flowers on the fireplace mantle, kitchen counter, and bedside table in the master bedroom.

Mary was skirting around the main level in a fit of excitement. She slid in her socks across the newly polished heart-pine floors. "Where is my bedroom, Mother?"

"We won't be going to the apartment today," Arthur said. "You'll be spending your first night in Petersburg in your new home."

Arthur turned to his true love. Lizzie's beautiful eyes were filled with tears of joy.

Bradsher's Petersburg Home at 320 So. Sycamore St.
~ Courtesy of Judy Hoyle

Forty-six

DELTA PHI RHO ALPHA

The success of every woman should be an inspiration to another.
We should raise each other up. Make sure you're very courageous;
be strong, be extremely kind, and above all be humble.
~ Serena Williams

IT WAS APRIL 1919, AND THE NEW PHONE RANG AT THE BRADSHER house at 320 S. Sycamore Street.

"Mr. Bradsher, this is Clara Barnett from Trinity College, do you have a minute?"

"Yes, Miss Barnett, how can I help you?"

"Sir, four of us want to start an honorary athletic sorority for women, similar to the Tombs Fraternity for men. I am calling you to get some advice on how to get this off the ground, and the best path to success."

"I'm excited for you and Trinity," he said. "The formation of a women's organization to serve the athletic association on campus is needed to better our relations with other colleges. The Tombs has served the college well, and today is one of the strongest organizations at the school. Do this, Miss Barnett, please call me at this time tomorrow night and I will have a list of suggestions for your team. Is that convenient for you?"

"That's great, Mr. Bradsher. I really appreciate your help. I've heard so many good things about you from the professors. I'll call you tomorrow night at seven." He hung up the phone and opened his desk drawer. He retrieved a yellow pad and some number two pencils. He scribbled notes for the next forty-five minutes.

Lizzie walked in and stood behind her husband. "Who was that dear?" she asked as she started to massage his muscular shoulders.

"That was one of the young ladies attending Trinity. She and some of her fellow students want to start a sister athletic society to the Tombs."

"What an exceptional idea to get the women involved," Lizzie said.

~

At SEVEN THE NEXT EVENING, the phone rang, and nine-year-old Mary Elizabeth slid across the newly polished hardwood floor in the kitchen in her sock feet. She loved to answer and talk on the phone. "Good evening, this is the Bradsher residence, how may I help you?"

"Young lady, is your father home?"

"Yes, ma'am, he's in his office."

"Would you go tell him that Clara Barnett is on the line?"

"Yes, ma'am, right away." Mary set the phone down and sprinted to her father's office. She slid across the floor and ended up next to him. She gave him a hug. "Daddy, Clara Barnett is on the phone."

"Thank you, darling. You are doing an excellent job handling my calls. Now, please go hang up the phone."

Arthur picked up the phone and was greeted by Clara's cheerful voice. "Do you have a few minutes, Mr. Bradsher?"

"It's a great time to talk, Clara. I have my notes right in front of me. I want to say how proud I am of you for taking the initiative of starting the women's athletic society."

"Thank you, sir. We're seeing an explosion of interest in sports on campus."

"Your timing is very good to start this organization," he said. "The word is out that the football program will be resumed in the fall of 1921. They are recruiting now. The fans will flock to the games and there will be a need for the Tombs and Delta Phi Rho Alpha to act as a support group. "

"Inner-class basketball and tennis have become a big deal for the women on campus," Clara stated. "Our goal at this point is to promote participation for women in golf, tennis, flag football, softball, basketball, badminton. We want to get women out of the dorms and on to the playing fields."

"Wow!" he exclaimed.

Bradsher chuckled and said to Clara, "You're too young to remember this. You would have been five or six. *The Saturday Evening Post* featured a cover on the magazine in 1906 that featured a young girl holding a basketball, in a short dress, instead of basketball shorts. She was about to shoot. That was the same year W.W. Card started the men's basketball program at Trinity and coached the first game to be played in the state of North Carolina against Wake Forest. When I saw the cover, I knew women's basketball would be played at Trinity. Clara, let me share my thoughts."

"Thank you for all this," she replied.

"First, you need to meet with President Few and get his approval. Be prepared! Have a list to give to him on who will be your first initiated class and their credentials. He'll need to get approval from the board members. I am friends with him. Feel free to tell him we have talked, and I stand behind you on this.

"After you hand him the list, be ready for him to present you three or four questions that were asked of me by Dr. Kilgo when I founded the Tombs. He may ask first, 'What's on your agenda?' Next, he'll question you, 'How will Delta Phi Rho Alpha benefit Trinity College?' And the last question that I feel he'll ask you is where you see Delta Phi in ten years."

"Mr. Bradsher, all this information is so helpful. I promise we won't let you or Trinity down."

Arthur could hear the emotion in her voice.

"Clara, make this experience fun. Come up with an initiation that captures the interest of the entire campus. The Tombs' first initiation was quite memorable; gaining the attention of everyone at the school from day one. Come up with a fun emblem or symbol, a different flower, and team colors that every sorority displays in the yearbook to represent your spirit. I'm going to let you figure out this on your own, but good colors for Delta Phi Rho Alpha would be black and blue."

"Pretty funny, Mr. Bradsher. I'll top that! Our chosen flower is going to be the wild onion, instead of a pretty rose, carnation, or daisy."

"You're catching on fast," he continued. "The success of any group depends on the commitment and organization of the team members. Choose potential inductees that are conscientious and are good planners. Everyone that's chosen has to have a deep love for sports and service."

"Do they have to play sports?"

"Absolutely not. When we started the Tombs, we had eight members, and only four played sports—two on the varsity baseball team and two on the class baseball team."

"How many people should we initiate each year?"

"I would keep it small at first. Your first-class initiation should have no more than nine people."

"I agree with you, Mr. Bradsher; I think we'll be more effective as a smaller group. This way we can get everyone in the group involved and give each member specific responsibilities."

"Let's do this. You gals work out a game plan and then meet with President Few. My wife, Lizzie, and I have planned to spend a couple of days in Durham for my reunion in mid-June. Why don't you and your three proposed officers meet me at Murphy's at noon, June fifteenth."

"That sounds swell," she excitingly answered.

He smiled. "Oh heck, bring all nine of you, and lunch will be on me."

"You're a dear man, Mr. Bradsher. You know people talk about you at Trinity."

"Well, I hope they're saying wonderful things." He laughed. "I've enjoyed our conversation and I'll see you on the fifteenth."

He looked over and Mary was standing beside him.

"Daddy, can I speak with her?"

"Yes, darling."

"Clara, this's Mary. I just want to say goodnight and remind you to say your prayers."

There was a wide smile on Clara's face when she hung up the phone.

Delta Phi Rho Alpha, 1921.
~ Courtesy of Duke University Library and Archives

Forty-seven

THE BLACK AND BLUE GIRLS

Our team colors are black and blue, our flower,
the wild onion, and our emblem will be a rolling pin.
Our goal is to get women on the playing fields
and have outrageous fun.
~ Clara Barnett, 1921

NINE OF THE BLACK AND BLUE GIRLS WERE SITTING AROUND a corner table when Arthur Bradsher, accompanied by his two children, walked in. The owner, Murphy, welcomed them at the front door. "It's been a long time since we've seen each other."

"Too long, Murph. These are my children, Mary and Charles."

Eight-year-old Charles extended his hand to shake with Murphy.

Mary, the oldest of the Bradsher children, said, "Nice to meet you, sir."

Arthur said with a smile, "Murphy, are you still serving hamburgers?"

"Of course. And they're the best in town," the owner responded proudly.

Bradsher pointed to the large round table. "What do you

recommend for the young ladies over there?"

"Well, that's a healthy-looking group. I imagine some of them are going to want beef. We also have good soups and stews."

Bradsher walked over to the table and greeted the girls. He introduced his children to them. After he sat down, he asked each of them to introduce herself and share interests, and how she was faring in college.

The team leader for Delta Phi, Clara Barnett, said, "Let Herminia Ursula Haynes begin. If she tells her whole story, we will be here all day."

"Hello, Mr. Bradsher, I'm Herminia. I came to Trinity from Lakeview, North Carolina. In my first two years, I have served on the *Chronicle* staff, been on the cabinet of the YWCA, and I am a member of the Athena Literary Society. I was past vice-president of the Citizenship Club and am now president-elect. I'm the VP of the League of Nations Club and a member of the World Fellowship Committee."

"Wow, that's very impressive," Arthur said. "Anything else?"

"Yes, sir! I play a mean game of badminton, and I have a keen interest in almost all sports."

Clara jumped in, "Well, the guys won't be able to say we're a bunch of dumb flappers." The women all drummed their hands on their knees and laughed.

Most were on the Women's Athletic Council, and they had a deep love for sports. Some played tennis, a few played golf, and two of the taller girls played on the class basketball team.

Arthur said, "Tell me how your meeting with Chancellor Few went."

Pearl responded, "It went very well. He was very receptive. I went with Clara. It was exciting to sit across the desk of the president of the college and speak to him. We were prepared for his questions. We explained that our purpose was to foster school spirit, leadership, and the promotion of athletics on campus. He called us to his office two weeks later and gave us his full approval. It was quite a day."

"And, by the way, Mr. Bradsher," Clara chirped, "President

Few had some very nice things to say about you. He told us the story about the famous 'Miracle at Mercer' game."

The waiter brought the food out on a wooden cart. Hamburgers, fries, and soups were placed on the table. The aroma was inviting. He cut a hamburger in half and brought it to a nearby table on two plates along with a couple of Cokes for Mary and Charles.

Charles stood and said, "Father, may I bless this food?"

"You sure may."

"Lord, thank you for this fine meal, my sister, my father, my mother, my family, and the Delta Phi girls. In Jesus's name, we pray. Amen." An "amen" for the young boy's blessing was heard from every nearby table in Murphy's Bar and Grill.

Halfway through the meal, Bradsher asked, "What's your game plan for Delta Phi Rho Alpha?"

Clara answered, "Sir, we are following many of the suggestions you gave me over the phone. We are going to initiate two sophomores and seven juniors every March. Our team colors are black and blue, our flower, the wild onion, and our emblem will be a rolling pin."

She continued, "Our initiation is going to be zany. The pledges will dress up annually in their outfit comprised of a white middy blouse, black skirt, white tennis shoes, and a white cotton nose. They will be nicknamed 'the goats.' After lunch, they will parade for an hour around the East Campus with their rolling pins, singing songs and making goat noises. The pledges will be required to wear their outfits to all their classes that day.

"We plan to have tournaments and give a trophy to the dorm that accumulates the most points. There will be a badminton tournament on the East Lawn that will be one of the highlights of the year. The best badminton players from all over the state will be invited. We'll also have a B level tournament where the other players can join in and compete."

Clara added, "A medal will be presented to the athlete that serves her school in the best manner over her four-year tenure. Mr. Bradsher, I understand you received the medal in 1904."

Arthur reached into his coat pocket and retrieved the medal that was presented to him by the Tombs in 1904. "I was so honored and humbled to receive this." It had a baseball player engraved on it. He handed his prized possession to Clara.

"This is neat." She turned it over and saw that it had been inscribed on the back. "Do you mind if I read the inscription aloud?"

"Please, do."

"It reads, 'Arthur Bradsher, the best that ever pitched in the South. He represented Trinity College with integrity between 1901-1904.'" She passed his special treasure around the table.

Bradsher smiled. "Well, ladies, Delta Phi Rho Alpha has been born. You are on your way to accomplishing remarkable things. I congratulate you for your worthy goals. It has been a real pleasure meeting all of you and getting to know a little bit about each of you. Now, I must go. I've got a reunion party I need to get ready for."

He stood and put two fives and three one-dollar bills on the table. "Thank Murphy for me." He held the hands of Mary and Charles and walked toward the exit.

Halfway to the front door, he heard a voice say, "Thank you, Mr. Bradsher, for the lunch and your time today. You're the best." The others agreed.

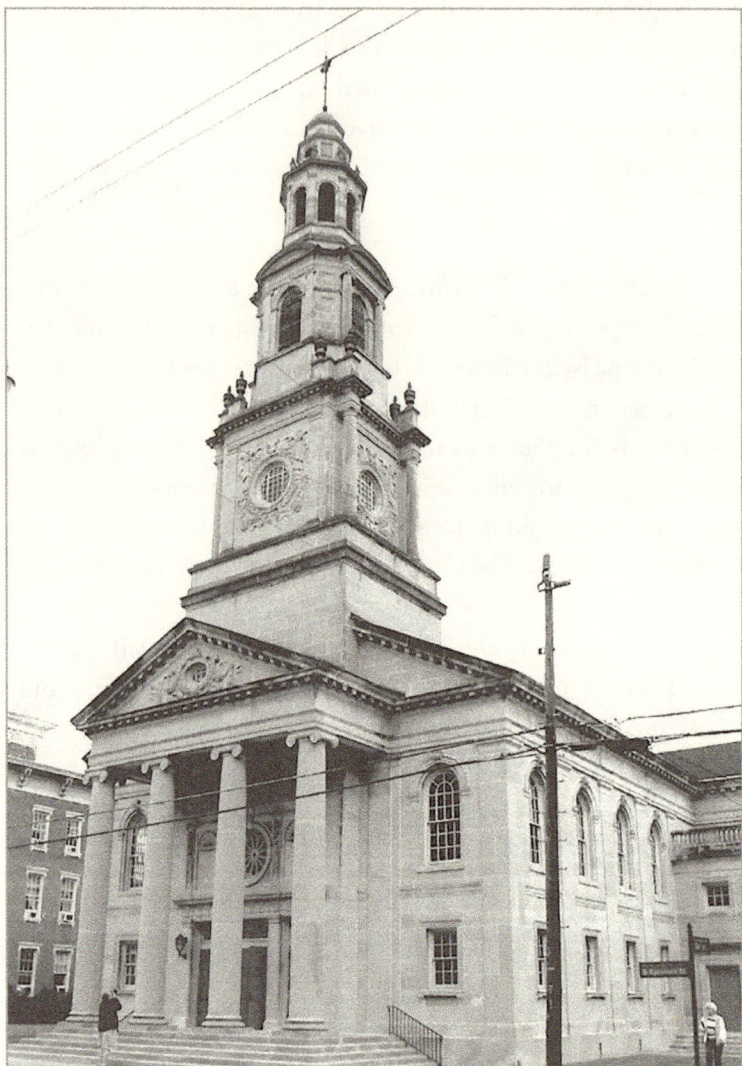

Trinity Methodist Church
Cornerstone laid August 26, 1921.
Initial services were held in a temporary sanctuary
on February 25, 1923.
The first meeting in the of the congregation
permanent sanctuary in March 1927.
~ Courtesy of Petersburg Historian Curtis Anderson.

Forty-eight

THE MOST BEAUTIFUL
CHURCH IN AMERICA

Learn the lesson that, if you are to do the work of a prophet,
what you need is not a scepter but a hoe.
~ Bernard of Clairvaux

IT IS THE SPRING OF 1920. WOODROW WILSON WAS IN HIS EIGHTH year as President of the United States. The economy was booming two years after the end of World War I. America had entered the era of prohibition.

"Gentlemen, we're going to build the most beautiful church in America," Arthur exclaimed to six of Petersburg's most prominent executives and respected citizens. They sat in the nineteenth century, ornate Queen Anne chairs which surrounded the handsome and richly inlaid mahogany desk.

He reached into his desk drawer to retrieve a humidor crafted in red maple. It had a print of the island of Cuba affixed to its lid. "Men help yourself to a fine cigar. We brought these back from our trip to Havana last fall. What a magnificent country." He smiled as fond memories had surfaced. He pulled a wooden matchstick out of the box on his deck and struck it across the heart pine floor. He smiled and lit his Monte Cristo.

As the men puffed their cigars, Arthur rolled out the architectural drawings for the Trinity Methodist Church to be built at 215 South Sycamore Street. "Construction is set to begin in January 1921. There are two proposed completion dates. We feel the church building will be finished in February 1923 and the sanctuary in early 1926. Our congregation will worship in the large thirty-two-hundred-square-foot auditorium until the sanctuary is completed. Afterward, that space will be converted to a gym area where our children and young adults can play basketball and badminton.

"Our building committee's selection of Russell Edward Mitchell as our architect for the church is an excellent choice. His design of our future place of worship is strongly influenced by the work of the architect James Gray's stunning Saint Martin-in-the-Fields, built in 1720 in London. The church will be built in Georgian Revival style and constructed out of Indiana limestone and brick. It will employ decorative vocabulary from ancient Rome and Greece."

C.M. Brister added: "No attention to detail will be spared. Our church will be magnificent. Here are a few highlights of its exterior design. Parishioners will be greeted by four columns as they enter the double front doors. The massive steeple, rising one hundred and twenty-five feet from the ground level, will truly be a highlight, as will the twelve Palladian windows and profuse detail to the cornices that will adorn the front and sides of the church. The spire will be visible for miles and be a drawing card.

"The building will be massive, with approximately twenty-six-thousand square feet of heated space. The sanctuary will seat close to a thousand people - six hundred and fifty on the ground floor and three hundred in the balcony. There will be a richly decorated parlor to serve as a meeting place for our men's and women's Bible studies on Sunday nights.

"We've developed a prolific Sunday school program at Market Street Church, where I've had the honor of serving as superintendent for the last ten years. With your blessings, I will continue my duties with Trinity Methodist, with the intent of doubling the size of the program for the benefit of the youngsters of Petersburg." He took a long draw from his stogie and blew a smoke ring that drifted across the desk. "There will be twelve classrooms on the third floor of the church, which will accommodate up to two-hundred-and-fifty children."

"Mr. Brister, I need you to find 250 chairs for the temporary sanctuary and 150 school desks for the Sunday school classrooms. Over the next year look for a school that may be closing. I remind you gentleman that we are on a strict budget and cutting costs without sacrificing quality is a priority."

Charles Guthrie said, "Brad, your Sunday school has served our kids well. I am glad to hear your ambitions for an expanded agenda. We need to get all hands on-board to help teach parents and young adults. The children are our future. Our program does an excellent job in planting the seeds that will grow into strong faith. We need teachers who are willing to be prepared every week to teach our children valuable lessons about our Lord and Savior."

"Charles," Brad responded, "I have a want list. I expect our wives to be a huge part of this major undertaking, and you men and your spouses to be the backbone of this church. As they lead our households, they can have the same strong influence in our sanctuary. Tell them the exciting news about our future and enlist their support.

"I want you and everyone in the church to ensure its future success by being generous financially. I am going to ask for some pledges from each of you—I need everyone in our congregation to tithe ten percent of his family income during the year.

Charles Graham spoke. "I would like to volunteer to head up a membership drive with a goal of attracting nine hundred members. I want everyone in the congregation to be involved in some significant way. I don't want people just to show up for the sermon. To be successful as a new church, we need our congregation to serve as teachers, deacons, ushers, and a group to continue to raise funds."

"Sign me up to join you as an everyday committed fundraiser for the church," Guthrie said. "Let's sit down next week and establish a plan that will support the goals of our fundraising campaign."

"Gentlemen, today I would like to discuss what thoughts the building committee has in the budget, fundraising, financing, and growth of the church," Bradsher said. "Your businesses are all related to financing and the construction of this church. I'd like each of you to share in how you'd like to participate."

President of the Petersburg Bank, Robert Johns, offered, "We just accepted a forty-thousand-dollar offer on the Market Street Church property. Our initial calculations on the cost to build the Trinity Methodist Church is $375,000. We all know estimates are usually low. Let's go with a figure of $395,000 to build."

"Business is booming at Export Leaf and Tobacco," said Arthur. "We are the largest handler of tobacco in the United States. I have a challenge for each of you today. My fine company has agreed to make a very generous donation of seventy-five hundred dollars to the building fund. Each one in this room is blessed by God for your business successes. I am asking that your companies consider matching that pledge. I would like to see us hit the ground running with fifty thousand dollars in the bank after our meeting today."

G.C. Wright, president of Virginia National Bank of Petersburg stood, puffed on his cigar and spoke. "I suggest we hit the biggest business owners in Petersburg. I can direct our fund-raising committee to the right people without abusing confidentiality. We hope to do the long-term financing of the church. Robert, you and the Petersburg Bank would be best suited to do the construction-loan financing. I will commit our bank for an eight-thousand-dollar donation."

John Wilson said, "We hope to supply the brick and the limestone." As president of Petersburg Lime and Stone, I commit eight-thousand-five-hundred dollars to the building fund."

Arthur smiled. "You men are generous souls." He stood and smashed the butt of his cigar in the ashtray on his desk. "Gentlemen, your hearts are full of the love of the Lord, as is mine. We are on our way to honor our Savior and bring others closer to His Word."

Before the afternoon meeting was adjourned, the seven men pledged $59,000 from their businesses.

August 26, 1921. The laying of the cornerstone for the church.
Three hundred were in attendance for the big event.
~ Courtesy of Petersburg Historian Curtis Anderson

Forty-nine

BRADSHER IS STILL MASTER OF THE BALL

If you did not know how old you were, how old would you be?
~ Satchel Paige

L ET'S GO, KIDS, " BRADSHER SAID AND HURRIED HIS KIDS ALONG. "We need to get to the ballfield." It was a warm summer day in Petersburg in the year 1922.

Twelve-year-old Mary had her baseball glove and eleven-year-old Charles had his track shoes. Rough and tough Arthur had a miniature football made from real pigskin that was given to him on his seventh birthday, a year earlier. Four-year-old Nancy, who had no interest in sports, came along per her father's wishes. She brought a stuffed animal that looked like a baby lion.

None of the four children had ever seen their father pitch in a baseball game.

Arthur had been invited to pitch on the Market Street Methodist Church team. He had turned thirty-nine in January. He'd stayed in great shape by tending to the small garden he enjoyed in his spare time. The average age of the players in the church league was twenty-three. The ace lefthander took the mound to pitch his first competitive inning of fastpitch baseball in eighteen years.

With his full head of grey hair, he was greeted by the sarcastic yells from the fans of the opposing Petersburg Catholic Church.

Before he'd thrown his first pitch, a fan screamed, "Come on, Gramps! Can't you move any faster than that?"

Another fan hollered, "Take it easy, Grandpa, don't hurt yourself!"

Mary frowned. She witnessed the opposition calling her father, "old man."

They shouldn't be talking about my daddy that way.

The Market Street Methodist Church southpaw rubbed the ball down and smiled at the excited rooters.

Umpire Williams bent over to sweep off the plate with his small brush. He brought himself back up. He spit out a cheek-full of tobacco juice and yelled, "Play Ball!"

His first inning was as sharp as any inning he'd pitched in college. His curveball, change of pace, and drop balls made the youngsters look silly. The southpaw hurler struck out the side in the first inning on eleven pitches.

Bradsher thought, *This is like having learned to ride a bike. Once you have acquired the skill, you do not forget how to do it.*

The fans on both sides of the field went wild for the "King of the Southern Diamond." The strikeout artist tipped his hat to them as he walked back to the Market Street Church team bench.

Bradsher batted third in the bottom of the first inning with two men on. A fan screamed, "Here he comes 'old man river.' He can't hit! He can't hit!"

Little does the loudmouth know that I batted .354 in my second year at Trinity, leading the team in hits and batting average.

In the summer league in 1901, he played first base for Roxboro, and against Boston, went six for eleven in a doubleheader and scored seven runs.

The Catholic team's obnoxious fan was relentless, and he screamed, "Batter, batter, no batter! Batter, batter, no batter!"

Bradsher smiled. It's time to shut this one up.

He drilled the first pitch a good hundred feet over the center fielder's head, and by the time the fielder reached the ball, Arthur rounded third and headed for home. His inside-the-park home run silenced the opposition's belligerent fans.

~

Young Arthur looked over to where his sister sat in the first inning. She was gone. She sprinted to the track where Charles ran and pumped his arms hard. Mary jumped in front of her brother and forced him to stop.

"Charlie! Charlie! Come quick! Father has mowed down the Catholics with his curveball. He has already struck out six batters. He has also hit a long home run."

They both dashed back to the ball field and joined Arthur and Nancy in the stands. They were their father's best cheerleaders for the next seven innings. The Bradsher children and the Market Street fans stomped the bleachers, blew their whistles, and rang their cowbells in support of their hero.

In the ninth inning, The Market Street marvel felt as good as he did at the beginning of the game. He struck out the first two batters on seven pitches.

It's time to get this last kid out, go home and get a tuna sandwich. Don't get careless. Put the next three pitches on the edge of the plate.

Mary put two fingers under her tongue and let out an attention-getting whistle. "Strike him out, Father," she shouted. He did just that with another strikeout of their clean-up hitter and finished with a shutout of the Catholics. The fans from both sides of the diamond applauded loudly as the Market Street Church wonder walked off the field.

~

Excited Mary jumped from the car. She pushed open the front door and raced to the kitchen. "Mother, Mother, Father is a star! He struck out twenty batters and only gave up one soft bloop hit. The Catholics were calling him 'Grandpa' because of his grey hair. He showed them, Mother. He struck out the side three times. Mother, he wasn't satisfied with starring in the game with his pitching heroics, he smashed the ball for three hits in four at-bats.

He had a homer, a two-bagger, and a single! By the end of the game, the fans on both sides were screaming, 'Bradsher! Bradsher! Bradsher!'"

~

A WEEK LATER, Bradsher almost repeated his previous week's performance. He struck out nineteen batters. His control was reminiscent of the old days at Trinity when he only walked one batter. His children were blessed with the opportunity to see their father pitch.

~

IN JULY OF 1922, headlines exploded in newspapers across the South: *"Trinity Strikeout King Again In His Togs"* - Raleigh News and Observer; *"King Of The Southern Diamond Hangs Up A Strikeout Record"* - The Charlotte Observer; and, *"Trinity Diamond Is Still At It"* - The Twin-City Daily Sentinel - Winston Salem

Arthur Bradsher Still Is Master Of The Ball

Famous College Pitcher Is Fanning 19 and 20 Men Right Along in the Virginia Sunday School League at Petersburg—Old Students Remember His Records.

BY HENRY BELK.

DURHAM, July 20.—Much water has run under the bridge since Arthur Bradsher won a national reputation and the title of "King of the Southern Diamond" with his strike-

TWILIGHT LEAGUE

STANDING OF TEAMS.

"Arthur Bradsher Is Still Master of The Ball"
The Charlotte Observer
Charlotte, North Carolina - July 21, 1922

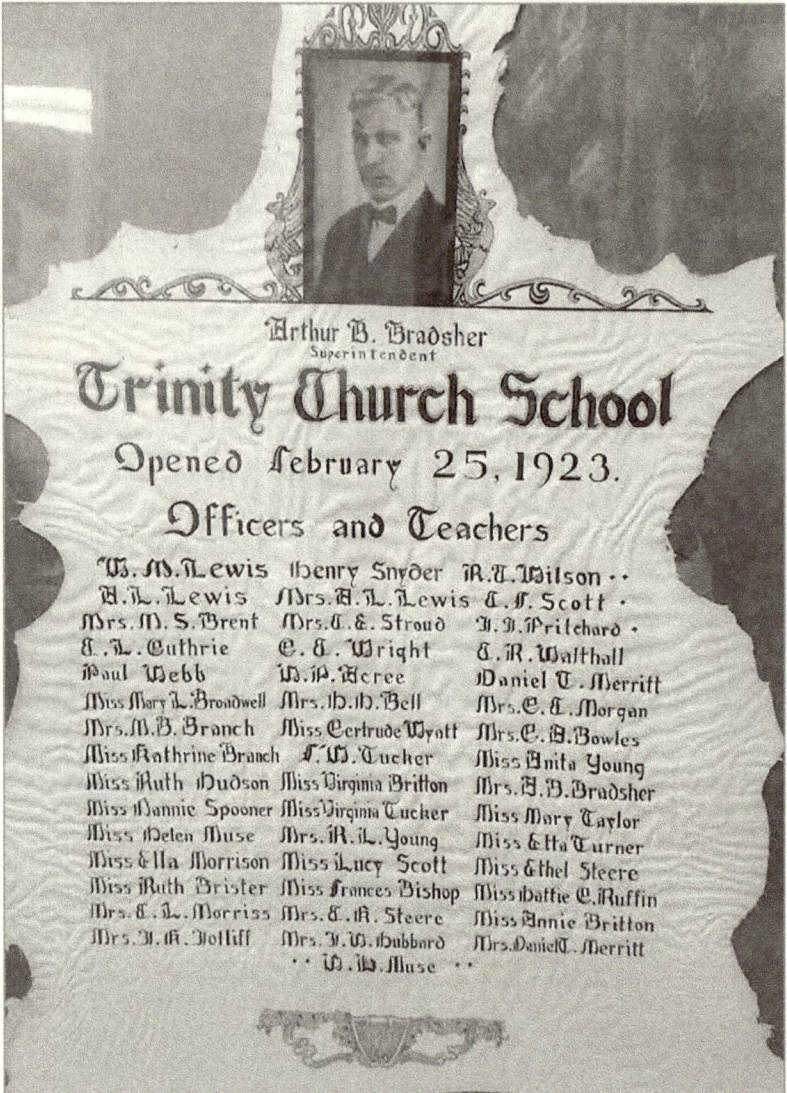

Trinity Methodist Church Opening Day Program in 1923,
Superintendent Arthur Bradsher.
~ Courtesy of Trinity Methodist Church

Fifty

OPENING DAY
AND SCRAMBLED EGGS

You always get a special kick on opening day.
You look forward to it like a birthday party when you're a kid.
You think something wonderful is going to happen.
~ Joe DiMaggio

FEBRUARY 25, 1923. THE BIG DAY HAD ARRIVED. IT WAS A COOL and clear morning in Petersburg, Virginia.

Mary was sitting at her father's handmade breakfast table. She looked at the bulletin for the first service to be held in a few hours at the newly constructed Trinity Methodist Church. She smiled as she saw her father's picture on the back of the program with the caption under it, Sunday school superintendent. There were forty-five names listed under her father's picture that would be officers and Sunday school teachers for the church.

The Sunday school, largest in Virginia, would serve 275 children, aged four to thirteen. They would be taught in twelve classrooms situated on the third floor of the twenty-six-thousand-square-foot church.

Lizzie cooked on the stove with an apron around her petit twenty-two-inch waist when her husband walked into the kitchen, handsomely dressed in a dark blue suit, white shirt, polished shoes, and a bowtie. He snuck up on her; she didn't hear him over the loud sizzle of the bacon.

He tip-toed past his thirteen-year-old daughter, sitting at the breakfast table. He winked at her, and she smiled back. Arthur put his arms around his wife's waist and kissed her on the neck. He could feel the bulge of the baby in her womb. She was six months pregnant and shuddered from his soft kiss and warm breath on her neck. The kiss made her lose track of time for a moment.

"Arthur, I am going to burn our food if you don't stop this," she said, blushing in front of Mary. "Please go get the rest of our children here for breakfast."

As he turned to leave the kitchen, his daughter said, "I'm proud of you, Father. What you are doing for the church and the children of Petersburg is terrific."

He walked over and kissed her forehead. "Thank you, my dear child, for saying that. It means a lot to me."

"Mom, can I help you with the scrambled eggs?" Mary asked.

"Sure, darling girl," her mother responded. "Go into the cupboard and get an apron. I don't want a speck of grease, butter, or food on your new print dress." *These are the moments when being a mother is so special, teaching your child something new,* she thought.

Lizzie cracked ten eggs in the glass bowl and whisked them furiously. She had the iron skillet on the gas stove. The time had arrived for Mary's first batch of scrambled eggs.

"Go ahead, honey, pour the eggs in the pan. Give them a minute to set up and then gently stir them."

"What's for breakfast?" were the words heard from a stocky seven-year-old Arthur Bradsher Jr. All he wanted to do was play football and eat. He was dressed in a suit and sported a bow tie. His voice was like a bear cub growl. "I'm hungry. Let's have some pancakes."

"There will be no pancakes this morning, Mr. Football. Please go and sit at the table," his mother instructed.

"Good morning, Mother," Charles and Nancy said as they entered the kitchen. They both walked over and gave her a hug.

"Sit down and let's eat. We have thirty minutes before we leave to walk to church. This is a very important day. Arthur, would you please bless this food?"

The four children and their two loving parents bowed their heads for grace.

~

THE BRADSHER FAMILY WALKED down South Sycamore Street, headed for the grand opening of the first phase on the construction of the Trinity Methodist Church. Each child wore a name tag with his or her name on it, their grade, and the Sunday teacher they would have for the year.

For three years, Arthur had worked diligently to bring his dream of building the "prettiest church in America" to fruition. He had Lizzie's total support along the way; she volunteered to teach Mary's class of twelve- and thirteen-year-old children. The hundred-by-forty-five-foot wing of the church had been completed the previous month and a hundred and fifty chairs placed in a large hundred by fifty-foot room to serve as the temporary sanctuary. The chairs were screwed to the floor. Each seat had a hook for the congregation to hang their hats. The large sanctuary and the parlors for adult Bible study would take four more years to complete.

"How are we doing?" Lizzie asked as they began their walk to the church. "You sure got in late last night."

"We're doing great," Arthur said. "With the help of your father and six or seven of the men in his Bible study, we brought the hundred-and-fifty school desks into the ten classrooms. Brister secured these from a school that recently closed in Richmond at an incredible price. We are ready to serve the children."

"Lizzie, I'd like to say one more thing. Your dad is a fine man. His leadership serving the men's Bible study at the Market Street Church and beginning today the Trinity Methodist Church has been such a blessing for all those who attend."

She smiled, "Thank you for saying that Arthur. It means a lot to me you acknowledge him in this way. Father has done a wonderful job raising the children in our family and leading us to the Lord after losing Mom at such an early age."

The two lovebirds held hands as they walked the two blocks to the church. Their children followed thirty feet behind them. Arthur suddenly stopped, as did the kids. He turned to Lizzie and gave her hand a gentle squeeze. He looked into her eyes and said, "I am so grateful for your bringing our fifth child into this world and the two of us having such a glorious place of worship to raise them in." He embraced her and lifted her a few inches off the ground. He placed a short, but tender kiss on her lips.

Their children were preoccupied with counting the cracks on the sidewalk, picking up rocks, throwing pinecones along the walk. Mary was throwing her stones at the metal lampposts that lined the street. The sound rang out, *Bang!*

She yelled out, "Strike!"

Her father stopped abruptly, turned to her, and said, "Let's leave our pitching for out on the ballfield."

~

THREE MONTHS LATER Lizzie gave birth to her fifth child, Mildred Elizabeth Bradsher, in their home at 320 S. Sycamore Street. Lizzie beckoned Arthur to come in the room during the delivery. A midwife delivered the baby in the second-story bedroom. Arthur stood by the bed during the birth, holding Lizzie's hand. He had never seen anything so miraculous as when Millie's head first appeared.

She would be a very special child.

Lizzie Muse's father led Bible studies from 1920-1931.
~ Courtesy of Trinity Methodist Church

Fifty-one

CRABBING AND FLOUNDERING IN THE NEUSE

A family that fishes together stays together.
~ Bradsher

GRANDFATHER BRADSHER, ALONG WITH HIS KIDS, MILLIE, Mary, and Charles, moved along slowly in calf to knee-deep waters of the Neuse River. It was late summer 1949. The water was a refreshing relief to the day's smoldering heat and had a cooling effect on the children's sunburn. It was not a night for storms; there was barely a breeze.

The river was almost mirror-like, catching the magnificence of the setting sun and rising golden moon in its picture frame. The eerie silence would not last, as the tree frogs began to chorus, and the night owl made its raucous territorial calls with long deep breaths.

The sixty-seven-year-old patriarch led the procession of adults and their children. Each was tied to something. Grandfather Bradsher led with a six-foot sharply pointed spear and carried an oil-filled lantern. They were in search of river flounder and crabs that night. Mary, his first-born daughter, had "little Bradsher" tied to her hip, and he bobbed up and down gleefully in a John Deere lawn tractor tire innertube. Her thirteen-year-old daughter, Liz, gripped her hand tightly.

Kirk, one of the oldest grandsons, also held a spear and a lantern. One of the lead hunters, he had inherited the skills and been taught the precision of the spear by his proud grandfather.

Millie had a beer tub tied to her waist and two of the grandchildren, Sandy and Artie, stayed carefully close, tugging at her hip. Five-year-old Dottie and her cousins, Marien and Trinka, were treated to a royal ride on an old rowboat that slowly drifted behind the body of a family moving along in the Neuse.

Oldest grandson Teddy, Millie's son, wore the boat rope around his waist. The rowboat would be the final resting place for the soft-shelled crabs they'd catch that night.

The children were barefoot, and the cool and slimy silt felt good between each of their toes. After her first step in the silt, Patti exclaimed, "It feels like I'm stepping in fresh dog poop." The kerosene lanterns carried by the adults reflected and shimmered in a beautiful way against the water. The sparkles in the river were mesmerizing to the children as were the brilliant display of stars.

"Look up, children. Look up," Grandfather said. "How can anyone claim that God isn't part of this very existence?"

The pungent kerosene created an oily smell that attacked the nostrils of those who were there that night.

Grandfather stopped sharply and slowly raised the gig out of the water. He whispered to Kirk, "Shine the flashlight." What they both saw looked like a doormat buried below them in an inch or two of sand and lying very still. He referred to the flounder as the underwater ghost of the night. There was a sudden swoosh as his weapon penetrated the water aimed at its head. He raised the gig out of the water with the two-pound beauty perfectly targeted. He beamed with pride.

"Kirk, I want you to claim the next one we see. Walk calmly and stay perfectly focused until it's time to thrust the spear. When you strike it, be sure you do it with true conviction, and you're in perfect control."

Kirk imagined, *this was exactly how he approached the hitters he'd faced during his glory days at Trinity: always remaining calm and composed, always using pinpoint accuracy when delivering to his target. Always staying in control when the unexpected came upon him.*

They moved a few more steps when Kirk said, "Do you see it?" There sat another, flat as a pancake, flounder buried an inch under the sand.

"There's a funny thing about this fish," Grandfather whispered to him, "do you know what it is?"

"No, I don't," he replied.

"Look closer with the flashlight, Kirk, and let me know if you see anything that strikes you as unusual."

The light from the flashlight pierced the water and gave him a very clear view of the flounder. Bradsher's first-born, Mary, edged closer to get a look at what she already knew.

"Wow!" Kirk responded in an excited manner. "There it is! I see the two eyes, and they are both on one side of its head. It's as if one of the eyes has migrated from the other side."

Grandfather coached Kirk, "When you gig you want to sink the spear in its head, not in the middle of the belly. If you hit it in the belly, it'll give you a terrible fight." Kirk hit his target in the sweet spot, and it resulted in a quick and fight less end for the fish, "Great job, Grandson."

Mary stepped in next as her father handed her the spear. Oldest of the Bradsher children, she was just as adventuresome as Bradsher's youngest daughter, Millie. Mary Elizabeth and Mildred Catherine would become and stay lifetime friends, and their children would become favorite cousins. Both families would spend summers fishing together in Morehead City, North Carolina after Grandfather passed away.

Mary had a steady hand and good judgment. She waited for the exact moment when she had the spear perfectly lined up with the flounder's head. She jabbed it down quicker than the snap of her father's curveball. She put the sharp tip of the gig right through the fish's brain, leaving it with no capacity to fight or suffer. Mary raised it high into the air to celebrate her trophy.

Meanwhile, behind the parents, the kids were working on gathering up soft-shelled crabs. Some crabs could be felt under their feet as they waded through the silt. The kids would reach down and pick each one out of the water with their hands.

An occasional squeal would be heard from one of the grandchildren when getting snipped by one of the crab claws. As they picked the crabs out of the water, the kids threw them in the bottom of the rowboat. The crabs frightened five-year-old Patti as they clattered and snipped at her ankles.

Millie was Bradsher's last-born child. She was born a month prematurely at home on South Sycamore Street. She would raise six very adventuresome and talented children. She had one child die at childbirth, which made her appreciate every minute of life.

The family kidded her that she couldn't wait to be born in the hospital because she didn't want to miss anything her life had in store.

Mary traded places with her sister, and she passed her the gig.

As Millie waded up to Mary's previous spot next to Grandfather, she suddenly whispered, "I think I got one." She bent over and reached down to the floor of the river and grabbed a one-pound blue crab. "He went for it," she proudly exclaimed, "he attacked the chicken bone I tied to the laces of my tennis shoe."

Millie wasted no time in spearing what would be the last flounder of the night. She too was precise with her spear and it pierced the unsuspecting fish. She brought him out of the water proudly, as her son Kirk said, "Fantastic job, Mom."

The kids had also set four or five crab traps on ropes extending out eight to nine feet from the rowboat. The traps were baited with shrimp and baitfish. At the end of the night, Charles, Bradsher's second-born child, pulled the traps into the rowboat. "We've hit the jackpot," he happily exclaimed. There were at least two crabs in each trap.

Charles, with a gentle voice, directed the grandchildren. "Sort through the traps, keep the male crabs and release the females back into the river." The grandchildren all liked Uncle Charles. He was a kind and soft-spoken man, like his father.

The night was full of fun. The Bradsher clan speared four flounders and captured ten soft-shelled crabs that were keepers. Grandfather motioned for all those in the river to look up the top of the bluff. Grandmother, Aunti Pearl, and Aunt Nancy had built a roaring fire. The sparks from the massive fire flew thirty feet into the evening sky.

Bradsher had built the fire pit for Lizzie out of an old oil drum he had cut in half. He finished it by setting it in a stand with large river rocks.

It was a signal to everyone in the river it was time to call it a night and head back to the shore. Kirk, always trying to get the attention of the younger cousins, asked them, "Did you see the alligator's eyes floating back up the Neuse River on the far side?" All the children's eyes widened.

Grandmother looked down from the top of the bluff as the family walked back towards the house and climbed the steep stairs up to her. Grandfather walked in the center of his two oldest grandsons with his right arm slung over the shoulder of Kirk and his left arm over the shoulder of Teddy.

"Boys, I cannot express enough to you how very important it is you are spending time with me and your grandmother. Someday you will look back on our adventures on the Neuse River as some the most special times of your life."

As they reached the top of the stairs, Lizzie was there to greet Arthur. She always had that look like she yearned for him. He gave her a long embrace and a soft kiss.

Dottie, only five years old, ran over to Grandmother and excitingly exclaimed, "Grandmother, Grandmother, I never realized that life could be this great!" The family broke out into rip-roaring laughter.

They all turned to walk the final fifty yards to the river house. Grandmother told the children, "We'll need to get up early in the morning to break down the crabs and gut some of the fish. Aunti Pearl will be cooking us eggs, a few pieces of fried fish, and her delicious crab cakes. She'll also treat us with her yummy and fresh homemade biscuits for our breakfast tomorrow."

~

THERE WAS ONE MORE SURPRISE, as Grandmother brought out a tray with marshmallows, pieces of chocolate, and graham crackers. "Smores for everyone," she joyfully hollered. She didn't have to say it twice to get the grandchildren running to her to enjoy their gooey symphony.

Grandfather gave his last instructions for the night, "Kids, go upstairs and bathe. Your grandmother will be up in a few minutes to read and tuck you in. Kirk and Teddy, why don't you help me put up the fishing gear and crab traps. Let's put the crabs in the blue cooler and the flounder in the red cooler. We can filet the fish and break down the crab meat in the morning." They finished around eleven and headed back to the big house to get some needed rest.

"Thank you, Grandfather, for tonight. It was fun," Kirk said.

Teddy said, "You are the best, Grandfather. It doesn't get any better than tonight."

In the dark walk back to the river house, the two boys did not see the tears streaming down his face. This had been one of the greatest moments in Arthur Bradsher's life.

Fifty-two

AUNTI PEARL
EATS WITH THE FAMILY

If you want to see the true measure of a man,
watch how he treats his inferiors, not his equals
~ J. K Rowling

G RANDFATHER, WHY HAS AUNTI PEARL NEVER EATEN WITH US
at the dinner table?" Nine-year-old Marien asked. It was
the Summer of 1949. One filled with many first-time experiences at
Summerlea.

He didn't have an immediate answer. Still, he did not want to
avoid the question. "Marien, many of the people in our country
are divided on what the fair rights for the Negro should be."

"How're they divided?"

"Back in the day, Negroes couldn't vote or hold public office.
Even today, they go to different schools than white kids. It may not
be right, and you might not understand. I appreciate your love for
Aunti Pearl."

"I do love her," Marien said.

Aunti Pearl loved the Bradsher grandchildren like a mother. She
had worked for his first child, Mary, for five years. Mary invited
her to join them and help the family all the years that the family
gathered at the farm, Summerlea, from 1946 to 1951.

The agreement between Mary and her housekeeper was: she

would cook and clean and keep a careful watch over Bradsher's dozen grandchildren at the river house for the summer.

~

"IN MY HOUSE, if you and the other children want to invite Aunti Pearl to join us at the dinner table tomorrow night, I'm in. I'd appreciate all of you volunteering to help her provide our dinner," he said with direction.

He had always spoken to her and treated her with kindness. She'd cooked for, bathed, thrown the ball with, clothed, and lent a caring ear to the children.

If they were worried about anything, she would be there for them. She played a motherly role at times to the kids, and they loved her.

~

SHE HAD LAID OUT all the food on platters and bowls on the large wooden table in the kitchen. She was about to bring them out to the family when Arthur greeted her. He said to her before she picked up the first platter, "I want you to sit down at the dining room table. The kids and I will bring the food in. We're going to serve you tonight."

She entered the dining room. Marien and Dottie remained seated at the dining room table, an empty chair between them. "Aunti Pearl, please sit between us," Marien said to her. She was a large woman. They spread the chairs an extra few inches to give her ample room.

As she seated herself, she noticed a small vase filled with wildflowers that were red, blue, yellow, and pink. "Marien and I picked these for you this afternoon," five-year-old Dottie said.

"They're quite colorful. You are very thoughtful."

Marien smelled lavender in the air. "Your perfume is nice."

"Thank you, my dear child of God."

Bradsher and the entire family entered the dining room carrying either a platter or bowl of the evening's dinner. The corn, okra, tomatoes, carrots were all fresh from the garden.

The blue-and-white Wedgewood platters and bowls were gifts when Arthur and Lizzie were married. The room was flooded with beautiful aromas. Each dish was placed on the sixteen-foot-long mahogany table.

Grandfather announced to the family, "Join hands and let's pray over this fine food." Each parent and child reached out to the one next to them. Marien grasped Aunti Pearl's right hand tightly, Dottie holding her left. Thirteen heads bowed and Grandfather began his blessing: "Dear Lord, our Heavenly Father, we're so grateful for this beautiful and hearty meal and the hands of Aunti Pearl who prepared it for us.

"We've been blessed with abundance while others go hungry. Guide us to be more charitable to the less fortunate and be willing to lend a helping hand. We have our health and the ability to go out and fish, crab, and swim in the river. You have allowed my children to bear my energetic and mindful grandchildren. I experience something new from them every day."

He continued his prayer, "Our Father, we join tonight as one family. We come to you forgetting some of our differences and focusing on the common love that binds us. In Jesus' name, we pray. Amen."

All those in the room followed with an enthusiastic, "Amen."

When Dottie turned to ask Aunti Pearl to pass the platter of biscuits, she saw her partially smiling but with tears streaming down her face. "Are you, all right?" she asked in a concerned little voice.

"This should be a moment of happiness," the head of the family said.

"It is very much so, Mr. Bradsher," she responded. "These are tears of immeasurable joy and gratitude. All of you have made me feel part of the family tonight, not just as a servant," she said, her voice shaky.

"We thank you for preparing this fine meal," the family patriarch said. He removed a few pieces of the fried chicken from the platter. "I understand you had some help from the kids."

She answered, "That I did, sir. Kirk and Teddy went out to the garden and picked the corn. They shucked it and cut the corn off the cobb. Marien sliced these tasty ripe tomatoes. I'll have to take responsibility for the fried chicken, fried okra, the creamed corn, and the biscuits and gravy," she said with great pride.

"It is certainly a fine dinner, and we are grateful. I'm sure the kids would love to help you with the dishes after we finish dinner."

As the family enjoyed the dinner, Grandfather asked Aunti Pearl, "How did you learn to cook?"

"From my grandmother. I was fortunate to live with her when my mother died," she began. "She passed when I was ten and I didn't have a father that I knew. I learned to cook at a very young age."

"What's your secret for this splendid cream corn?" Bradsher asked. "It's the best I've ever had."

She smiled and answered. "Fresh corn, homemade butter, and cream."

"How did you cook it?"

"I combine the fresh corn with cream, salt sugar, and butter and put it in a cast iron skillet over medium heat. Next, I whisk in flour and milk into the corn mixture and stir until it thickens, and the corn is cooked through. I put it in an oven-safe dish and sprinkle the top with Parmesan. After five minutes in the oven, it's ready to serve."

"Who would like seconds?" Grandfather asked. He reached to the middle of the table to get the pot of creamed corn. As he strained to reach it, he exclaimed, "Excuse my Southern reach." His comment brought laughter from those at the table.

"What does that expression mean?" Elizabeth asked.

"It's a term I learned from the renters at my mother's boarding house in Durham. It originated when one of the borders would break with good manners, and overreach across the table to help themselves." Grandfather chuckled.

"I made your favorite carrot cake with crème cheese frosting you like so much, Mr. Bradsher. I added pineapple, pecans, and fresh coconut to the recipe," she said proudly.

"Elizabeth and Sandy spread the crème cheese frosting on the cake."

"What did little Bradsher do to help?"

"We let him lick the spoon after we frosted the cake," Marien chimed in. The whole table broke out in laughter.

Grandfather pushed himself back from the dinner table and stood. "Kids, take the plates to the kitchen and give Aunti Pearl a hand. We'll meet on the screened porch in twenty minutes."

After all the kids left the room, he walked over to where Lizzie was sitting. "I want to thank you for giving me all of this and want to tell you how deeply I love you," he whispered. He bent over and gave her a soft kiss.

~

FIFTEEN MINUTES LATER, the grandchildren retreated to the screened porch, knowing that Aunti Pearl was close behind with the carrot cake and plates.

"Kids, I need some help," Arthur explained. "There're three buckets in the shed. Two of the buckets have different sized stones in them and one is filled with sand. Kirk, Teddy, and Thor! Get the buckets and bring them to me."

"Yes, sir," the three oldest grandchildren responded.

As Aunti Pearl brought Arthur his cup of coffee, he said to her, "Please bring two of the biggest jars you have in the kitchen for pickling."

She brought the cake and the plates and set them at the end of the large table. She began slicing a piece for each of the children. She also set the two large pickle jars on the table.

He reached into one of the buckets and took out two sets of rocks the size of and roughly shaped like a small potato. He now had their attention.

Bradsher said to his story-time audience, "This jar and everything I'll put in it represents my life. I want to share it with my family."

Fifty-three

TIME IS SO PRECIOUS

A man who wastes one hour of time
has not discovered the value of life.
~ Charles Darwin

O N THAT SUMMER NIGHT IN 1949, GRANDFATHER BRADSHER
shared a life lesson with his family.

"In life, children, time is the great equalizer in that each minute
has sixty seconds, each hour of the day has sixty minutes, and each
day has twenty-four hours. Time is a very valuable commodity in
our life. Sometimes, life is cut short without a moment's notice."

He scratched his chin. "In your teenage years, you need to
start recognizing what is truly important in life. On rare occasions,
some teenagers do this very well and use their time to accomplish
remarkable things. Many do not and waste a lot of precious time.

"One of the first priorities I put into place in my teenage
years was to strive to achieve an important level of education.
Your grandmother and I were very fortunate to have mothers that
believed in the value of education and set the standard of excelling
in college, which we both did.

"Your grandmother was smarter than me, but I did manage to
graduate with honors, cum laude, my senior year. I got my master's
degree my fifth year." He placed a rock in the jar.

"At seventeen, playing baseball was very important to me. I
wanted to be recognized. I was willing to work hard to become a

great pitcher. At first, I didn't know how difficult it would be, but I stuck with it. I felt like the challenging work in learning to pitch would teach me discipline.

"It was a terrific opportunity to make new friends and represent Trinity College with honor." He put another rock in the jar to represent his five years of achievements in baseball.

Arthur picked the largest rock out of the bucket. It was the size of a baseball. "What priority do you think this rock represents? As you can see by its size, it is the most important accomplishment in my life."

"Marrying Grandmother," they screamed out in unison.

"Exactly," he continued. "It turned out to be the most crucial decision I ever made in my life." Grandfather walked over to Lizzie and gave her a warm kiss. The grandchildren cheered him on.

Marien thought, *their deep love is immeasurable.*

"At the time I was considering marrying your grandmother, I had to make a tough decision—whether or not to go into major league baseball. Boy, was I recruited to do so! The owners came a-courting, and most said just name your price. There were offers of ten thousand dollars to play with the pros.

"There was one problem. There was no price that could be put on having a happy marriage with Lizzie and having a large family. I felt like I would lose her if I took their offers, so I declined them.

"So, instead of putting a rock in the jar for a major-league career, I am putting five rocks in to represent the five fine children that were born to your grandmother and me, and we would have the opportunity to raise and educate." He looked over to his firstborn, Mary, and winked at her.

"Grandchildren, you're probably too young to understand some of our summer talks and the importance I hope they play in your later life. I want you to feel like I told you the story of my life.

"One of the great loves of my life, besides your grandmother, life on the Neuse River, and baseball, has been my and Lizzie's involvement with the churches wherever we lived. We've been evenly yoked in our Christian beliefs."

"What does evenly yoked mean?" five-year-old Dottie asked.

"Imagine you have two oxen pulling a wagon," he began. "If the oxen are tied into their harnesses an equal distance from the cart, then they can pull the cart in a straight line without struggling. But if one of the oxen was tied into the harness eight feet from the cart and the other was four feet from the cart, he would be very difficult to pull the cart without veering off the road. There would be conflict.

"Your grandmother and I are equally yoked in that we both share the same beliefs in serving God and the right way we raise our children. You might say we're the same distance from the cart."

The patriarch continued, "I was inspired by your grandmother's belief in the Lord and her commitment to serve her church shortly after I met her. She told me about her summers spent at Morehead City training to supervise the Sunday school program at her church.

"I was called by my faith to lead and be to be a superintendent of a major church's Sunday school program that would be a terrific way to help forty other churchgoers make it successful."

He walked over and gently squeezed Lizzie's hand. "I learned a lot from your grandmother."

"Thank you, Arthur," she responded with a smile.

"We would serve our churches in Durham, Petersburg, and in Montreal," he said. "The next rock I'm putting in the jar signifies the priority your grandmother and I have placed on our Christian beliefs and serving the church."

"What should the next rock represent, children?"

Elizabeth, who was one of the most outgoing of the grandchildren, answered enthusiastically, "Family adventures on the Neuse River during the summers in our childhood."

"You're very smart, Liz. I made a great decision to buy this hundred-acre farm six years ago. Having our children and grandchildren spend summers at Summerlea has brought us closer together as a family.

"Children, the last rock is for my forty-five-year career in the tobacco business. Most people feel it would be the first rock you'd put in the jar because your career is all about the money. It's my last choice because my wife and family come first to me."

He grinned. "I have tried to be aware of crossing the line with your grandmother and my career, by not putting my job above my family. It was a tough act to balance, and a few times I've failed," he said.

"What do you see?" he asked. "Is it full?" The jar was filled to the top with eleven stones.

Sandy answered, "Yes, Grandfather, it is full."

He went over to the corner of the porch and picked up the bucket of marble-sized stones and brought them over to the table. "Every day in our lives on this earth, we are faced with decisions on what we should do each day. Sometimes, we avoid the most important things we should be focused on.

"The smaller rocks signify the other things you deeply care about or are interested in."

"Things less important than you described with the larger rocks," Patti offered.

"Yes, indeed," he responded.

He put handful after handful of the small pebbles into the pickle jar and shook it. The pebbles started to fall into the gaps between the larger rocks. He looked at them and broke out in a wide grin. "Is the jar full now?"

The kids answered, "Yes, it is full!"

He brought over a bucket of bone-dry river sand to the table. He started putting handful after handful into the jar. He shook the jar and the sand filtered down into finding every possible crevice. "The sand represents the insignificant things in life like reading comic books, listening to music, and talking on the phone.

"Listen carefully, children. If you put the sand in the jar first, there will be no room for all the rocks and pebbles. The same can be applied to our lives. If you spend all your time and efforts on the small stuff, you'll have no room for the things that are truly important."

He smiled at his ten-year-old grandchild, Patti, and asked her, "What does this mean to you?"

"Grandfather," she began, "I think we need to decide what are our five or six priorities and focus on them every day."

"Elizabeth, what did you learn from this lesson?"

"Don't get bogged down with the small stuff, and let it eat up all your time during the day. Work on being a master of the big stuff."

He stood up. "Well, it looks like you both learned a valuable lesson tonight. Gather around and let's hold hands and pray before we turn in for bed.

"Lord, our Heavenly Father, guide us to know what the most important things in life are and move us to focus on those things that you would find pleasing. We know that our love and faith in you and our prayers to you are one of those important things in life. Lord, thanks for this wonderful family. Please keep them safe, healthy, and in your sight always. In Jesus's name, we pray."

Each of the children squeezed the hand they were holding and joined in, "Amen."

"Okay, children, go get ready for bed."

~

AFTER HE HAS READ TO THE GRANDCHILDREN, he gave them a kiss goodnight and tucked them in. He headed down the long staircase of the river house.

Halfway down, he heard Patti's tiny voice. "I love you, Grandfather."

Sixty-six-year-old Lizzie Muse,
a week after her loss of beloved Arthur Bradsher.
~ Courtesy of the Bradsher Family

Fifty-four

THE FINAL INNING

I consider myself the luckiest man on the face of the earth
~ Lou Gehrig

IT HAD BEEN A SCARY WEEK. TWO OF DURHAM'S FINEST HEART doctors had traveled to Beaufort, North Carolina, to try to save Arthur's life. He had experienced constant chest pains and dizziness for the past six days. His blood pressure was highly elevated at 190/99. His physical existence was teetering on the edge.

Lizzie was a very strong woman. This was one time she felt the outcome was out of her control. She was frightened she was going to lose her loving husband and best friend. It was time for her to let go. She prayed to God for his salvation.

In between doctor's visits, the two lovers held hands, shared warm kisses, and talked about their life together almost every minute of their waking days. As they held hands, they reminisced about great college memories, his heroics on the baseball field, rich life in Petersburg and Montreal, and the wonderful experiences of raising their children.

"Gosh, we had some great times, Arthur. The tapestry of all those life events has truly been a blessing from God. I am going to miss you, my dear man. You will be in the air I breathe every day for the rest of my life. Just know I'll be with you someday in Heaven."

Arthur was feeling faint. He reached for Lizzie and said, "I feel so lucky to have shared so many things with you, my dear."

"Your records on the diamond may never be equaled. It was such fun watching you perform. You were the best and still are. What may be just as important when your story is told is the honor you brought to Trinity and Duke University, and the admirable example you set on the playing field. Generations will learn from your extraordinary life."

"Thank you, Lizzie. Your love means so much to me."

They revisited the adventures of the six summers spent with their children and grandchildren at the farm on the river.

"Look at the picture of little Artie on the tractor with you at Summerlea," Lizzie said. "He was six in this picture. He so loved to follow you around the farm during those summer days. He felt he was your buddy."

"Arthur, you've been such a leader in the church. Being the Sunday school superintendent in three cities for over forty years helped so many children know the word of the Lord. Your being on the board and your leadership of the YMCA in Montreal really made a difference in the organization being very successful."

She brought out the scrapbook she had compiled through the years. It was three inches thick and documented the beautiful memories they shared over the past forty-seven years.

When the river house burned to the ground the previous year, it was the only thing she took with her, as Arthur carried her out through the smoke and flames, exiting through the front door. They were looking at it the evening before the fire broke out, and it was on the bedside table.

She handed Arthur the scrapbook as he sat in the recliner resting. She sat down beside him. He opened it to the first page and gazed with a broad smile at one of his favorite pictures. It was taken on the night of the ATO gala ball on their first date. It was a night that he relived in his mind often. It was her first date and a night of her first kiss. In the picture, the two were standing next to Governor Aycock.

"Lizzie, you were the prettiest girl at the ball that evening."

"It was the most exciting night I had ever experienced. I felt so lucky to be with you," she said, reaching out to grasp his hand.

To the right of the picture was a newspaper clipping from the day he first met her. The headlines of the article read, "Bradsher misses shutout by one pitch. He pitches a three-hitter and strikes out thirteen batters."

"I'll never forget my first glimpse of you. You were unbelievably pretty. You took my breath away. The headline in the paper should have read, 'Bradsher loses shutout but wins the prettiest girl in America.'"

"Oh, Arthur, you have always treated me and our family so well." She leaned over and gave him a soft kiss. She held his hand as he turned the pages to one of his favorite pictures. It was a beautiful picture of her, their first-born child, Mary Elizabeth, and their son, born two years later, Charles Kilgo.

"Those two were inseparable as kids, and dearly loved each other," Arthur said.

"The picture was taken in 1914, during a time when people being photographed rarely smiled," Lizzie commented.

"Look at Charlie's grin," he said. "What a happy child he was."

"I think he got a lot of his good disposition from you, Arthur." She squeezed his hand. "You've always been so happy and pleasant. I've watched you greet each day with a smile on your face since the first time I met you."

"Lizzie, you have been such a big part of my happiness. I have always been so proud to be your partner in life. I love you so much," he whispered. She drew closer to him and could feel his warm breath on her cheek. They kissed.

Another clipping featured bold headlines: "Arthur Bradsher Is Still Master of The Ball." The article read, "The King of the Southern Diamond is at it again. He strikes out twenty and nineteen batters in two straight games in the Petersburg Church league."

"It was so nice that our children got to see you pitch and appreciate how great you were," Lizzie said proudly. "Those were great times we had in the twenty-five years we lived in Petersburg."

Arthur turned to another page and smiled. He showed her a clipping from 1931. "Do you remember this night, Lizzie?"

"Oh, my goodness," she exclaimed, "it was a night of all nights." The clipping was entitled, "Plenty Fast."

Arthur displayed his famous smile, but he was becoming increasingly short of breath. "Please read it to me, Lizzie."

The article read: "Winning highest honors scholastically and athletically. In twenty-eight minutes and traveling twelve miles between the two distinctions is the record of Charlie Bradsher, a track star at Duke University, Durham, N. C. At nine o'clock at night Bradsher was awarded a Phi Beta Kappa key, the highest honorary scholarship honor at the university. At 9:28, he was twelve miles away breaking the tape for a new record in the Southern Conference indoor half-mile." - *The Winnipeg Tribune*

"I was parked at the door. Charlie and you raced to the car and off we raced to Chapel Hill. Charlie took off his suit and put on his track shorts and running shoes in the car."

As they sped towards Chapel Hill, Arthur spoke to his son. "Charlie, this reminds me of when we played Mercer. We arrived ten minutes before game time. You're in the same boat. Start stretching now because you'll be competing in the 880-meter run within five minutes of us reaching the gymnasium."

"You always show up, Dad," Charlie said, "Thanks for getting me here."

Charlie jumped out of the car and sprinted to the gymnasium. He heard his father's scream: "Run like the wind, Charlie, run like the wind."

Charlie has been a great son, but all my children have had special qualities, he thought.

"You know, Lizzie, I think one of my greatest contributions was starting the Order of The Tombs at Trinity. From 1904 to 1942 we initiated over eleven hundred members into the Tombs Honorary Athletic Society. For most of those years, the Tombs was the strongest organization on campus. We made a difference in promoting athletics and sportsmanship. We also succeeded in improving our relations with the colleges we competed against.

"The Rose Bowl held on the Duke University campus in 1942 may have done us in. Most of the Tombs members were football players that year. They made significant efforts to accommodate the Oregon players and fans who attended the game.

"So much, it led Wallace Wade to say after their surprising defeat in the hands of Oregon, 'We spent too much time being the host and too little time preparing the team.' The Tombs morphed into the Varsity Club in 1945. It was time for a name change and to evaluate some new goals and direction."

"Arthur, you have been such a fine father to your children and grandchildren. Charlie was right. You did always show up and support them. You offered a safe place to visit if one of them needed to talk about something that was troubling them. Your door was always open." She gently ran her fingers through his thick grey hair.

Arthur smiled as he looked at the next picture in the scrapbook. He was feeling weak and his vision was becoming somewhat blurred. "Lizzie, the day we were married was one of the happiest days of my life." The picture was shot from the back of the room with Lizzie and Arthur turned sideways speaking their vows. "Dr. Kilgo was so honored to perform the ceremony."

Lizzie smiled at Arthur and slid her chair up to get a closer look at the photograph. "That was the most magical day of my life. I was so in love with you and feel the same way at this very moment. On that day, I knew I was marrying a man that would be a loyal husband, a great father, and a person of adventure. And, I was right," Lizzie said as she gently stroked his forearm.

Arthur spoke. "I'm fading a little bit and having a few chest pains. My time is nearing to join the Lord. Will you sing the fourth stanza of 'How Great Thou Art' to me?"

Lizzie leaned towards Arthur and kissed him warmly. "I love you, Arthur, and always will. I will be with you again in eternity." The emotion of losing him caused her hand to tremble when she gently stroked his forehead.

She sat on the bench at the piano and began to play their favorite hymn:

Oh Lord my God
When I, in awesome wonder
Consider all the worlds
Thy hands have made

I see the stars
I hear the rolling thunder
Thy power throughout
The universe displayed

Lizzie looked to the heavens as she sang with all her might. Tears were streaming down her face:

Then sings my soul
My Savior, God, to Thee
How great Thou art
How great Thou art

Then sings my soul
My savior, God to thee
How great Thou art
How great Thou art

The scrapbook fell from Arthur's lifeless hands and landed on the floor.

Lizzie hurried over to her beloved husband. His eyes were closed, and he still had a smile on his face. She felt his pulse and there was none. Life had left his body, and his spirit had gone to join his Lord and Savior in Heaven.

"Oh, Arthur, I will miss you, my darling man. I know you are at peace now. I'll join you in that eternal place someday." Her tears soaked his shirt as she laid her head on his warm chest and wept.

A. B. BRADSHER, 68, DIES IN CAROLINA

Former Executive of Imperial Tobacco Well·Known in Montreal

A. B. Bradsher, former vice-president of the Imperial Tobacco Company of Canada Ltd., Montreal, died Saturday in Beaufort, North Carolina. He was in his 69th year.

Born in Rexoboro, N.C., and a graduate (M.A.) of Duke University, Durham, N.C., Mr. Bradsher joined the Imperial Tobacco Company in Montreal in 1935. Associated mainly with the company's leaf tobacco operations, he was elected a director in 1936 and appointed a vice-president in 1939.

He retired in 1945 and returned to North Carolina.

Prominent in Church Work

In Montreal he was interested in church and Y.M.C.A. work. He was an elder of Erskine-American United Church and of the national executive council of the Y.M.C.A.

He was a member of the Royal Montreal Golf Club.

A son, Arthur, attended McGill University, was graduated in medicine and is married to the former Elinor Montgomery of Montreal West.

Mr. Bradsher is survived by his wife, the former Elizabeth Muse; two sons, Dr. Charles Bradsher, professor of chemistry at Duke University, and Dr. Arthur Bradsher of Philadelphia; and by three daughters, Mary, Mildred and Nancy.

Funeral arrangements will be announced later.

A. B. BRADSHER

Article honoring Arthur Bradsher the day after he died.
January 29, 1951.
~ Courtesy of *The Gazette*, Montreal, Quebec, Canada.

Arthur Bradsher, '04, Great Trinity Pitcher, Dies

Arthur Brown Bradsher, '04, one of the greatest collegiate pitchers in the nation in the early 1900's, died at his home in Beaufort, N. C., on January 27, of a heart attack.

As the ace southpaw for Trinity College, Mr. Bradsher rolled up an amazing strike-out record and was known throughout the land as "King of the Southern Diamond." In each of his years at Trinity, Mr. Bradsher made an outstanding reputation for himself on the baseball diamond, becoming one of the top collegiate pitchers of all time. In 1901 he fanned 70 opposing players, and in 1903 there were 99 who could not touch one of his pitches. 1904 brought an even more spectacular season, for Arthur Bradsher pitched 14 winning games and lost only one. Facing 427 hitters he allowed only 48 safe hits, struck out 166 batters, and pitched a 9-0 no-hitter against Oak Ridge. During his final year he allowed only 38 hits in 13 games, striking out 169 would-be hitters. Two no-hit games were pitched by him that season. A versatile ball player, Mr. Brasher played regularly in the outfield or at third base when he was not pitching.

As a young boy, Arthur Bradsher moved to Durham with his family. Having received his elementary education in the Durham city schools, he entered Trinity.

After graduating from college, he declined a $10,000 job (an unheard of sum at that time) to play professional ball, choosing instead to be employed by the old American Tobacco Company. Later he became market supervisor for the Export Leaf Tobacco Company located in Petersburg, Va. At the time of his retirement in 1945 he was a director and vice-president of the Imperial Tobacco Company of Canada, Montreal, Canada.

After his retirement in 1945, Mr. Bradsher made his home on Summerlea Farm near New Bern, N. C., until September, 1950, when he moved to Beaufort.

Funeral services for Mr. Bradsher were held at the Howerton-Bryan Funeral Home in Durham, and interment was in Maplewood Cemetery, annex B.

Surviving are his widow, Mrs. Elizabeth Muse Bradsher, '05; three daughters, Mildred Bradsher Voorhees (Mrs. E. H.), '46, Garden City, Long Island, N. Y.; Mary Elizabeth Bradsher Hayes (Mrs. F. L.), '31, Charlotte, N. C.; and Mrs. F. A. Gill, Jr., Petersburg; two sons, Dr. Charles K. Bradsher, '33, former Duke track star hailed as one of the greatest half-milers in the school's history, who is now teaching chemistry at Duke; and Dr. A. B. Bradsher, Jr., '38, Philadelphia, Pa.; and a half brother, Gordon M. Carver, '15, Carolina Beach, N. C., and sixteen grandchildren. In addition to his immediate family, Mr. Bradsher is survived by a large number of relatives and in-laws, many of whom came to Duke University.

DUKE ALUMNI REGISTER, February, 1951   [Page 43]

Arthur Bradsher's obituary posted in the Duke Register.
February 16, 1951.
~ Courtesy of Duke University Library and Archives

Duke University honored Arthur Brown Bradsher one week after the school placed a long obituary in the Duke Register. President Arthur Edens addressed the entire assembled student body in the chapel.

"Last week Duke University and Trinity College lost one of its finest student athletes to ever attend our schools. Arthur Bradsher, whom many referred to as the 'King of the Southern Diamond' passed away quietly at his home in Beaufort. He's survived by five children, four that went to Duke and sixteen other decedents that also attended our University. Arthur Bradsher was Duke Blue through and through. He will be missed.

"Please, let's take a minute of silence to honor and pray for his family."

February 1951

~ Courtesy of Duke University Library and Archives

EXTRA INNINGS

John Heisman
1869-1936

John William Heisman called Arthur Bradsher the "King of the Southern Diamond" after Bradsher started the 1904 season pitching twenty-five consecutive no-hit innings. Few recognize Heisman for his successes on the baseball diamond. His overall record as a baseball coach was 219-119-7, and his finest baseball team which was comprised of all-stars Chip Robert, team captain, shortstop Tommy McMillan, and pitchers Ed Lafitte, and Craig Day. went 23-3, winning the SIAA in 1906.

Heisman's contract for the 1903 season to coach baseball and football at Clemson was $300 plus room and board. It was a year he went ten and three in baseball and in football beat Georgia, twenty-nine to zero. He defeated his soon-to-be employer, Georgia Tech, seventy-three to zero on the way to the SIAA championship.

Georgia Tech had lured Heisman away from Clemson to coach the Gold and White in football, baseball, and basketball, and be Tech's athletic director. He was paid with an enormous salary for that era of $2,250 a year plus thirty percent of attendance fees.

Heisman won 77 percent of his football games at Georgia Tech from 1904 to 1919 and won a national championship in 1917. From 1916 to 1917, his teams compiled a thirty-three-game win streak. Heisman coached like a czar on the playing fields and shouted instructions to his players through a megaphone that he was never without.

John Heisman was one of the great innovators in College football along with Pop Warner, Walter Camp, and Amos Alonzo Stagg. He is credited with several changes to the game of football including legalizing the forward pass, reformatting the game into four quarters instead of two halves, and created the hidden ball trick, and jump shift (later known as the Heisman shift) in his arsenal of weapons.

Georgia Tech coach was described as the master of the surprise element pulled off in a ball game. On the eve of a big game between his team, Clemson against Ga. Tech, while his team was quietly resting in log cabins outside of Atlanta, he brought in a team of scrubs who stayed up until dawn drinking and partying. Thinking they would have an easy time with the hung-over Clemson team, they were trounced by Clemson 44-5.

In 1909 Heisman became the president of the Atlanta Crackers minor league baseball team. The Crackers captured the Southern Association title the same year.

Off the playing fields, Heisman's interests were acting and he was a part of several acting troupes in the offseason. He was known for his grand theatrical speeches to his players often with the accompaniment of his megaphone. The Tech coach enjoyed walks with his beloved poodle, Woo, who he often fed ice cream as a special treat.

Heisman left Atlanta in 1926 after divorcing his wife. The fabled coach died from pneumonia in New York City on October 3, 1936. He was preparing a history of college football which he never completed.

Two months after his death, the Downtown Athletic Club Trophy, given to the most outstanding college of the year in college football was renamed The Heisman Memorial Trophy.

He was inducted in the second class of the College Football Hall of Fame in 1956.

Washington Duke
1820-1905

Washington Duke, industrialist and philanthropist, was born in 1820 on his parents' farm, located on the Little River in what was then part of Orange County, in North Carolina. He once said that he considered himself very poor twice in his life—first, when he began making a living with nothing but "willing hands and a stout heart" and second, upon returning to his home after the Civil War. In the first instance he made a modest living farming, and in the second, he grew wealthy by turning to the manufacture of tobacco products.

After returning home from the Civil War Duke decided to give up his farming business and go down a different road...That being tobacco., with the assistance of his two sons, Benjamin Newton and James Buchanan, referred to as Buck,, and his daughter, Mary Elizabeth, Washington Duke's early manufacturing business consisted of beating cured tobacco by hand with sticks, sifting it through a fine wire sieve, and packing it in small bags for sale. Selling the finished product of pipe tobacco, took Duke or his boys through thirty-two states.

In the mid 1870's Washington Duke and his sons realized that the biggest market for tobacco would be on the sale of cigarettes. Cigarettes came to the United States in the 1860. After becoming very popular in Europe. In 1880, Washington Duke retired from the day by day involvement of the tobacco business and turned business over to his sons Benjamin and James, common referred to as Buck, who would become president. In that pivotal year James Duke decided to move forward with full steam in the production of cigarettes. They also move their production facilities to Durham, N.C. and built two factories in this fast growing and bustling city.

The production and sale of cigarettes was clearly the roadmap for a profitable and growing business. However, the major drawback to the production of cigarettes at that time was the time-consuming task to roll each cigarette. Early hand-rolling of cigarettes was slow and tedious.; an expert could roll about four per minute. To speed up the process, Duke, at first began to hire immigrants from Eastern Europe who were skilled cigarette rollers, but as cigarette popularity began to boom, a faster process was needed.

In 1884 decided on a different path and leased two Bonsack cigarette rolling machines. With an eye on the future James B. Duke created more warehouse space in Durham, expanded the company with a branch in New York City and continued to invest in Bonsack rolling machines. By 1885, W. Duke, Sons was emerging as the leading cigarette producer in the country, fueled by mechanization, advertising and Buck Duke's leadership.

By 1890, James B. Duke controlled the largest tobacco industry in the world and the combined firms continued to grow over the next two decades. By the turn of the century, however, public anti-trust sentiment increased rapidly in the United States,

After his retirement in 1880, at the age of sixty Washington Duke retired from the business, and devoted himself to his family, his church and the Republican Party. In 1901, Duke and his sons

established Durham's first hospital for African Americans, Lincoln Hospital on Proctor Street. His civic-mindedness and love of the Methodist Church coalesced in 1890 with the successful campaign to persuade the Methodist-related Trinity College to relocate to the bustling New South city of Durham from Randolph Macon.

Duke's offer of $85,000 and later donations totaling $300,000 for the

College's endowment began a family philanthropic pattern that was continued by his sons and daughters and their children. In 1896, while Trinity College was struggling financially, he offered Trinity an endowment of $100,000 on the condition that women be admitted as residential students "placing them in the future on an equal footing" with the male students. This act attracted widespread attention. The National Suffrage Association offered Duke its vice presidency (which he declined).

In the Spring of 1902, James B. Duke, per the direction of Washington Duke, met with Trinity President Kilgo to get a recommendation of what student from Trinity would be the most eligible candidate to do an internship at American Tobacco Company. His recommendation was Arthur Brown Bradsher. Washington Duke mentored Bradsher until his death three years later. He died the morning of May 8th, 1905 the day Arthur Bradsher was to pitch his last game at Trinity College. Upon word of his death Both Kilgo and Bradsher notified Wake Forest and all interested parties that the game would have to be postponed to a later date.

Arthur Bradsher began work at American Tobacco during the summers of 1902, 1903, 1904. He received his master's degree in business in 1905 and wrote his thesis entitled, "The Growing of Tobacco in the State of North Carolina. American Tobacco hired him in 1906 and he prospered with them until a Supreme Court dissolved the American tobacco Company in 1911. Arthur Bradsher was hired by Export Leaf and Tobacco out of Petersburg Virginia in that year.

In the 1910's members of the Duke family began to plan what would become The Duke Endowment of Trinity College. After the indenture for the $40,000,000 was signed in December 1924 by Washington's youngest son, James B. Duke, Trinity College renamed itself Duke University in honor of Washington Duke. Today, a statue of Washington Duke sits on Duke University's East Campus.

O. Maxwell Gardner
1882-1947

O. Maxwell Gardner was a true renaissance man. He was the youngest in a family of ten children. His mother died when Max was nine years old, and his father passed when he was sixteen.

Max Gardner wrote for the News and Observer to put himself through undergraduate school at North Carolina A&M (State). He selected Arthur Bradsher as the top player in the state of North Carolina for the year 1904. Wooten was also selected on that team.

Gardner majored in chemical engineering, was involved in ROTC, managed the baseball team, served as the president of the senior class, and was a member in the Sigma Nu Fraternity. John Heisman picked Gardner on his all SIAA football team in 1903.

After graduating from A&M (North Carolina State) in 1903, he studied law in graduate school at the University of North Carolina. He was Captain, a strong debater, and a star athlete for both schools' football teams.

Oliver Maxwell Gardner's later life was spent deeply involved in politics. Maxwell was a twice-elected senator, lieutenant governor, and governor of the State of North Carolina.

Gardner was a speechwriter for Franklin Delano Roosevelt and served President Truman as Under Secretary of Treasury. He was his appointed ambassador to Great Britain. Gardner died of a heart attack on his cruise to England.

Billy Laval
1885-1957

Billy Laval was born to coach. The State magazine called him "the greatest collegiate coach in the history of the state of South Carolina."

Laval held positions at Furman, South Carolina, and Newberry college where he coached baseball, basketball, and football. He is the only South Carolina football coach to have seven consecutive winning seasons. He never played football but was a true student of the game.

Billy Laval lost to Arthur Bradsher in one of the most anticipated games in Southern baseball college history. He was 7-0 going into the contest and Bradsher was 12-1. Trinity and Bradsher prevailed, 3-1. They had an important level of respect for each other and remained friends until their deaths

During the 1904 season, he proposed to his girlfriend Elizabeth, who responded, "If you beat Clemson today, I will marry you." Laval pitched Furman to a win, 2-1, and the two were married soon after. He would later joke in speeches, "She has hated Clemson ever since and I'm glad I didn't make that bet against Bradsher and Trinity."

Laval played five years in the minor leagues. During his last year in baseball in 1907, the manager of the Greenville Mountaineers, Tommy Slouch, signed Shoeless Joe Jackson. To evaluate him, he had Laval pitch against Jackson for five days of batting practice. He chose Laval for his assorted repertoire of curveballs and spitballs.

Laval was inducted into South Carolina's Hall of Fame in 1961 and Furman Hall in 1981.

Denton True "Cy" Young
1867-1955

Cy Young was the winningest pitcher in major league history, compiling a 512-316 record over twenty-two seasons.

The talented hurler won thirty games or more in five seasons and twenty games or more ten times. He holds the major league records for most strikeouts (7,356), most career games started (815), and most complete games (749). He had a lifetime 2.63 era and pitched a major league fourth best, seventy-six career shutouts.

In addition, he threw three no-hitters, including the third perfect game in baseball history in 1904.

Young was an assistant coach for Mercer University, helping the pitchers in the spring between 1903 and 1905 before the major league seasons commenced. He witnessed Bradsher's "Miracle at Mercer."

In 1999, eighty-eight years after his final performance, editors at The Sporting News ranked Young fourteenth on their list of "Baseball 100 Greatest Players."

Young was not inducted in his first year of eligibility to the Hall of Fame in 1936, a year that Ty Cobb, Babe Ruth, Honus Wagner, Walter Johnson, and Christy Mathewson were honored. He was inducted the next year, as the eighth member voted in the first two years.

One year after his death, the Cy Young Award was created to honor the previous season's best pitcher. The first recipient of the Award was Don Newcombe of the Dodgers. In 1957, Warren Spahn became the first left-hander to be honored.

Lizzie Chadwick Muse
1885-1970

At the turn of the twentieth century, many people said Lizzie Muse was one of the prettiest and smartest girls in the state of North Carolina. Lizzie was an accomplished pianist and operatic singer.

She was the first born in a family of eight children and was the number one honor roll student in the Durham public school system. At age fifteen she was accepted at Trinity College and enrolled the next year as the youngest female to attend the school. Taking seven courses a semester, she excelled with magna cum laude average of 90. She was one of only two women to receive a full scholarship for her sophomore year.

She left Trinity in 1903 to teach in the Durham public high school system. Her heart was with the underprivileged.

She married Arthur Bradsher in 1907, a year that her mother died of pneumonia at the age of 43. Arthur and Lizzie were married for forty-three years and had five children, four of whom attended their alma mater, Duke University.

Both Lizzie and Arthur were devout participants to the Trinity Methodist Sunday school programs in Durham, Petersburg, and Montreal, Canada.

Lizzie would write a letter to her children every Sunday after church. She bought and ran the Beaufort Inn for ten years in the late fifties and early sixties.

In 1970, Lizzie Muse was laid to rest next to her husband, Arthur Bradsher, in the Maplewood Cemetery.

Walter Chadwick
1882-1948

Walter Chadwick's .321 lifetime batting average at Trinity College ranks him 15th of all-time hitters at Trinity/Duke University. He batted .309 in 1902, .312 in 1903, and .338 in 1904.

Arthur Bradsher batted a team-high .354 in 1903, hitting ahead of Chadwick, who batted in the four-spot. "I was successful because with Walter following me, I always got good pitches to hit." Trinity and Bradsher were 27-3 in the games the two all-stars were battery mates in the years 1902-1904.

Chadwick was one of the best defensive catchers in the South and committed only two errors in Trinity's 1904 championship season and four errors in 1903. No one framed a pitch or fielded a bunt better than Chadwick. He possessed a rocket for an arm, and opponents were reluctant to try and steal against him.

The savvy backstop taught Arthur Bradsher the mechanics of pitching. He took a pitcher that was not on an organized team in high school and mentored him into being one of the best baseball hurlers and players in the history of college baseball.

He was an ATO at Trinity

He did not return for his senior year at Trinity College because of academic problems. Most feel Trinity would have won their second straight SIAA championship if he and Wooten had been in the lineup for the 1905 season.

After college, he went into the fishing business in Beaufort, N.C.

Craig Day
1894-1952

Craig Day pitched for Georgia Tech between 1903 and 1906, compiling a 24-8 record.

John Heisman picked Day as back-up pitcher to Arthur Bradsher on the 1905 All-Southern team. His most notable win was against Bradsher that year. Day and Tech prevailed, 3-2. The game was called "the greatest game ever pitched in Dixieland," and both pitchers went the distance of twelve innings.

In the 1905 season, the Tech pitcher won eleven of the thirteen contests he started, and twelve of those were complete games.

The next year, he led Georgia Tech to one of the best seasons in its history, with a team record of 23-3. His record for 1906 was 8-2. Craig Day is honored in the Georgia Tech information guide, which points out a few of his records: complete games in 1904 (7), complete games in 1905 (12), complete games in 1906 (9), and most innings pitched in a season (108).

In four years, Day struck out 202 batters in 268 innings. The hurler from Georgia Tech was also an excellent hitter and baserunner. He also played end on the football team.

Craig Day was inducted in the first Hall of Fame induction class at Georgia Tech in 1962.

1906 Ga. Tech S.I.A.A Championship Team with a 23-4 Record.

Tommy McMillan
1888-1966

Tommy McMillan was a member of one of Georgia Tech's all-time best baseball teams. Between the years 1905 and 1906, the team compiled a 37-6 record.

He was chosen by John Heisman as his starting shortstop on his 1905 All-Southern-Conference team along with teammates Gager and Craig Day. Heisman nicknamed him "Rebel." At five-foot-five-inches and 130 pounds, he was pound for pound the toughest player in the league and certainly one of the most difficult to pitch to.

Arthur Bradsher said after the 'Greatest game ever played in Dixieland,' "If there was one walk, I gave up in my college career I regretted, it was the leadoff walk to Tommy McMillan. I remember to this day all eleven pitches I threw to him. He stole second, stole third and scored on a ball thrown over the third baseman's head."

The 1906 squad had one of the most successful years of a Tech team ever, winning twenty-three games out of twenty-six and capturing the SIAA championship. All-stars McMillan, Day, Chip Robert, and Ed Lafitte manned the Tech team.

McMillan played five seasons in Major League Baseball (MLB) from 1908-1912 for the Brooklyn Superbas (Dodgers), Cincinnati Reds, and the New York Highlanders.

He passed away at seventy-eight years of age in 1966.

Wilbur Wade Card
1873-1948

W. W. Card was a star athlete at Trinity College in 1895. A hard-hitting outfielder, he set several batting records, was Captain of the 1899 team, and eventually earned the nickname "Cap."

After graduating in 1900, Card attended the School of Physical Education at Harvard University for two years. In the fall of 1902, Card was invited by John Carlisle Kilgo, Trinity president, to return to his former college and become the director of the new physical education program there.

He instructed Card to meet with Bradsher on his first day on campus. Separated by only two years, the two developed a brotherly relationship until their deaths.

Card is known as the "Father of intercollegiate basketball in North Carolina," as he coached Trinity against Wake Forest in the first game played in the state in 1906 until 1912 and compiled a 30-17 (.638) record.

Wilbur Wade Card was honored in 1946 with a portrait painted by Paul Whitener, a 1938 graduate and former football player from Hickory, North Carolina. He donated the painting to Duke with an agreement that the portrait be hung between two of his favorite athletes, Arthur Bradsher and Bob Gantt.

The building in which the portraits were hung was named the Card Gymnasium in 1956. He served as athletic director at Trinity/ Duke until his death.

The gravesites of Card and Bradsher sit fifty feet apart in Maplewood Cemetery.

Walter Clarkson
1878-1946

Walter Clarkson was born into a baseball family. Two brothers, "Dad" and John played in the majors. John won 328 games between 1882 and 1895. In 1885, John became Chicago's principal starting pitcher and appeared in 70 games, pitched 623 innings and 68 complete games. He also won 53 games. He was elected into the MLB Hall of Fame in 1963.

Walter Clarkson played for one of the strongest college teams to ever take the field. He pitched for Harvard between 1901 and 1904. He had a won-loss record of 24-7. Many Northern writers proclaimed him the best twirler in college baseball.

At times Clarkson had bouts of wildness, some say because of his smaller five-foot-eight-inch stature to overthrow the ball.

His first game for the Harvard varsity was as a twenty-three-year-old during his sophomore year. Highlights of his career included beating rival Yale all five times he faced them.

He was kicked off the Harvard team and stripped of his Captainship after admitting he was playing in college as an amateur but had taken money from the New York Highlanders months earlier.

Clarkson's record in professional baseball was mediocre. He left baseball after five years with an 18-16 record.

After his brief career, he became a shoe salesclerk.

Walter Clarkson was inducted in the Harvard Club Hall of Fame in 1972.

John Carlisle Kilgo
1861-1922

After the hard times of the depression of 1893, the trustees at Trinity turned to John Carlisle Kilgo (1861-1922), then financial agent of Wofford College, and a preacher of great renown.

Kilgo became the fourth president at Trinity College in August. He was the second president on the Trinity campus and served until 1910. He caught the eye of the search committee because of his success at Wofford College. In 1888 Kilgo was made financial agent of Wofford College, which was owned by the South Carolina Conference of the Methodist Church.

At thirty-three years of age, he had a reputation as a committed Methodist churchman, fiery orator, an educator with high academic standards, and a firm belief in academic freedom.

Well-known for his staunch defense of the Bassett Affair, where Trinity professor John Spencer Bassett praised African-American leader Booker T. Washington, Kilgo invited Washington to speak on the Trinity campus in 1896. Washington's appearance at Trinity was his first on a white Southern college campus.

Additional principles firmly established during Kilgo's presidency include high standards in admissions, quality over numbers, hiring the best possible faculty, and the equal education of women with men.

Today, a quad on the Duke University campus is named after him.

After leaving Trinity in 1910, Kilgo was elected as a bishop of the Methodist Episcopal Church, South. As bishop, Kilgo oversaw many annual conferences.

Dr. Kilgo married Arthur Brown Bradsher and Lizzie Chadwick Muse at her father's home on August 25, 1907. They named their first son, Charles, with the middle name Kilgo in his honor.

John C. Kilgo died on August 10, 1922, at the age of sixty-one.

BASEBALL GLOSSARY
A-Z

Banjo Hitter • A batter who lacks power. A banjo hitter usually hits bloop singles, often just past the infield dirt, and would have a low slugging percentage. The name is said to come from the twanging sound of the bat at contact, like that of a banjo.

Bases Loaded • Runners on first, second, and third base.

Bat on the Ball • To hit the ball with the bat — whether into fair territory or foul.

Batter's Box • A rectangle on either side of home plate in which the batter must be standing for fair play to resume.

Battery • The pitcher and catcher considered as a single unit.

Batterymates • A pitcher and catcher from the same team.

Bazooka • A strong throwing arm. A gun, a cannon, a rifle.

Beanball • A pitch intentionally thrown to hit the batter if he does not move out of the way, especially when directed at the head (or the "bean" in old-fashioned slang).

Bender • A curveball.

Big as a Grapefruit • When a hitter sees the pitch so well that it appears to be larger than its actual size, he may describe the ball as being "as big as a grapefruit". "After hitting a 565-foot home run, Mickey Mantle once said, 'I just saw the ball as big as a grapefruit'. During a slump, Joe 'Ducky' Medwick of the St. Louis Cardinals said he was 'swinging at aspirins'."

Bingle • A single. A base hit that ends up with the hitter on first base.

Bleeder • A weakly hit ground ball that goes for a base hit. A scratch hit.

blistered • A ball that is hit so hard that it seems to generate its own heat may be said to have been blistered.

Block the Plate • A catcher who puts a foot, leg, or whole body between home plate and a runner attempting to score, is said to "block the plate". Blocking the plate is a dangerous tactic.

Blooper • A blooper or bloop is a weakly hit fly ball that drops in for a single between an infielder and an outfielder. Also known as a bloop single, a dying quail, or a duck snort.

Blue Darter • A hard-hit line drive. Also referred to as a "frozen rope."

Booted • Made an error, kicked it – typically referring to a misplay on a ground ball.

Bottom Dropped Out of It • Sometimes said of a sinker or drop ball, implying that a pitch suddenly moved downward as if it fell through a trap door or rolled off a table.

Baseball Glossary

Brushback • A pitch intentionally thrown close to a batter to intimidate him, i.e., to "brush him back" from the plate. Also referred to as a duster, a purpose pitch or chin music.

Buck and Change • A player batting between .100 and .199 is said to be batting "a buck and change" or, more specifically, the equivalent average in dollars (bucks) and cents (change). Example: A batter batting .190 is said to be batting "a buck ninety."

Bullpen • The area off the field used by pitchers and catchers to warm up before taking the mound.

cannon • A strong arm. Also, a gun.

can of corn • A high, easy-to-catch, fly ball hit to the outfield. The phrase is said to have originated in the nineteenth century and relates to an old-time grocer's method of getting canned goods down from a high shelf. Using a stick with a hook on the end, a grocer could tip a can so that it would fall for an easy catch into his apron.

caught looking • A term used when the third strike is called on a batter without the batter attempting to swing at the pitch.

chatter • To verbally challenge or taunt to distract the opposing batter. Fans and players alike participate in chatter. "Heybattabattabatta" is an example of common baseball chatter.

chin music • A high and tight, up and in pitch meant to knock a batter back from home plate to avoid being hit on the chin. Also known as a brush-back or purpose pitch.

choke up • A batter "chokes up" by sliding his hands up from the knob end of the bat to give him more control over his bat. It reduces the power and increases the control.

comebacker • A ball batted directly back to the pitcher.

command • The advanced skill of a pitcher's ability to throw a pitch where he intends to. Contrast with control, which is just the ability to throw strikes, command is the ability to hit particular spots in or out of the strike zone.

complete game • The act of a pitcher pitching an entire game, without the benefit of a relief pitcher. A complete game can be either a win or a loss. It can be awarded to a pitcher even if he pitches less than or more than nine innings, if he pitches the entire game.

corners • When runners are "at the corners," they are at first base and third base on the baseball   diamond, with no runner on second base.

count • The number of balls and strikes a batsman has in his current at bat. Usually announced as a pair of numbers, for instance "3–0."

crack of the bat • The sound of the bat hitting the ball.

crooked number • A number other than a zero or a one, referring to the appearance of the actual number. A team which is able to score two or more runs in an inning is said to "hang a crooked number" on the scoreboard.

crowd the plate • When a batter sets his stance extremely close to the plate, sometimes covering up part of the strike zone. A player that crows the plate should expect a brushback from the pitcher.

crush the ball • A batter who hits a ball extremely hard and far might be said to crush the ball, as if he had destroyed the baseball or at least changed its shape. Smacked, murdered, clobbered the ball are terms also used.

curveball • A pitch that curves or breaks from a straight or expected flight path toward home plate. Also called a curve, a bender, Uncle Charles, the deuce, the hook, a yacker and number two.

cut • A swing of the bat.

cut-off man • A fielder that "cuts off" a long throw to an important target. This tactic increases accuracy over long distances and shortens the time required to get a ball to a specific place.

Often the shortstop, second baseman, or first baseman will be the "cut-off man" or "relay man" for a long throw from the outfield to third base or home plate.

dark one • A pitch that is difficult to see, much less hit. "Throw him the dark one" is an encouragement to the pitcher, typically given with two strikes, to throw a strike past the batter.

deliver •   To deliver is to pitch. Announcer: "Koufax delivers. ... Strike three!!!"

deuce • A curveball, because the catcher's sign is usually made by extending the first two fingers.

diamond • The layout of the four bases in the infield. It's actually a square 90 feet (27 m) on each side, but from the stands it resembles a parallelogram or "diamond."

deep in the count • When a lot of ball have been thrown to a batter and the count reaches three ball and two strikes.

dinger • A home run or round-tripper.

double • A hit where the batter makes it safely to second base before the ball can be returned to the infield. Also, a two-base hit.

double play • A play by the defense where two offensive players are put out as a result of continuous action resulting in two outs. A typical example is the 6-4-3 double play.

drop ball • A sinkerball. Extreme 12-to-6 curveballs are also referred to as "drop balls", since they start high and dive as they reach the plate. They appear to drop off or roll off the table.

duck snort • A softly hit ball that goes over the infielders and lands in the outfield for a hit. Originally called a "duck fart."

ducks on the pond • Runners on second or third base, but especially when the bases are loaded.

duster, dust-off pitch • A brushback pitch, often thrown so far inside that the batter drops to the ground and hits the dust.

This tactic increases accuracy over long distances and shortens the time required to get a ball to a specific place.

dying quail • A batted ball that drops in front of the outfielders for a hit, often unexpectedly (like a shot bird). Also known as a blooper, a chinker, bloop single, a bleeder, or a gork.

earned run • Any run for which the pitcher is held accountable (i.e., the run did not score as a result of a fielding error or a passed ball). Primarily used to calculate the earned run average. In determining earned runs, an error charged to a pitcher is treated exactly like an error charged to any other fielder.

error • An error is an act of a fielder misplaying a ball in a manner that allows a batter or baserunner to reach one or more additional bases, when that advance could have been prevented by ordinary effort by the fielder. Because the pitcher and catcher handle the ball so much, some misplays by them are called "wild pitch and passed ball" and are not counted as errors. Also referred to as bobble, blooper, muff, miscue, flub, kick or boot.

expand the strike zone • When a pitcher gets ahead in the count, he "expands the strike zone" because the hitter will be more likely to swing at a pitch that's at the edge or out of the strike zone or in some other location where he can't hit it.

fall off the table • A pitch is said to "fall off the table" when it starts in the strike zone or appears hittable to the batter and ends low or in the dirt. This term is mainly used for change ups and split-fingered fastballs, and occasionally for an overhand curveball.

fan • To "fan" a batter is to strike him out, especially a swinging strike three.

framing a pitch • "Framing is very subtlety sliding that ball back into the strike zone, so the umpire will call it for a strike. The catcher needs to work with the finesse of a highly skilled jewel thief." You put his hands against his chest with his thumbs touching and quickly moved them two inches to the left. You steal balls that are off the plate and making them look like strikes to the ump.

fencebuster • A slugger.

flashing the leather • Making an outstanding or difficult defensive play. A player who regularly makes difficult defensive plays may be described as a "leather flasher."

freeze the batter • Pitcher fools the batter so badly that he does not swing at a good pitch.

four-bagger • A home run. Never mind that the 4th "bag" is actually a plate.

free pass • A base on balls or a walk.

gap • The space between outfielders. Also, alley. A ball hit in the gap is sometimes called a flapper or a gapper.

gap hitter • Hits with power up the alleys and tends to get a lot of doubles. A doubles hitter.

gas • A fastball. "Give him [the batter] the gas"; as in stepping on a car's gas pedal to accelerate.

gem • A very well-pitched game, almost always a win, in which the pitcher allows few if any hits and at most a run or two.

get on one's horse • When a fielder (usually an outfielder) runs extremely fast towards a hard-hit ball in an effort to catch it.

go quietly • When a team fails to mount a strong offense, such as going 1–2–3 in an inning, it may be said to have "gone quietly gone.

A ball hit over the wall, a home run. Announcer: "That ball is gone." That's a reduction of the timeless phrase, "Going . . . going . . . gone."

good eye • A hitter who has excellent awareness of the strike zone and is able to lay off pitches that are barely out of the strike zone, is said to have a "good eye."

goose egg • A zero on the scoreboard.

got a piece of it • When a batter hits a foul ball or foul tip, perhaps surviving a two strike count and remaining at bat.

grand slam • Home run hit with the bases loaded. Also, called a granny.

green light • Permission from the manager for a batter or runner to be aggressive. Examples include permission for the batter to swing away on a 3–0 count or for a runner to steal a base

gun down • To throw out a runner.

hammer • To hit the ball hard, typically for extra bases.

handcuff • A hard-hit ground ball that bounces directly at an infielder may be difficult for him to get his hands up in time to grab. Also a pitch thrown high and inside may handcuff a batter because he can't get his hands far enough away from his body to swing the bat.

heart of the plate • Middle of home plate.

help his own cause • Said of a pitcher who knocks in runs as a hitter, thereby helping himself to earn credit for a win.

high and tight • A location pitch thrown above the strike zone and close to the batter. Also known as high cheese, high hard one, and high heat.

hill • The pitcher's mound.

hit the deck • When a batter drops or dives to the ground to avoid being hit by a pitch.

home • Home Plate.

home cooking • When a player for the home team gets a favorable or generous call from the official scorer, the players may refer to the scorer's call as "home cooking." For example, the scorer may credit a batter for a base hit on a batted ball that a fielder bobbled briefly and then failed to make a putout.

hook slide • A foot-first slide to a base in a baseball game in which the runner with both legs extended throws the body to either side to avoid the fielder covering the base and hooks the base with the inside foot.

hurler • A pitcher.

immaculate inning • A half-inning in which the pitcher strikes out all three batters he faces on exactly nine pitches—that is, throwing nothing but strikes.

insurance run • A run scored by a team already in the lead. These surplus runs do not affect the game outcome but serve as "insurance" against the team giving up runs later.

in the hole • The spaces between the first baseman and second baseman and between the shortstop and the third baseman, one of the usual places where a ground ball must go for a hit.

jam • To pitch a ball in on the hands of a batter to keep him from extending his arms on his swing.

jerk • To hit the ball hard, typically used to refer to pulling the ball over the fence for a home run. "He jerked one of his patented doubles into the left-field corner." Also yank.

K • The traditional abbreviation for a strikeout. A backwards K is often used to denote a called strikeout. Invented by Henry Chadwick in 1869 by taking the "most prominent" letter of "struck" and reinforced by inference of "knockout" or "K.O." That connotation still exists, when the announcer says the pitcher "punched out" the batter, a play on words that also refers to "punching" a time clock and the punching motion that the home plate umpire usually makes on a called third strike.

keep the hitter honest • A pitcher needs to mix up his pitches and thereby "keep the hitter honest" by making it difficult for the hitter to anticipate the type, speed, and location of the next pitch.

kicked • A player who makes an error fielding a ground ball may be said to have "kicked the ball" or "kicked it".

knockout pitch • Strikeout pitch

laugher • A game in which one team gets a large lead, perhaps early in the game, and it appears that the other team has no chance at all of catching up. An easy win; a romp; a blowout.

left on base • A baserunner is said to be left on base (LOB) or stranded when the half-inning ends.

letter high • Is one that crosses the plate at the height of the letters on the batter's chest. Also see at the letters.

line drive • Also known as a liner, a line drive is a batted ball that is hit hard in the air and has a low arc. See also frozen rope.

live on the corners • A pitcher who "lives on the corners" throws most of his pitches on the inside or outside black edges of home plate. He's not inclined to try to overwhelm the hitter with hard pitches down the center of the plate.

lord charles • A slang term for a "12-to-6" curveball. Similar to Uncle Charlie.

lumber • A baseball bat. Timber Sometimes used in reference to a powerful offensive showing.

meat of the bat • On the barrel or fat end of the bat, but not too close to the end, is the "meat of the bat" where a hitter tries to make contact with the pitched ball.

mechanics • Proper use of hips and legs and the right stride and windup.

meat of the order • Refers to the 3, 4, 5 and sometimes 6 hitters in the lineup and usually the strongest hitters.

mound • The pitcher's mound is a raised section in the middle of the diamond where the pitcher stands when throwing the pitch. From 1903 through 1968 this height limit was set at 15 inches.

murdered • To hit a ball with great force. Smacked, scalded, smashed, swatted.

nibble • When a pitcher focuses on pitching just at the left or right edges of home plate rather than throwing a pitch over the heart of the plate where a batter can get the meat of the bat on the ball, he's said to nibble at the edges.

no-hitter • A game in which one team does not get any hits, a rare feat for a pitcher, especially at the major league level.

no-no • A no-hitter and a shut-out. Thus, no hits, no runs.

on-deck • The next batter due to bat after the current batter.

on his horse • Running at full speed, especially in reference to an outfielder tracking down a fly ball.

on the black • The edge of home plate derived from the black border of the plate that is buried when the plate is correctly installed.

A pitch that just nicks the edge of the zone for a called strike.

one-two-three inning • Side retired in order. Three up, three down.

out-dueled • Out pitched the opposition.

to paint • To throw pitches at the edges of the strike zone. Paint the black or paint the corner.

park • To hit a home run. "He parked a three-run homer."

passed ball • A catcher is charged with a passed ball when he fails to hold or control a legally pitched ball which, should have been held or controlled with ordinary effort, and which permits a runner or runners to advance at least one base.

pine tar • A sticky substance used by batters to improve their grip on the bat.

pinpoint control • A pitcher who is able to throw the ball to a precise spot in the strike zone.

pitch • A baseball delivered by the pitcher from the pitcher's mound to the batter.

pitcher's best friend • A nickname for a double play.

pitchout • A defensive tactic used to pick off a baserunner, typically employed when the defense thinks that a stolen base play is planned. The pitch is thrown outside, and the catcher catches it while standing, and can quickly throw to a base.

plunked • Hit by a pitch. Also beaned.

power hitter • A powerful batter who hits many home runs and extra base hits, but who may not have a high batting average, due to an "all or nothing" hitting approach

punch-out • A strikeout. Named such because the umpire will typically make a punching-like signal on the third strike, especially if the batter does not swing at the pitch.

receiver • Another term for catcher. Also backstop, signal caller.

relay • A defensive technique where the ball is thrown by an outfielder to an infielder who then throws to the final target. This is done because accurate throws are more difficult over long distances and the ball loses a considerable amount of speed the farther it must be thrown. Also called cut-off.

retire the batter • To get the batter out.

ring him up • A strikeout. The phrase is probably drawn by analogy to cashiers who ring up the total on the cash register when a customer is ready to pay up. It also comes from the "cha-ching" motion that plate umpires use to signal a strikeout. "Outside corner, ring him up, strike three called!"

rip • To hit a hard line drive.

robbed • When a fielder makes a spectacular play the denies the batter a hit or a home run, the batter may be said to have been "robbed" by the fielder — as if the fielder had taken away something that belonged to the hitter.

rope • A hard line drive. Also see "frozen rope." Sometimes used as a verb: "He roped one up the middle."

round-tripper • A home run. The analogy is to a commuter who buys a round-trip ticket from home plate to second base and back again to home. A dinger.

rubber • The rubber, formally termed the pitching plate, is a white rubber strip the front of which is exactly sixty feet six inches (18.4 m) from the rear point of home plate. A pitcher will push off the rubber with his foot in order to gain velocity toward home plate when pitching.

rubber arm • A pitcher is said to have a "rubber arm" if he can throw many pitches without tiring. Relief pitchers who can pitch consecutive days with the same effectiveness tend to be known as "rubber arms."

runners at the corners • runners on 1st and 3rd, with 2nd base open.

sack • Synonymous with bag. 1st, 2nd, or 3rd base. A player who plays a particular base might be called a sacker. Most often this is the second sacker (second baseman).

saw off • When a pitcher gets a batter to hit the ball on the handle, and the batter hits the ball weakly or even breaks his bat, the pitcher may be said to have sawed off the bat.

sacrifice bunt • A sacrifice bunt is the act of deliberately bunting the ball in a manner that allows a runner on base to advance to another base, while the batter is himself put out.

seeing-eye ball • A batted ground ball that just eludes capture by an infielder, just out of infielder's range, as if it could "see" where it needed to go.

send a runner • If a coach signals for a runner to attempt to steal a base, he is "sending" a runner.

set the table • To get runners on base ahead of the power hitters in the lineup.

shake off the sign • A pitcher who disagrees with the catcher's call for the next pitch may shake off the sign by shaking his head "no," thereby telling the catcher to call for a different pitch.

shoestring catch • When a fielder, usually an outfielder, catches a ball just before it hits the ground ("off his shoe tops"), and remains running while doing so.

shutout • A pitcher shuts out his opponent when he prevents them from scoring any runs in a given game.

shuts the door • When a pitcher, generally the closer, finishes the ballgame with a save or makes the last out.

side retired • When the third out of an inning is called, the "side is retired" and the other team takes its turn at bat.

sign • A catcher is said to call the game by sending signs to the pitcher calling for a particular pitch. After he moves into his crouch, the catcher gives the sign by placing his non-glove hand between his legs and using his fist, fingers, wags, or taps against his inner thigh to tell the pitcher what type of pitch to throw (fastball, curve, etc.) as well as the location.

slide • A slide is when a player drops to the ground when running toward a base, to avoid a tag.

small ball • A strategy by which teams attempt to score runs using bunting and sacrifice plays; usually used in a situation where one run will tie or win the game; manufacturing runs.

southpaw • Left-hander, especially a pitcher.

spaldings • **Baseballs.**

stanza • An inning.

swiped • Stole a base.

stolen base • In baseball, a stolen base (or "steal") occurs when a baserunner successfully advances to the next base while the pitcher is delivering the ball to home plate.

strike out the side • A pitcher is said to "strike out the side" when he retires all three batters in a half inning by striking them out. All three batters who made outs were out on strikes, no matter what other batters did in that half inning.

struck out looking • A batter called out on strikes without swinging on the third strike is said to have "struck out looking." Labeled with a backwards "K" by some scorecard keepers. Commentators have also been known to use the slang term "just browsing" or "window shopping."

struck out swinging • A batter called out on strikes when swinging at the third strike is said to have "struck out swinging." Usually labeled with the traditional forward "K" on scorecards.

through the wickets • When a batted ball passes through the legs of a player on the field (most commonly an infielder) it's often said, "That one went right through the wickets." Usually ruled an error by the scorer.

tore the cover off the ball • Hit the ball so hard that the batter figuratively tore the cover off the ball.

turn two • To execute a double play.

triple • A three-base hit.

twin killing • A double play

twirler • An old-fashioned term for a pitcher. In the early years, pitchers would often twirl their arms in a circle one or more times before delivering the ball, literally using a "windup," in the belief it would reduce stress on their arms. The terms "twirler" and "twirling" faded along with that motion. The modern term "hurler" is effectively the substitute term.

two-bagger • A double.

two in the well • Two outs.

uncle charles • A curveball. A hook, A bender.

walk • A base on balls. A free pass.

waste a pitch • When a pitcher gets ahead in the count, he may choose to throw a pitch that is outside the strike zone in hopes that the batter will chase a pitch he can't hit.

wheelhouse • A hitter's power zone. Usually a pitch waist-high and over the heart of the plate.

wheels • Legs. A player who runs the bases fast has great wheels.

whiff • A swinging strike (referring to the bat whiffing through the air without contacting the ball).

window shopping • Caught looking for strike three.

worm burner • A hard-hit ground ball that "burns" the ground. A daisy cutter.

ACKNOWLEDGMENTS

Without the following people's encouragement, help, and guidance this book would not have been possible.

Best friends are those that always have your best interests in mind. I thank you Shelby White for your hours spent reading and reviewing my work, many phone calls, and your honest feedback.

This has been a work of passionate love and has brought our family closer together. Appreciation fills my heart for all the Bradsher family who shared their stories and for your interest and involvement in honoring our grandparents.

Special thanks to Liz, my sister, who inherited my grandmother's kindness. The memories you have shared are priceless and are the backbone of my story of the summers spent at the farm/river house, Summerlea.

Milam Propst was my first mentor. Her inspirational talks and guidance on the steps necessary to improve my writing skills were invaluable

The brilliance and caring of my gracious friends Gray and Cynthia Oliver are applauded. You listened to what I was trying to convey and helped me make it happen. Thank you for letting me bend your ear. Cynthia your critique and review of my full manuscript helped me make valuable changes to my work.

I give special thanks to my editor Gerald Shaw for his good eye and thoroughness and the willingness to go the extra mile to make things right. Working with you has been a fruitful journey. Lisa Margolis, I am very appreciative of the excellent job you did in constructing the Wikipedia on Arthur Brown Bradsher. Your work on this piece was a home run.

My hat goes off for Art Chase at Duke University for the gracious offer to put Arthur Bradsher on the Hall of Fame ballot at Duke in the year 2020.

Amy McDonald at the Duke library you have been a loyal

friend and so helpful in my research. Your digging deep for hundred-year-old pictures, transcripts and records have brought a special light and truth to my book.

Enough credit cannot be given for the marvelous job my graphic designer, Ned Kandul achieved in the formatting of "King of the Southern Diamond." The challenging task of the proper placement of over seventy-six photographs was done with a keen eye and brought a handsome and inviting look to my work. Steve Slaton and North Georgia Reprographics were great closers to my project. I could not be more pleased with the printing of my book.

I applaud the members of the Atlanta Writers Club and the president George Weinstein, past presidents Ron Aiken, and officer Emerita VP of programs, Valerie Connors. Your monthly programs are well planned, and the guest speakers are very informative.

Gelia Dolcimascolo, the leader of our writers circle you have in so many ways helped expand our knowledge of the craft of writing. You have brought us together every Friday for years and we are better writers for that.

I salute my friends putting pen to paper: Ed, Harry, Michael, Susan, Freddie, Alexandra, Elizabeth, Jayna, Mike, Gary, and Josh in my writer's circles. We will never win without teamwork. Your writing and constructive advice always inspires me.

Michael March you are a talented writer and have been a wonderful friend in the journey of writing "King of the Southern Diamond." Your daily check-ins, writing tips and suggestions have been so helpful.

Finally, I would like to acknowledge all those that have the courage to write. I hope I can be there for many of you and give back as much that has been given to me in this exciting trip around the bases.

REFERENCES

All Fifty-Nine Games Bradsher Pitched In

1. "Hobbs Brothers Defeat Trinity and Bradsher 1-0." The Greensboro Patriot. March 29, 1905. P.4. Retrieved July 1. 2018 via Newspapers.com.

2. "Bradsher and Trinity Lose to Lafayette. William Barre Times Leader, the Evening News. P.8. March 30.1905. Retrieved July 1, 2018, via Newspapers.com.

3. "Trinity and Bradsher Shut Out Wake Forest 4-0." The Morning Post (Raleigh, North Carolina) p.2. April 2, 1905. Retrieved June 15, 2018, via Newspapers.com.

4. Bradsher and Trinity Defeat W. & L. 9-3. Bradsher Pins 2 Hitter. The Times-Dispatch (Richmond Virginia). April 5, 1905. p.7. Retrieved June 15, 2018, via Newspapers.com.

5. "Crack Trinity Twirler Fanned 22 Men Without A Hit." Macon News Saturday Evening. April 8, 1905. Retrieved June 15, 2018, via Newspapers.com.

6. "Champion Game Goes to Tech." The Atlanta Constitution. P.10. April 11, 1905. Retrieved July 1, 1905, via Newspapers.com.

7. "Clemson Took Trinity's Scalp." The Greenville News. April 13, 1905. p.1. Retrieved July 15, 2018, via Newspapers.com.

8. "Trinity Defeats Wofford." The Charlotte Observer. April 15, 1905. p.8. Retrieved July 22, 2018, via Newspapers.com.

9. "Bradsher Mows Down 18 Orangemen." The Atlanta Constitution. April 19.1905. p.11. Retrieved June 15, 2018, via Newspapers.com.

10. "A Twin Goose Egg. No Runs No Hits." News and Observer (Raleigh, North Carolina). April 26, 1905. p.1. Retrieved June 15, 2018, via Newspapers.com.

11. "In the Baseball World. Bradsher Spins Four Hitter." The Charlotte News. April 28, 1905. p.6. Retrieved May 30, 2018, via Newspapers.com.

12. "Trinity and Bradsher Beat Wake 2-1. Neither Team Had an Earned Run." News and Observer (Raleigh, North Carolina). May 2, 1905. p.5. Retrieved June 15, 201, via Newspapers.com.

13. "Wake Wins Over Bradsher in Final Game 1-0." The Times-Dispatch (Richmond Virginia). May 16, 1905. p.7. Retrieved April 15, 2018, via Newspapers.com.

14. "Trinity Beat Wake in a Great Pitchers Battle." The Morning Post (Raleigh, North Carolina). May 3, 1905. p.6. Retrieved May 1, 2018, via Newspapers.com.

15. "Bradsher No-Hits Trinity Park 9-0." The Durham Sun. March 26, 1904. p.1. Retrieved April 15, 2018, via Newspapers.com.

16. "Bradsher No-Hits Oak Ridge." The Durham Sun. March 19, 1904. p.4. Retrieved

April 10, 2018, via Newspapers.com.

17. "Bradsher Pitches Seven No-Hit Innings Against Guilford." The Atlanta Constitution. March 27, 1904. p.8. Retrieved April 1, 2018, via Newspapers. Com.

18. "Bradsher and Trinity Whip Lafayette." News and Observer (Raleigh, North Carolina). March 30, 1904. p.5. Retrieved April 1, 2018, via Newspapers.com.

19. "Bradsher 2 Hits Strong Syracuse Team." The Durham Sun. April 4, 1904. p.4. Retrieved April 1, 2018, via Newspapers.com.

20. "Bradsher and Trinity Defeat Gettysburg and Plank." News and Observer (Raleigh, North Carolina). April 5, 1904. p.5. Retrieved April 1, 2018, via Newspapers.com.

21. "Close and Exciting Game. Trinity Defeats Guilford 2-1." The Morning Post (Raleigh, North Carolina). April 7, 1904. p.1. Retrieved April 1, 2018, via Newspapers.com.

22. "Trinity Outlasts Wake in the Rain 11-9." The Morning Post (Raleigh, North Carolina). April 21, 1904. p.5. Retrieved April 1, 2018, via Newspapers.com.

23. "Bradsher Shuts Out Wake 1-0." The Charlotte Observer. April 24, 1904. p.8. Retrieved April 1, 2018, via Newspapers.com.

24. "A.&M. Wins Over Trinity." The Morning Post (Raleigh, North Carolina). April 26, 1904. p.5. Retrieved April 1, 2018, via Newspapers.com.

25. "Bradsher Defeats A.&M. and Strikes Out 18." The Charlotte Observer. April 30, 1904. p.8. Retrieved April 1, 2018, via Newspapers.com.

26. "Bradsher Downs Wofford and Strikes Out 17." The Charlotte Observer. May 5, 1904. p.8. Retrieved April 1, 2018, via Newspapers.com.

27. Bradsher Beats Billy Laval 3-1. Loses a Shutout with Two Strikes, Two Outs.: Greenville Times. May 7, 1904. p.1. Retrieved April 1, 2018, via Newspapers.com.

28. "Bradsher Shuts Out Wofford." Retrieved April 1, 2018, via Newspapers.com. "Bradsher

29. Bradsher Gets Win Over Trinity Park. Pitches 5 Innings. The Durham Sun. March 15, 1903. p.1. Retrieved April 1, 2018, via Newspapers.com.

30. Trinity Park and Trinity Defeat a Strong Lafayette Team 6-3. Bradsher in Perfect Control." The Durham Sun. March 26, 1903. p.1. Retrieved April 1, 2018, via Newspapers.com.

31. "Bradsher and Trinity Defeat a Strong Gettysburg Team." The Morning Post (Raleigh, North Carolina). April 26, 1904. p.5. Retrieved April 1, 2018, via Newspapers.com.

32. "Bradsher Lose First Game of Season, Trinity Commits 10 Errors." News and Observer (Raleigh, North Carolina). April 11, 1903. p.1. Retrieved April 1, 2018, via Newspapers.com.

33. "Bradsher Defeats South Carolina 5-4." Spins a 5 Hitter. The Durham Sun. April 18, 1903. p.4. Retrieved April 1, 2018, via Newspapers.com.

34. "Bradsher Defeats Charlotte Pro Team and Gets 3 Hits." The Morning Post (Raleigh, North Carolina). April 26, 1904. p.5. Retrieved April 1, 2018, via Newspapers.com.

35. "Bradsher Strikes Out 17 and Defeats Davidson 4-2." The Atlanta Constitution. April 30, 1903. p.1. Retrieved April 1, 2018, via Newspapers.com.

36. "Trinity Defeats Davidson 5-2." Bradsher Strikes Out 13. The Durham Sun. April 28, 1903. p.4. Retrieved April 1, 2018, via Newspapers.com.

37. "Bradsher Pitches Only Game of Relief in His 5 Year Career. Pitches 6 Perfect Innings and Strikes Out 12." The Atlanta Constitution. May 5, 1903. p.12. Retrieved April 1, 2018, via Newspapers.com.

38. "Bradsher Roughed Up by Tech 10-0." The Atlanta Constitution. May 5, 1903. p.9. Retrieved April 1, 2018, via Newspapers.com.

39. "Trinity and Bradsher Defeat Wofford 8-4." The Atlanta Constitution. May 7, 1903. p.4. Retrieved March 1, 2018, via Newspapers.com.

40. "Bradsher Shuts Out Horner in Season Opener." The Durham Sun. March 24, 1902. p.1. Retrieved April 1, 2018, via Newspapers.com.

41. "Bradsher and Trinity Defeat Trinity Park 13-0." The Morning Post (Raleigh, North Carolina). March 25, 1902. p.2. Retrieved February 15, 2018, via Newspapers.com.

42. "Bradsher Runs Out of Gas Against Lafayette." The Morning Post (Raleigh, North Carolina). March 27, 1902. p.2. Retrieved February 15, 2018, via Newspapers.com.

43. "Davidson Defeats Trinity and Bradsher 6-2." The Charlotte Observer. April 1, 1902. p.1. Retrieved April 1, 2018, via Newspapers.com.

44. "Bradsher with Chadwick Defeat Hobart 4-2." The Durham Sun. April 5, 1902. p.1. Retrieved April 1, 2018, via Newspapers.com.

45. "Trinity Commits 12 Errors. Bradsher Beats A.& M. 10-7." The Morning Post (Raleigh, North Carolina). April 11, 1902. p.5. Retrieved February 1, 2018, via Newspapers.com.

46. Bradsher No-Hits Wake and Strikes Out 19." The Morning Post (Raleigh, North Carolina). April 15, 1902. p.6. Retrieved February 15, 2018, via Newspapers.com.

47. "Bradsher Pitches Second Shutout in 3 Days. Trinity Beats Guilford 13-0." The Durham Sun. February 15, 1902. p.1. Retrieved April 1, 2018, via Newspapers.com.

48. "Bradsher Has the Baptists At His Mercy. Allows 2 Hits." The Charlotte Observer. April 23, 1902. p.4. Retrieved February 1, 2018, via Newspapers.com.

49. "Bradsher Beats Durham Professionals." The Morning Post (Raleigh, North Carolina). April 26, 1902. p.1. Retrieved February 1, 2018, via Newspapers.com.

50. "Wofford Wins Bradsher's 6 Game Winning Streak Halted." The Charlotte Observer. May 2, 1902. p.2. Retrieved February 1, 2018, via Newspapers.com.

51. "Bradsher and Trinity Defeat Horner in Season Opener." The Charlotte Observer. March 24, 1901. p.3. Retrieved February 1, 2018, via Newspapers.com.

52. "Lafayette Defeats Trinity. Seven Errors Costly." The Charlotte Observer. March 28, 1901. p.5. Retrieved January 15, 2018, via Newspapers.com.

53. "Bradsher and Trinity Win A Laugher Over Bingham." The Charlotte Observer. April 2, 1902. p.8. Retrieved February 1, 2018, via Newspapers.com.

54. "Bradsher Pitches First Career Shutout." The Durham Sun. April 6, 1901. p.4. Retrieved January 21, 2018, via Newspapers.com.

55. "Bradsher Leaves Game in Third Inning with Sore Arm." The Charlotte Observer. April 11, 1901. p.4. Retrieved February 1, 2018, via Newspapers.com.

56. "Harvard Smashes Trinity 12-0." The Durham Sun. April 18, 1901. p.4. Retrieved January 21, 2018, via Newspapers.com.

57. "Wake Beats Trinity and Bradsher in the Slop." The Morning Post (Raleigh, North Carolina). April 21, 1901. p.2. Retrieved February 15, 2018, via Newspapers.com.

58. "Bradsher Defeats Georgia 13-1. Spins A 3 Hitter." The Charlotte Observer. April 27, 1901. p.1. Retrieved February 1, 2018, via Newspapers.com.

59. "Bradsher Finishes Season with 5 Shutout Innings After Rough Start." The Charlotte Observer. May 5, 1901. p.8. Retrieved February 1, 2018, via Newspapers.com.

~

Arthur Bradsher Five Complete Game No-Hit Performances

1. "Crack Trinity Twirler Fanned 22 Men Without A Hit." Macon News Saturday Evening. April 8, 1905.

2. "A Twin Goose Egg. No Runs No Hits." News and Observer (Raleigh, North Carolina). April 26, 1905. p.1. Retrieved June 15, 2018, via Newspapers.com.

3. "Bradsher No-Hits Trinity Park 9-0." The Durham Sun. March 26, 1904. p.1. Retrieved April 15, 2018, via Newspapers.com.

4. "Bradsher No-Hits Oak Ridge." The Durham Sun. March 19, 1904. p.4. Retrieved April 10, 2018, via Newspapers.com.

5. Bradsher No-Hits Wake and Strikes Out 19." The Morning Post (Raleigh, North Carolina). April 15, 1902. p.6. Retrieved February 15, 2018, via Newspapers.com.

~

Arthur Bradsher Two Non-Complete Game No-Hitters

1. Bradsher Pitches Seven No-Hit Innings Against Guilford." The Atlanta Constitution. March 27, 1904. p.8. Retrieved April 1, 2018, via Newspapers. Com.

2. "Bradsher Pitches Only Game of Relief in His 5 Year Career. Pitches 6 Perfect Innings and Strikes Out 12." The Atlanta Constitution. May 5, 1903. p.12. Retrieved April 1, 2018, via Newspapers.com.

References

~

Arthur Bradsher 15 Shutout Performances

1. "Bradsher Pitches First Career Shutout." The Durham Sun. April 6, 1901. p.4. Retrieved January 21, 2018, via Newspapers.com.

2. Bradsher No-Hits Wake and Strikes Out 19." The Morning Post (Raleigh, North Carolina). April 15, 1902. p.6. Retrieved February 15, 2018, via Newspapers.com.

3. Bradsher No-Hits Wake and Strikes Out 19." The Morning Post (Raleigh, North Carolina). April 15, 1902. p.6. Retrieved February 15, 2018, via Newspapers.com.

4. "Bradsher Pitches Second Shutout in 3 Days. Trinity Beats Guilford 13-0." The Durham Sun. February 15, 1902. p.1. Retrieved April 1, 2018, via Newspapers. com.

5. Bradsher No-Hits Wake and Strikes Out 19." The Morning Post (Raleigh, North Carolina). April 15, 1902. p.6. Retrieved February 15, 2018, via Newspapers.com.

6. "Bradsher No-Hits Oak Ridge." The Durham Sun. March 19, 1904. p.4. Retrieved April 10, 2018, via Newspapers.com.

7. "Bradsher No-Hits Trinity Park 9-0." The Durham Sun. March 26, 1904. p.1. Retrieved April 15, 2018, via Newspapers.com.

8. "Bradsher 2 Hits Strong Syracuse Team." The Durham Sun. April 4, 1904. p.4. Retrieved April 1, 2018, via Newspapers.com.

9. Bradsher Shuts Out Wake 1-0." The Charlotte Observer. April 24, 1904. p.8. Retrieved April 1, 2018, via Newspapers.com.

10. "Bradsher Downs Wofford and Strikes Out 17." The Charlotte Observer. May 5, 1904. p.8. Retrieved April 1, 2018, via Newspapers.com.

11. "Trinity and Bradsher Shut Out Wake Forest 4-0." The Morning Post (Raleigh, North Carolina) p.2. April 2, 1905. Retrieved June 15, 2018, via Newspapers.com.

12. "Crack Trinity Twirler Fanned 22 Men Without A Hit." Macon News Saturday Evening. April 8, 1905. Retrieved June 15, 2018, via Nespapers.com.

13. "Bradsher Mows Down 18 Orangemen." The Atlanta Constitution. April 19.1905. p.11. Retrieved June 15, 2018, via Newspapers.com.

14. "A Twin Goose Egg. No Runs No Hits." News and Observer (Raleigh, North Carolina). April 26, 1905. p.1. Retrieved June 15, 2018, via Newspapers.com.

15. "Trinity Beat Wake in a Great Pitchers Battle." The Morning Post (Raleigh, North Carolina). May 3, 1905. p.6. Retrieved May 1, 2018, via Newspapers.com.

References

~

Chapter References

Chapter 1 - Stop That Train

"A Long Tie Game at Macon. The Miracle at Mercer." The Atlanta Constitution. April 8.1905. p.9. Retrieved June 15, 2018, via Newspapers.com.

"Letter from Arthur Bradsher to W.W. Card." Letter dated May 15, 1943." Retrieved from the W.W. Card Collection. Courtesy of the Duke University Library. April 8, 2019.

Chapter 2 - The Miracle at Mercer

"A Long Tie Game at Macon. The Miracle at Mercer." The Atlanta Constitution. April 8.1905. p.9. Retrieved June 15, 2018, via Newspapers.com.

"Bradsher Made A Fine Record. Crack Trinity Twirler Fanned 22 Men Without A Hit." Macon News Saturday Evening. April 8, 1905. Retrieved June 15, 2018, via Nespapers.com.

Chapter 3 - Grandfather's Farm

"Family Stories with Liz Bradshaw." Retrieved 2017-2019.

Eugenia Bradsher. "A History of the Bradsher Family." Retrieved June 1, 2017.

Chapter 4 - The Reunion

Eugenia Bradsher. "A History of the Bradsher Family." Retrieved June 1, 2017.

"Family Stories with Liz Bradshaw, the Voorhees family, the Hayes family, and the Bradsher family." Retrieved June 15, 2018.

"Letter from Arthur Bradsher to daughter, Millie Bradsher." Mailed from Cuba and dated May 15, 1943.

Chapter 5 - Greatest Game Ever Played in Dixieland

"Champion Game Goes to Tech." The Atlanta Constitution. p.10. April 11, 1905. Retrieved July 1, 1905, via Newspapers.com.

Chapter 6 - Heisman Steals the Game from Trinity

"Champion Game Goes to Tech." The Atlanta Constitution. p.10. April 11, 1905. Retrieved July 1, 1905, via Newspapers.com.

Chapter 11 - The Curveball

Author. Verducci, Tom. "The Curveball's Resurgence is Changing Starting Pitching." Sports Illustrated. May 27, 2017.

Chapter 14 - Eight Days in April

"Bradsher No-Hits Wake and Strikes Out 19." The Morning Post (Raleigh, North Carolina). April 15, 1902. p.6. Retrieved February 15, 2018, via Newspapers.com.

"Bradsher Pitches Second Shutout in 3 Days. Trinity Beats Guilford 13-0." The Durham Sun. February 15, 1902. p.1. Retrieved April 1, 2018, via Newspapers.com.

Chapter15 - Best Friends

"Bradsher Has the Baptists At His Mercy. Allows 2 Hits." The Charlotte Observer.

References

April 23, 1902. p.4. Retrieved February 1, 2018, via Newspapers.com.

Chapter 17 - A Bright Orange Moon

"Family Stories with Liz Bradshaw." Retrieved 2017-2019.

Chapter 18 - The Order of the Tombs

"Tombs Staged a Dinner Last Night." Durham Morning Herald. April 19.1922. p.9. Retrieved June 15, 2018, via Newspapers.com.

Tombs 1909 picture: Courtesy of Duke Library Archives.

"The Tombs 1937." The Chanticleer 1937. p. 351. Retrieved June 15, 2018.

"The Tombs 1939." The Chanticleer 1939. p.163. Retrieved June 15, 2018

Chapter 19 - The Tombs Starting Nine

"Tombs Staged a Dinner Last Night." Durham Morning Herald. April 19.1922. p.9. Retrieved June 15, 2018, via Newspapers.com.

"The Tombs 1939" The Chanticleer 1939. p. 163. Retrieved June 15, 2018.

Chapter 20 - Playing the Pros

"Bradsher Defeats Charlotte Pro Team and Gets 3 Hits." *The Morning Post* (Raleigh, North Carolina). April 26, 1904. p.5. Retrieved April 1, 2018, via Newspapers.com.

Chapter 21 - Playball

"Bradsher Defeats Charlotte Pro Team and Gets 3 Hits." *The Morning Post* (Raleigh, North Carolina). April 26, 1904. p.5. Retrieved April 1, 2018, via Newspapers.com.

Chapter 22 - The Play at the Plate

"Bradsher Defeats Charlotte Pro Team and Gets 3 Hits." *The Morning Post* (Raleigh, North Carolina). April 26, 1904. p.5. Retrieved April 1, 2018, via Newspapers.com.

Chapter 24 - No Hits

"Bradsher Pitches Seven No-Hit Innings Against Guilford." *The Atlanta Constitution*. March 27, 1904. p.8. Retrieved April 1, 2018, via Newspapers. Com.

Chapter 25 - Bradsher Takes Himself Out

"Bradsher Pitches Seven No-Hit Innings Against Guilford." *The Atlanta Constitution*. March 27, 1904. p.8. Retrieved April 1, 2018, via Newspapers. Com.

Chapter 27 - The Furman Game and Billy Laval

"Bradsher Beats Billy Laval 3-1. Loses a Shutout with Two Strikes, Two Outs.": Greenville Times. May 7, 1904. p.1. Retrieved April 1, 2018, via Newspapers.com.

Chapter 28 - First Meeting with Lizzie Muse

"Bradsher Beats Billy Laval 3-1. Loses a Shutout with Two Strikes, Two Outs.": Greenville Times. May 7, 1904. p.1. Retrieved April 1, 2018, via Newspapers.com.

Chapter 29 - The ATO Gala Ball

"ATO Fraternity Gala Event." The North Carolinian (Raleigh, North Carolina) June 8, 1905. p.3. Retrieved June 15, 2018, via Newspapers.com.

Chapter 34 - Winners Never Quit

Heisman quotes after Mercer-Ga. Tech game." "Champion Game Goes to Tech." *The Atlanta Constitution*. p.10. April 11, 1905. Retrieved July 1, 1905, via Newspapers.com.

Chapter 35 - The Final Game

"Wake Wins Over Bradsher in Final Game 1-0." The Times-Dispatch (Richmond Virginia). May 16, 1905. p.7. Retrieved April 15, 2018, via Newspapers.com.

Chapter 36 - The Interview

"Heisman quotes after Mercer-Ga. Tech game." "Champion Game Goes to Tech." *The Atlanta Constitution*. p.10. April 11, 1905. Retrieved July 1, 1905, via Newspapers.com.

Chapter 37 - The Answer

Trinity College Team Batting and Fielding Statistics for the years 1901-1905.

Chapter 38 - The Best Pitcher in the Country

"Heisman quotes after Mercer-Ga. Tech game." "Champion Game Goes to Tech." *The Atlanta Constitution*. p.10. April 11, 1905. Retrieved July 1, 1905, via Newspapers.com.

"Heisman names Bradsher his Shining Star." *The Atlanta Constitution*. p.10. April 11, 1905. Retrieved July 1, 1905, via Newspapers.com.

Chapter 40 - Train Ride to New Bern

"Family Stories with Liz Bradshaw and Mary Bradsher Hayes." Retrieved June 15, 2018.

Chapter 43 - The Proposal

"Popular College Athlete Marries." Times-Dispatch. September 2, 1907. p.3. Retrieved February 15, 2018, via Newspapers.com.

"Family Stories with Liz Bradshaw and Mary Bradsher Hayes." Retrieved 1995-1997.

Chapter 44 - The Petersburg Years

Trinity Methodist Church program dated February 23, 1923, with a picture on the back, listing Arthur Bradsher as Superintendent. Retrieved February 15, 2018, via Trinity United Methodist Church.

Chapter 45 - Delta Phi Rho Alpha

"The Duke Chanticleer. p.259. Retrieved April 1, 2018, via Newspapers.com.

Chapter 46 - The Black and Blue Girls

"Delta Phi Rho" The Duke Chanticleer. p.260. Retrieved April 1, 2018, via Newspapers.com.

Chapter 47 - The Prettiest Church in America

"Bradsher is moving spirit in constructing a $375,000 Church which will be moving which will be the most beautiful in America." The Twin- City Daily Sentinel (Winston-Salem, North Carolina). June 22, 1922. p.16. Retrieved June 15, 2018, via Newspapers.com.

Chapter 48 - Bradsher is Still Master of the Ball

"Trinity Diamond King is Still at It." The Twin- City Daily Sentinel (Winston-Salem, North Carolina). June 22, 1922. p.16. Retrieved June 15, 2018, via Newspapers.com.

References

"Trinity Strike-Out King Again in His Baseball Togs." News and Observer (Raleigh, North Carolina). June 21, 1922. p.8. Retrieved June 15, 2018, via Newspapers.com.

"Arthur Bradsher Still is Master of the Ball." Charlotte Observer. June 21, 1922. p.12. Retrieved June 15, 2018, via Newspapers.com.

"King of the Southern Diamond Hangs Up a Strike Out Record." Durham Morning Herald. July 19, 1922. p.7. Retrieved June 15, 2018, via Newspapers. com.

Chapter 50 - Crabbing and Floundering in the Neuse

"Family Stories with Liz Bradshaw." Retrieved June 15, 2018.

Chapter 51 - Aunti Pearl Joins the Family for Dinner

"Family Stories with Liz Bradshaw and Mary Bradsher Hayes." Retrieved 1959-2019.

Chapter 54 - The Final Inning

"Former Athlete Dies" The Daily Times-News (Burlington, North Carolina) January 31, 1951. p.6. Retrieved June 15, 2018, via Newspapers.com.

"Arthur Bradsher, '04, Great Trinity Pitcher, Dies." Duke University Alumni Register, (Durham, North Carolina). February 1951. p. 43. Retrieved May 15, 2018, via Newspapers.com.

"Trinity Strike-Out King Again in His Baseball Togs." News and Observer (Raleigh, North Carolina). June 21, 1922. p.8. Retrieved June 15, 2018, via Newspapers.com.

Trinity Methodist Church program dated February 23, 1923, with a picture on the back, listing Arthur Bradsher as Superintendent. Retrieved February 15, 2018, via Trinity United Methodist Church.

"Plenty Fast" The Winnipeg Tribune. Winnipeg, Manitoba, Canada) on April 6, 1933. p. 13. Retrieved June 15, 2018, via Newspapers.com.

~

References for Extra Innings

Lizzie Chadwick Muse (1885-1970)

Elizabeth Chadwick Muse receives freshman honors at Trinity commencement." *The Durham Sun.* June 4, 1902. p.1. Retrieved July 1, 2018, via Newspapers.com.

"Arthur Bradsher and Lizzie Attend Lavish ATO Banquet." *The Durham Sun.* June 8, 1904. p.4. Retrieved July 1, 2018, via Newspapers.com.

"Popular College Athlete Marries." Times-Dispatch. September 2, 1907. p. 3. Retrieved July 1, 2018, via Newspapers.com.

Eugenia Bradsher. "A History of the Bradsher Family."

"Family Stories with Liz Bradshaw." Retrieved June 15, 2018.

Trinity College Transcripts for the years 1901-1902.

References

"Lizzie Muse Participates in Sunday School Training." The Wilmington Messenger (Wilmington, North Carolina). June 16.1906. p.9. Retrieved August 6, 2016, via Newspapers.com.

John Heisman

"Heisman names Bradsher his Shining Star." *The Atlanta Constitution*. p.10. April 11, 1905. Retrieved July 1, 2017, via Newspapers.com.

"All Southern Team 1905 Picked by John W. Heisman." Atlanta Constitution. June 4, 1905. p.3. Retrieved July 1, 2017, via Newspapers.com.

John Heisman-Wikipedia

Heisman- New World Encyclopedia

"Heisman quotes after Mercer-Ga. Tech game." "Champion Game Goes to Tech." *The Atlanta Constitution*. p.10. April 11, 1905. Retrieved July 1, 2017, via Newspapers.com.

Oliver Maxwell Gardner (1881-1947)

O. Maxwell Gardner picks 1904 North Carolina All-Star Team. Names Bradsher as Top Star, and credits Chadwick" *The Durham Sun*. August 14, 1904. p.4. Retrieved July 1, 2018, via Newspapers.com.

Gardner, Oliver Maxwell by Richard L. Watson. NCPedia 1986.

Oliver Maxwell Gardner - Wikipedia

Oliver Maxwell Gardner 1881-1947 Ancestry.

Billy Laval (1885-1957)

Wikipedia - Billy Laval

WikiVisually - Billy Laval.

Morris: "Laval knew how to win no matter the sport." The State.

Denton True "Cy" Young (1867-1955)

Wikipedia - Cy Young

Browning, Reed. Cy Young: A Baseball Life. University of Massachusetts Press. 2003.

Walter Chadwick (1882-1948)

O. Maxwell Gardner picks 1904 North Carolina All-Star Team. Names Bradsher as Top Star, and credits Chadwick" *The Durham Sun*. August 14, 1904. p.4. Retrieved July 1, 2018, via Newspapers.com.

Trinity College Transcripts for the years 1902-1904.

Trinity College Team Batting and Fielding Statistics for the years 1902-1904.

"Trinity Defeats Hobart 4-2. Chadwick is Starting Catcher." *The Durham Sun* April 5, 1902. p.1. Retrieved June 15, 2018, via Newspapers.com.

Craig Day (1894-1952)

"All Southern Team 1905 Picked by John W. Heisman." Atlanta Constitution. June 4, 1905. p.3. Retrieved July 1, 2017, via Newspapers.com.

Tommy McMillan (1888-1966)

"All Southern Team 1905 Picked by John W. Heisman." *The Durham Sun* April 19.1922. p.9. Retrieved June 15, 2018, via Newspapers.com.

References

Wilbur Wade Card (1873-1948)

Wikipedia - Wilbur Wade Card.

"Wilbur Wade Card Papers: 1876-1943/Collection Guide." Duke University Archives.

Wilbur Wade Card - Wikidata.

Walter Clarkson (1878-1946)

"Clarkson and Harvard Defeat Yale 5-2 before 10,000 Fans." Boston Post (Boston, Massachusetts). June 19, 1903. p.3. Retrieved June 15, 2016, via Newspapers.com.

"Harvard Shut Out by Georgetown. Clarkson is as Wild as a Ribbon Clerk at the Seashore. He Walks Seven and Throws Six Wild Pitches." The Washinton Times. April 17, 1904. p.8. Retrieved June 15, 2018, via Newspapers.com.

"Clarkson and Mathews are heroes as Harvard defeats Yale 6-5." The Times (Philadelphia, Pennsylvania). June 29, 1902. p.18. Retrieved June 15, 2018, via Newspapers.com.

Clarkson Loses to Princeton 7-0. He Walks Nine. The New York Times. (New York, New York). June 12, 1902. p. 10. Retrieved June 1, 2016, via Newspapers.com.

"Clarkson Has Broken His Amateur Status by Signing with the Pros." The Washinton Times. April 19, 1904. p.8. Retrieved June 15, 2018, via Newspapers.com.

"Clarkson Continues to Leak Pro Signing is Near." Detroit Press (Detroit Michigan). April 4, 1904. p.8. Retrieved June 15, 2018, via Newspapers.com.

~

Baseball Glossary A-Z References

"Baseball: Glossary of Baseball Terms and definitions." Ducksters Education Site. Retrieved June 15, 2018, via Newspapers.com.

Baseball Terms/Baseball Terminology." Just Bats.com. Retrieved June 15, 2018, via Newspapers.com.

"Glossary of Baseball" Wikipedia. Retrieved June 15, 2018, via Newspapers.com.

"Baseball Glossary and Terms." Epic Sports. Retrieved June 15, 2018, via Newspapers.com.

"Baseball for Beginners." Baseball- A film by Ken Burns. Retrieved June 15, 2018, via Newspapers.com.

"Glossary of Baseball Term." Sports Genius. Retrieved June 15, 2018, via Newspapers.com.

"Baseball Slang-Baseball Lingo-Terminology." Lootmeister Sports. Retrieved June 15, 2018, via Newspapers.com.

References

~

Books Used as References and Research

Schlabach, Mark. "Heisman- The Man Behind the Trophy."

Spence, Hersey Everett (1954). "I Remember Recollections and Reminiscences of Alma Mater." Seeman Printery.

Duke University (2018-2019). Duke University Baseball Media Guide. P. 86-89. Retrieved June 15, 2018.

Eugenia Bradsher. "A History of the Bradsher Family." Retrieved June 1, 2017.

Muse, Amy. My Grandfather Was a Whaler: Story of the Carteret Chadwicks. Published by Papamoa Press. 2018.

Deford, Frank. "The Old Ballgame: How John McGraw, Christy Matheson, and the New York Giants Created Modern Baseball." Atlantic Monthly Press.

The Duke Chanticleer 1921 "Delta Alpha Rho" p. 259-260.

Sullivan, Dean, A. Middle Innings: A Documentary Story of Baseball, 1900-1948. Published in 2001.

The Duke Chanticleer 1937. "The Tombs." p. 351.

The Duke Chanticleer 1939. "The Tombs." p. 163.

Browning, Reed. Cy Young: A Baseball Life. University of Massachusetts Press. 2003.

Sports Illustrated: The Baseball Book. Introduction by Tom Verducci. Edited by Rob Fleder. Design by Steven Hoffman.

Sullivan, Dean, A. Early Innings: A Documentary Story of Baseball, 1825-1908. Published in 1997.

~

Links

https://www.arthurbradsher.com

https://www.kingofthesoutherndiamond.com

https://library.duke.edu/rubenstein

https://www.ncpedia.org/bibliography/card-wilbur-wade

https://www.si.com/mlb/2017/05/23/curveball-clayton-kershaw-lance-mccullers

www.lbrary.gatech.edu/archives/

https://www.antiqueathlete.com

https://www.digitalcollections.detroitpubliclibrary.org

www.umc.org/find-a-church/church/45798

References

~

Photographic Credits

Author's Collection: Book Cover portrait of Arthur Bradsher, Trinity Church School first program, Lizzie Muse at Seventy-two, Lizzie and her Family, Lizzie with Mary and Charles, Bradsher and his family at Summerlea, Bradsher with Sandy in wheelbarrow, Bradsher home in Petersburg, Original ticket of last game Arthur Bradsher pitched, dated May 8, 1905.

Duke University Archives and W.W. Card Collection: Wilbur Wade in baseball uniform, Wilbur Wade doing floor exercises, Portrait of Wilbur Wade, Wilbur Wade standing and wearing a Fedora, Bradsher's yearbook picture for 1904, Delta Phi Rho Alpha group picture, Alpha Tau Omega group picture for 1904. Trinity Baseball Team-Champions for 1904, Cropped Picture of Chadwick, the Ball boy, Bradsher, and Wooten. Hanes Field, Grandstands at Hanes Field, Bradsher gripping the baseball, Lizzie Muse's 1901-1902 class picture, Trinity Campus in 1904, Trinity Library built in 1903.

Trinity Methodist Church: William Muse plaque, sanctuary with view of assentation, two exterior pictures of the church, group picture of laying of the cornerstone in 1921.

Courtesy and special thanks to historian Curtis Anderson: Picture of sanctuary balcony, picture with view to front of sanctuary, picture in sanctuary with view of assentation, William Muse plaque, chairs in temporary sanctuary, picture of bell, group picture of laying of the cornerstone in 1921.

North Carolina Postcards: Courtesy of the Wilson Library at the University of North Carolina: postcard of Neuse River Bridge, postcard of Neuse River, postcard of Trinity campus in 1904, postcard of Trinity Library built in 1903.

The Duke University Chanticleer: Group picture of Delta Phi Rho Alpha of 1921, group picture of Tombs in 1937, group picture of Tombs in 1939.

Detroit Public Library Digital Collections: Picture of 1910 Packard 30 Model UC touring car, left side view, top lowered.

Antique Athlete: Pictures of baseball glove, baseball bat, catcher's mask and chest protector. Permission given per Corey Leiby, Antique Athlete, 4040 Village Road, Orwigsburg, PA 17961.

INDEX

*Page numbers in italics refer to illustrations
and chapter heading quotes*

ABOUT
BRADSHER HAYES

Bradsher Hayes is a Southern Gentleman and Writer who has a deep love for the game of baseball. He is a foremost authority of Southern college baseball at the turn of the twentieth century after years of study and research. The basis for this non-fiction work is three hundred and fifty newspaper articles, diaries, family letters and documents from the Duke University library and archives. He knows baseball and is well paired to the game from his playing time, being a spectator for sixty years and coaching. He played on two state championship baseball teams at Westminster in Atlanta, played college ball at the University of North Carolina, and coached youth programs for ten years. The author has two children Bo and Jenny. His first grandchild, Lilian Pearl, was born in September 2019.

ABOUT THE TYPE

This book is set in Sabon, a typeface designed by the well-known German typographer Jan Tschichold (1902-74). Sabon's design is based upon the original letter forms of Claude Garamond and was created specifically to be used for three sources: foundry type for hand composition, Linotype, and Monotype. Tschichold named his typeface for the famous Frankfurt typefounder Jacques Sabon, who died in 1580.